Scotland
The Facts

COMPILED BY

Michael T R B Turnbull

D.G. Wood

Citizenship Prize

Laura Stark

Chambers

Published 1991 by W & R Chambers Ltd,
43–45 Annandale Street, Edinburgh EH7 4AZ

© W&R Chambers 1991

**British Library Cataloguing in
Publication Data**

A catalogue record for this book is
available from the British Library

ISBN 0-550-11833-0

For Lucy

Cover design by John Marshall
Typeset by Alphaset Graphics Ltd, Edinburgh
Printed and bound in Great Britain by Richard Clay, St Ives plc

Contents

Physical Statistics

Places to Visit

Calendar

People

Miscellany

Acknowledgments

This book was compiled from many sources, including reference books, record books, quiz books, official statistics and the daily press.

In addition, I should like to acknowledge the help freely given by many individuals and organizations in my research, and in particular the staff of the Mitchell Library, Glasgow, the National Library of Scotland and the Central Library, Edinburgh, without whose consistent patience I would have been unable to trace much vital information.

I am also very grateful for the co-operation and assistance I received, in particular, from the departments I approached, in the Scottish Office, the Scottish Tourist Board, the Scottish Arts Council, the Scottish Development Agency, Historic Scotland, the Scottish Local Government Information Unit and the Scottish Sports Council. The selection and arrangement is, of course, my own.

Every effort has been made to trace and acknowledge copyright holders, but if any have inadvertently been overlooked the publishers will be pleased to make the appropriate arrangements at the earliest opportunity.

Preface

The creation of this book came from a thirst for greater knowledge of
Scottish life and history: the trivial as well as the important. It was born out
of a conviction that countries may well be the sum of all their parts.

If the arrangement of the book appears rhapsodic, it is because the
governing principle behind its construction is lateral thinking or, as the old
definition of metaphor has it, 'the joining of like with unlike'. The lists reflect
the diversity of Scotland itself.

'Facts alone are wanted in life' declares Thomas Gradgrind, in Charles
Dickens's *Hard Times*. Here then are facts and statistics, lists of places to
visit and things to do; a calendar of festivals and traditions, plus a catalogue
of the rich and colourful achievements of the Scots in most fields of
endeavour and misdemeanour. The book ends with a pot-pourri of the
marvellous, the cultural and the disastrous.

From these pages the reader will glean the heights and the depths of life in
Scotland – the extremes of first and last; largest, smallest; most famous and
infamous; oldest, youngest; and lists of people from all walks of life,
together with details of the numerous and infinitely varied attractions of
Scotland past and present.

Physical Statistics

Benjamin Disraeli warns us that, 'There are three kinds of lies – lies, damned lies and statistics.'

Although statistics may not always give the whole truth, they do not necessarily have to be one-sided versions of reality. Raw numbers give us the dimensions of the land, the vagaries of the notorious Scottish weather, who Scotland's visitors are and where they come from.

They also tell us how the very individual Scottish legal system operates, something about the produce of the country, what kinds of jobs the Scots have, how local and national government works, how Scottish children are educated and what Scottish religious beliefs would appear to be.

THE LAND

Area – 77 700 sq km/*30 405 sq miles* (Scotland is around 34% of Britain and 60% the size of England)
Greatest distance from north to south of the mainland – 440 km/*275 miles*
Maximum width – 248km/*154 miles*
Minimum width – 41 km/*25 miles* (between Firths of Forth and Clyde)
Situation – between 55 and 60 degrees north (Scotland's central belt is almost the same latitude as Moscow, Shetland being closer to the Arctic Circle than to the South of England)
Coastline – 10 000 km/*6214 miles*
Western seaboard – 416 km/*260 miles* long in a straight line; over 3680 km/*2300 miles* along the indented coastline
Islands – 790 (big rocks to large islands); 130 are inhabited
Western Isles – there are 550
Mainland sealochs – there are 40
Finest waterfalls – Eas a' Chual Aluinn (the highest at 211 m/*692 ft*); Glomach (highest unsupported leap, 112 m/*367 ft*); An Steall Ban (105 m/*344 ft*); Grey Mare's Tail (cascades of 60 m/*197 ft*); Lealt (60 m/*197 ft*); Reekie Linn (24 m/*79 ft*); Kirkaig (18 m/*59 ft*); Badan Mosach; Bruar; Measach; Clyde; Foyers
Landscape –
    above 120 m/*400 ft*   65%
    above 60 m/*200 ft*   20%
    above 600 m/*2000 ft*   6%
Landscape eroded over last 13 million years – 76.57%
Mainland above 152 m/*500 ft* – 66%
Most westerly point – Ardnamurchan Point
Most northerly point – Dunnet Head
Most easterly point – Budian Ness
Highest sea-stack in Britain – Old man of Hoy (137 m/*450 ft*)
Largest stretch of fresh water on mainland Britain – Loch Lomond
Last point of Pennine Way – Kirk Yetholm

Land Cover (1989)

	%
Arable and ley pastures	25.5
Heather moorlands	22.2
Grasslands	13.4
Peatlands (blanket bog)	13.1
Plantation woodlands	12.5
Montane (high-lying heaths and bogs)	4.4
Built-up area	3.0
Inland water	2.3
Native woodlands	1.8
Rock	0.5

Total agricultural area – 5 853 000 hectares/ *14 632 500 acres* (1988)
Farms – there are 5550 (1988)
Forestry Commission area – 726 000 hectares/ *1 815 000 acres* (1988)
Private woodlands – 494 000 hectares/ *1 235 000 acres* (1988)
Largest remaining portion of Caledonian pine forest – 48 hectares/*120 acres* at Glen Affric (Coille Ruigh na Cuileige) with trees over 150 years old. There has been continuous tree cover in the area for 10 000 years

Area under Crops (1988)

	hectares 000	acres 000
Rough grazing	4 033	10 082.5
Crops and grazing	1 702	4 255
Barley	388	970
Wheat	99	247
Oilseed rape	41	102.5
Oats and mixed grain	36	90
Vegetables	12	30
Soft fruit	9	22.5

Ten Highest Mountains

	m	ft
Ben Nevis*	1344	4408
Ben Macdui	1309	4296
Braeriach	1296	4252
Cairn Toul	1293	4241

continued

Ten Highest Mountains – continued

	m	ft
Cairn Gorm	1245	4084
Aonach Beag	1236	4054
Carn Mor Dearg	1223	4012
Aonach Mor	1219	3999
Ben Lawers	1214	3984
Beinn a' Bhuird	1196	3924

* highest mountain in Britain

Munros – 278 peaks over 914 m/*3000 ft* of which 12 are over 1219 m/*4000 ft*

Corbetts – 217 peaks at 762–914 m/*2500–3000 ft*

The Cairngorm Mountains is the most extensive area of Britain over 914 m/*3000 ft*

Ten Longest Rivers

	km	miles
Tay	193	120
Spey	172	107
Clyde	171	106
Tweed	156	97
Dee	137	85
Don	132	82
Forth	105	65
Findhorn	101	63
Deveron	98	61
Annan	79	49

Ten Largest Freshwater Lochs

	sq km	sq miles
Lomond	71.1	27.5
Ness	56.4	21.8
Awe (Etive)	38.5	14.9
Maree	28.6	11.0
Morar	26.7	10.3
Tay	26.4	10.2
Shin	22.5	8.7
Shiel	19.6	7.6
Rannoch	19.1	7.4
Ericht	18.7	7.2

WEATHER

Temperature

Mean Daily Temperature	1989	Mean Daily Sunshine	Total Rainfall
	°C	hours	mm
Aberdeen	8.5	4.3	514
Dundee	9.3	4.4	470
Edinburgh	9.3	4.3	529
Glasgow	9.1	4.1	1076

Hottest place in Scotland – Dumfries, 32.8°C/*91°F* (2 July 1908)

Coldest place in Britain – Braemar −27.2°C/−*43.41°F* (11 Feb 1895 and 10 Jan 1982)

Greatest temperature changes in Britain – Tummel Bridge, Tayside, a change of 29°C/*52.2°F* from −7°C/*19.4°F* to 22°C/*71°F* (9 May 1978)

Lowest temperature in Britain for a day – Blackadder, Borders, −30°C/−*23°F* (4 Dec 1879)

Lowest barometric pressure in Britain – Ochtertyre, 925.5 mb/*27.33 in* (26 Jan 1884)

Sunshine

Lowest sunshine in Britain – Lochranza, Isle of Arran (from 18 Nov to 8 Feb each year the south-east end of the village is in shadow)

Wind

Highest surface windspeed in Britain – 278 kph/*172 mph* (Cairn Gorm summit on 20 March 1986)

Rain

Mean annual rainfall (eastern Lowlands) – 500-700 mm/*20-28 in*

Mean annual rainfall (western Lowlands) – over 1000 mm/*40 in*

Rain days (minimum) – 175 (East Fife)

Rain days (maximum) – over 250 (parts of West and Western Islands)

Snow

Average days of snow in south-west – 10
Average days of snow in north-east – 40
Average days of snow at the coast – 5
Average days of snow inland at Braemar – 70
Oldest snow-bed in Britain – 50 years at
  Braeriach (1295 m/*4249 ft*)

Longest fogs in the world – around 300 days a
  year (Ben Nevis)
Most frequent Aurorae ('Northern Lights') –
  Shetland (high 203/low 58)

Recording the Weather

**First-class metereological station above 152 m/
  *500 ft*** – Eskdalemuir, Dumfriesshire (350
  m/*1148 ft*)
Longest series of accurate weather records –
  Edinburgh (1731)

FLORA

World's largest collection of rhododendrons –
  Royal Botanic Garden, Edinburgh
Highest hedge – Meikleour beech hedge near
  Perth
Best hedge in Scotland (1990) – Humbie beech
  hedge (Planted 19th century: now 4.3 m/
  14 ft high and up to 4.6 m/*15 ft* thick.
  Stands on both sides of the road for over
  0.4 km/*¼ mile*)

Tallest Trees

	m	ft
Beech – Hallyburton House, Perthshire	46	*150*
Birch – Taymouth Castle, Perthshire	34	*111*
Chestnut – Tyninghame, East Lothian	36	*118*
Copper Beech – Dalguise House, Perthshire	38	*124*

	m	ft
Cypress – Strone House, Argyll	41	*133*
Douglas Fir – The Hermitage, Perthshire	61	*200*
European Larch – Glenlee, Dumfries and Galloway	46	*150*
Grand Fir – Strone, Cairndow, Argyll	62	*203*
Hemlock – Murthly Castle, Dunkeld, Perthshire	52	*170*
Silver Fir – Arninglas House, Strathclyde	54	*176*
Sitka Spruce – R Findhorn, Nairn	59	*195*
Walnut – Garth House, Aberfeldy, Perthshire	30	*98*
Wellingtonia – Castle Leod, Strathpeffer	53	*173*

Trees, Vegetables and Flowers

Oldest tree in Europe – c 3500 years old
  (churchyard yew at Fortingall)
Deer forests – cover more than 2 500 000
  acres (more bare mountain than trees)
Largest broad bean in Britain – 59.3 cm/*23.4 in*
  (Jedburgh and Irvine, 1963)
Largest gladiolas in Britain – 2.6 m/*8 ft 4.5 in*
  (Roxburgh, 1981)
Largest peapod in Britain – 25.7 cm/*10.1 in*
  (Jedburgh, 1964)
Largest turnip in Britain – 16.8 kg/*37 lb*
  (Tillyfourie, 1987)

DEER and FISH

Deer (1989)

Fallow Deer	1 000 – 2 000
Red Deer	300 000
Roe Deer	200 000
Sika Deer	10 000

Fish Landings (1988)

	(tonnes)
Mackerel	161.3
Haddock	91.2
Herring	87.5
Cod	43.0
Whiting	34.9
Sand-eels	30.2
Norway lobsters	19.2
Monkfish	7.3
Plaice	6.9
Edible crabs	6.1
Dogfish	5.9
Scallops	4.2
Queen scallops	3.7
Periwinkles	2.2

Salmon and Sea Trout Catches (1988)

	Salmon (tonnes)	Sea Trout (tonnes)
Rod and line	96.5	47.8
Net and cable	79.8	37.7

Most expensive fish in Britain – the wrasse (£2 each) which eats salmon lice and is used in fish-farming

First wrasse fisherman in Britain – Dougie Lamont (Lochaline, Ardnamurchan)

TRANSPORT and TOURISM

First scheduled airmail flight in Britain – Inverness-Kirkwall (1934)

First keep left national regulation – applied to all towns under Traffic (Scotland) Act (1772)

First PO box numbers – Edinburgh Post Office (1830)

First road fatality involving self-propelled vehicles – five killed by John Russel's steam coach, Paisley (1834)

First automobile road fatality – Paisley (1834)

First women taxi-drivers – Edinburgh, Cardiff, Manchester (1917)

Last public service tramcar in Scotland – Glasgow (1962)

Bridge over the Atlantic – between Seil Island and Argyllshire mainland

First road to be snowbound each winter – Cockbridge to Tomintoul

Airports

	Operated by
Aberdeen (Dyce)	Aberdeen Airport Ltd
Barra	Loganair Ltd
Benbecula	Highlands and Islands Airports Ltd
Cumbernauld	Cumbernauld Aircraft Services Ltd
Dounreay	UK Atomic Energy Authority
Dundee	Tayside Regional Council
Eday (Isle of)	Orkney Islands Council
Edinburgh	British Airport Authority
Errol	in private ownership
Fife (Glenrothes)	Fife Airport Management Ltd
Flotta	Occidental Petroleum (Caledonia)
Glasgow	British Airport Authority
Hoy (Longhope)	Orkney Islands Council
Inverness (Dalcross)	Highlands and Islands Airports Ltd
Islay (Port Ellen)	Highlands and Islands Airports Ltd
Kinloss	Royal Air Force
Kirkwall	Highlands and Islands Airports Ltd
Lerwick (Tingwall)	Shetland Islands Council
Leuchars (MEDA)	Royal Air Force
Lossiemouth	Royal Air Force
Machrihanish	Royal Air Force
Montrose	in private ownership
North Ronaldsay	Orkney Islands Council
Oban (North Connel)	Strathclyde Regional Council
Papa Westray	Orkney Islands Council

continued

Airports – continued

	operated by
Prestwick	British Airport Authority
Strathallan	in private ownership
Tiree	Highlands and Islands Airports Ltd
Westray	Orkney Islands Council
Wick	Highlands and Islands Airports Ltd

Top Ten Paying Visitor Attractions (1989)

Edinburgh Castle	1 078 120
Magnum Leisure Centre, Irvine	800 253
Perth Leisure Pool	704 000
Edinburgh Zoo	542 020
Aquatic Ice Age/Water Complex, Motherwell	499 500
Culzean Castle/Country Park, Maybole	365 679
Loch Ness Monster Exhibition	350 000
Palace of Holyroodhouse, Edinburgh	316 679
Old Blacksmith's Shop Visitor Centre, Gretna Green	300 000
Stirling Castle	264 734

Top Ten Free Visitor Attractions (1990)

Glasgow Museum and Art Gallery	1 008 180
Burrell Collection, Glasgow	878 772
Royal Botanic Garden, Edinburgh	785 591
Museum of Transport, Glasgow	535 938
Royal Museum of Scotland, Edinburgh	508 299
City Art Centre, Edinburgh	484 697
People's Palace Museum, Glasgow	466 695
Glasgow Botanic Garden	350 000
Aberdeen Art Gallery	346 757
Scottish United Services Museum, Edinburgh	309 940

Visitors by Country of Origin (1989)

	trips 000
United States	339
West Germany	155
Canada	113
Irish Republic	110
Australia	102
France	94
Italy	71
Netherlands	54
Spain	40
Belgium/Luxembourg	35
Norway	27
Japan	22
Switzerland	21
New Zealand	21

Tourism as percentage of Scotland's gross domestic product (1990) – 5% (£1.44 billion)
Scotland's largest industry (1990) – tourism

RELIGION

Denominations

Church of Scotland	822 985 (1987)
Roman Catholic	793 620 (1988)
Scottish Episcopal	59 940 (1987)
Muslim	20 000 (1988)
Evangelical	17 800 (1984)
Baptist	16 000 (1988)
Congregational	14 257 (1988)
Conservative Presbyterian	12 250 (1988)
United Free	8 636 (1988)
Methodist	7 035 (1988)
Salvation Army	5 300 (1988)
Hebrew	4 200 (1988)
Quakers	550 (1988)
United Reform	500 (1988)
Hindus	(n/a)
Sikhs	(n/a)
Buddhists	(n/a)

IMMIGRATION (1981)

(by country of birth)

Old Commonwealth	15 292
New Commonwealth	
East Africa	4 408
Rest of Africa	3 603
Caribbean	1 547
India	9 097
Bangladesh	646
Far East	9 116
Mediterranean	3 127
Remainder	979
Pakistan	6 459
Other countries in Europe	9 816
Other countries in EC	20 810
Other foreign countries	28 299

LEGAL SYSTEM

Courts

High Court of Justiciary – final court on criminal matters: Lord Justice-General; Lord Justice-Clerk; Lords Commissioners

Court of Session – supreme court in Scotland for civil matters: Senators of the College of Justice/Lords of Council and Session (Inner House – 1st Division/2nd Division; Outer House)

House of Lords – final appelate court for civil matters

Sheriff Courts – criminal/civil jurisdiction (sentences limited to three years)

Other courts
Registration of Voters Appeal
Lands Valuation Appeal
Restrictive Practices
Court of the Lord Lyon King of Arms
Church Courts (eg General Assembly, Synods)
Licensing Boards

Verdicts – Guilty, Not Guilty, Not Proven.

Lawyers

Lawyers – Solicitors (6921 practising 1989) Advocates (266 practising 1990) advise, draft writs and appear in supreme court

First British judge appointed to European Court of Justice – Lord Mackenzie Stuart (1973)

First Scottish lawyer to pass New York Bar exams – solicitor Valerie Macadam (1990)

First free state legal aid – Act of James I (1424)

First women law professors in Scotland – Sheila McLean (Law and Ethics in Medicine), Glasgow University (1990); Noreen Burrows (European Law), Glasgow University (1990)

Largest law school in Scotland – Edinburgh University (837 students, 1990)

Case that changed the world – Mrs May Donohue, a Glasgow shop assistant, went to the Well Meadow Café, Paisley in 1928. She found a dead snail in her ginger beer and sued the manufacturer. The case (Donohue v Stevenson) became the foundation for the modern law of negligence

Only Scot to win an appeal in person before the House of Lords – teacher Jack Malloch (1971)

Crimes and Offences (1988)

Housebreaking	91 411
Theft (opening lockfast places)	77 503
Breach of the peace	55 900
Fraud	22 392
Drunk driving	11 353
Serious assault	7 694
Handling offensive weapons	4 487
Robbery	4 150
Fire-raising	3 657

Prisons

Prisons and their capacity – Aberdeen (151); Barlinnie (983); Cornton Vale (177); Dumfries (27); Dungavel (146); Edinburgh (547); Friarton (82); Glenochil (496); Inverness (87);

continued

Prisons and their capacity – continued

Low Moss (400); Noranside (115); Penninghame (400); Perth (519); Shotts (528)
Young offenders institutions and their capacity – Cornton Vale (41); Castle Huntly (114); Greenock (176); Polmont (408)
Detention centre and its capacity – Glenochil (182)
Prisoners (average daily populations, 1986) – persons on remand: 1107; adult prisoners: 3448; young offenders: 912

The Police

Police forces – Central; Dumfries and Galloway; Fife; Grampian; Lothian and Borders; Northern; Strathclyde; Tayside
Total police strength (1987) – 13 400

Public Disorder

Food riots (high food prices) – Edinburgh, 1784, 1800, 1812; Glasgow, 1800
Clearances – Kildonan (against sheep-farming), 1813
Mutiny – Perth, 1813. Last naval mutiny in British territorial waters (Invergordon: HMS Valiant, HMS Rodney), 1931
Scottish Militia Act (1797) Riots – Eccles, Berwickshire, Selkirk, Kirkcudbright, Stirling, Aberdeen, West Lothian, Tranent (massacre of 12 people)
Anti-Recruitment Riots – Uig, Lewis, 1793 Campbeltown, 1795 (against the Press Gang)
Industrial – handloom weavers strike, Glasgow, 1787; seamen, Aberdeen, 1792; navvies against townspeople, Pollockshaws, 1810
Political – Scottish Convention of Societies of Friends of the People, Edinburgh, 1792; George Square Riot, Glasgow 1919, 20 000 demonstrators ringed by armed troops

ADULT PARTICIPATION in ACTIVE SPORTS and GAMES (1986)

		%
Outdoor	walking/rambling/hiking	20.7
	athletics	4.0
	football	2.8
	golf	2.3
	cycling	1.5
	bowls	1.4
	swimming	1.3
	fishing	0.8
Indoor	billiards/snooker/pool	8.8
	darts	3.5
	keep fit/yoga	2.3
	badminton	0.9
	squash	0.9

SCHOOLS

State Schools (1989)

Type	Number	No Pupils 000
Nursery	612	40.9
Primary	2 386	433.2
Secondary	435	326.4
Special	349	9.3

Number of teachers (1984–85) – men: 18 516; women: 32 330
Independent schools (1989) – 121

Educational Landmarks

Oldest high school – Royal High School, Edinburgh (1128)
Oldest grammar school – Lanark Grammar School (mentioned in a Papal Bull of Pope Lucius III in 1183)
Education compulsory for sons of Scottish barons and freeholders – 1496
First Act requiring establishment of parish schools – Scotland (1696)

First school cookery class in Britain – Dumfries Burgh School (1753)

First art school to teach industrial design – The Trustees Academy, Edinburgh (1760)

First British deaf and dumb school – Thomas Braidwood's Academy for the Deaf and Dumb, Edinburgh (1765)

First books for the blind published in Britain – St John's Gospel in raised type produced by James Gall, Edinburgh (1834)

First state secondary school in Britain – burgh and parochial schools passed under control of School Boards under Scottish Education Act (1872)

First free state primary education in Britain – fees in Scottish board schools abolished for all pupils up to Standard V class

Highest school enrolment – 2317 (Our Lady's RC High School, Motherwell in 1977)

First regional council to ban corporal punishment in schools – Lothian Regional Council (1984)

School with most languages spoken by its pupils – Tollcross Primary, Edinburgh (16 nationalities)

HIGHER EDUCATION

Universities

	dates of foundation
St Andrews	1411
Glasgow	1451
Aberdeen	1495
Edinburgh	1583
Strathclyde	1796/1964
Heriot-Watt	1821/1966
Dundee	1881/1967
Stirling	1967

Full-time students (1987–8) – 41 579

Full-time post-graduates (1987–8) – 6 762

University staff (1987–8) – professors 636 others 3 859

The leading university in Britain for debate since 1953 – Glasgow

First Chair of Celtic in Scotland – Edinburgh (1882)

First Professor of Parapsychology in Britain – Dr Robert Morris, Edinburgh (1986)

First Chair of Microelectronics in Britain – Edinburgh (1980)

First American nun to be a Professor of Nursing in Britain – Professor Penny Prophit, Edinburgh (1983)

First university in Britain to offer degree courses in nursing – Edinburgh

Youngest professor – Colin MacLaurin (1698–1746), Professor of Maths at Marischal College, Aberdeen at the age of 19

Youngest undergraduate – William Thomson, Lord Kelvin (1824–1907) who entered Glasgow University at the age of ten

Further Education Students (1987–8)

	Advanced	Non-Advanced
Central institutions	31 679	19 668
Colleges of education	906	77
Local authority colleges	31 993	172 752

POPULATION (1988)

Total – 5 094 million
Male: 2 462.3
Female: 2 631.7

First statistical social survey – John Sinclair (1754–1835)

First census – Rev Alexander, Moderator of the General Assembly (1775)

Ten Most Populated Towns (1990)

Glasgow	765 000
Edinburgh	420 200
Aberdeen	190 450
Dundee	174 300
Paisley	84 900
East Kilbride	70 700
Greenock	59 000
Dunfermline	52 200
Kirkcaldy	52 000
Clydebank	51 850

Labour Force (1988)

	000
Services	1290
Production and construction	592
Education, health, other	449
Manufacturing	408
Wholesale distribution, hotel, catering	193
Public administration, defence	188
Retail distribution	180
Banking, insurance, finance	165
Construction	126
Transport and communication	115
Energy and water supply	58
Agriculture, forestry, fisheries	29

PARLIAMENTARY CONSTITUENCIES (1987)

	electorate
Aberdeen North	63 214
Aberdeen South	62 943
Angus East	61 060
Argyll and Bute	48 700
Ayr	66 450
Banff and Buchan	62 149
Caithness and Sutherland	31 279
Carrick Cumnock and Doon Valley	56 360
Clackmannan	49 083
Clydebank and Milngavie	50 152
Clydesdale	61 620
Cumbernauld and Kilsyth	45 427
Cunninghame North	54 817
Cunninghame South	49 842
Dumbarton	58 968
Dumfries	59 347
Dundee East	60 805
Dundee West	61 926
Dunfermline East	51 175
Dunfermline West	51 063
East Kilbride	63 097
East Lothian	65 046
Eastwood	61 872
Edinburgh Central	59 529
Edinburgh East	48 895
Edinburgh Leith	60 359
Edinburgh Pentlands	58 125
Edinburgh South	63 842
Edinburgh West	62 214
Falkirk East	52 564

Falkirk West	50 222
Fife Central	56 090
Fife North-East	52 266
Galloway and Upper Nithsdale	53 429
Glasgow Cathcart	49 307
Glasgow Central	51 137
Glasgow Garscadden	47 958
Glasgow Govan	50 616
Glasgow Hillhead	57 836
Glasgow Maryhill	52 371
Glasgow Pollok	51 396
Glasgow Provan	43 744
Glasgow Rutherglen	57 313
Glasgow Shettleston	53 604
Glasgow Springburn	51 563
Gordon	73 479
Greenock and Port Glasgow	57 756
Hamilton	62 205
Inverness, Nairn and Lochaber	66 743
Kilmarnock and Loudon	62 648
Kincardine and Deeside	63 587
Kirkcaldy	53 439
Linlithgow	59 542
Livingston	56 583
Midlothian	60 549
Monklands East	49 644
Monklands West	50 874
Moray	62 201
Motherwell North	57 632
Motherwell South	52 127
Orkney and Shetlands	31 047
Paisley North	49 487
Paisley South	51 127
Perth and Kinross	63 443
Renfrew West and Inverclyde	56 189
Ross, Cromarty and Skye	52 369
Roxburgh and Berwickshire	43 140
Stirling Central	57 836
Strathkelvin and Bearsden	62 676
Tayside North	53 985
Tweeddale, Ettrick and Lauderdale	37 875
Western Isles	23 507

Largest parliamentary constituency by area –
Ross, Cromarty and Skye (954 680 ha/
2 472 260 acres)

cottish Office
Jepartment of Agriculture and Fisheries
ndustry Department for Scotland
cottish Development Department
cottish Education Department
cottish Home and Health Department

EUROPEAN PARLIAMENT CONSTITUENCIES (1989)

	electorate
ilasgow	487 199
Iighlands and Islands	313 877
othians	523 506
cotland Mid and Fife	534 638
cotland North-East	554 408
cotland South	491 865
trathclyde East	494 274
trathclyde West	493 067

REGIONS

egional Councils

	Area (ha)	Population (1989–90)
orders	470 458	102 592
Central	263 609	272 077
Jumfries and Galloway	636 360	147 036
ife	130 708	344 590
irampian	870 400	502 863
Iighland	2 539 122	201 866
othian	175 509	743 700
trathclyde	1 385 716	231 600
ayside	750 318	393 748

Functions and Responsibilities of Regional Councils

Airports
Careers
Civil defence
Coast protection
Consumer
  protection
Diseases of
  animals
Education
Electoral
  registration
Ferries
Fire
Flood prevention
Harbours
Highways
Industrial
  development

Industrial
  promotion
Lighting
Police
Public transport
Registration of
  births, marriages
  and deaths
Roads and road
  safety
Social work
Strategic planning
Valuation and
  rating
Water and sewerage
Weights and
  measures

DISTRICTS

District Councils

	Area (ha)	Population (1989–90)
Aberdeen City	18 447	215 300
Angus	203 309	94 407
Annandale and Eskdale	155 342	35 945
Argyll and Bute	2 506	65 737
Badenoch and Strathspey	232 000	10 003
Banff and Buchan	152 634	83 174
Bearsden and Milngavie	3 647	40 365
Berwickshire	87 553	18 833
Caithness	177 576	27 098
Clackmannan	16 099	47 412
Clydebank	3 560	49 000
Clydesdale	132 505	58 436
Cumbernauld and Kilsyth	10 298	62 547
Cumnock and Doon Valley	80 105	43 107
Cunninghame	87 859	137 265

continued

District Councils – continued

	Area (ha)	Population (1989–90)
Dumbarton	47 703	76 937
Dundee City	23 504	175 748
Dunfermline	30 108	129 049
East Kilbride	27 738	81 750
East Lothian	68 117	82 821
Eastwood	11 563	57 185
Edinburgh City	26 524	438 232
Ettrick and Lauderdale	135 618	33 441
Falkirk	29 141	143 229
Glasgow City	19 778	715 621
Gordon	221 444	70 788
Hamilton	13 091	107 108
Inverclyde	15 779	96 382
Inverness	278 875	61 077
Kilmarnock and Loudon	37 813	81 200
Kincardine and Deeside	254 805	48 402
Kirkcaldy	24 835	147 963
Kyle and Carrick	132 156	113 081
Lochaber	446 830	19 369
Midlothian	35 803	81 440
Monklands	16 384	106 187
Moray	222 420	85 910
Motherwell	17 280	147 542
Nairn	42 194	10 310
Nithsdale	143 313	57 293
North-East Fife	75 982	66 720
Perth and Kinross	523 698	123 607
Renfrew	30 885	201 295
Ross and Cromarty	497 582	47 897
Roxburgh	154 048	35 060
Skye and Lochalsh	269 103	11 526
Stewarty	167 000	23 136
Stirling	216 989	81 436
Strathkelvin	16 706	89 475
Sutherland	586 578	13 199
Tweeddale	89 938	14 608
West Lothian	42 300	141 684
Wigtown	171 275	30 410

Functions and Responsibilities of District Councils

Administration of district courts
Allotments
Building control
Burial and cremation
Cleansing
Community centres
Conservation areas
Countryside development control
Employment of young persons
Environmental health
Food, hygiene, standards and labelling
Health and safety at work
Housing
Industrial development

Leisure and recreation
Libraries
Licensing of dogs, betting and gaming, theatres and cinemas, taxis and liquor
Listed buildings and ancient monuments
Local planning
Markets
Museums and art galleries
Nature conservation
Parks
Public conveniences
Refuse collection and disposal
Shop hours
Slaughterhouses
Tourism
Urban development
War memorials

Youngest chief executive in British local government – Rory Mair (33), Ross and Cromarty District Council (1990)
Youngest director of leisure in Scotland – Rory Mair (27), Clydesdale District Council (1984)
Only sitting Asian district councillor in Scotland – Mustaq Ahmad (Hamilton) (1991)

ISLANDS

Island Authorities

	Area (ha)	Population (1989–90)
Orkney	97 489	19 33
Shetland	140 800	22 91
Western Isles	289 758	31 04

Places to Visit

In the following chapter the reader will find a heterogeneous collection of castles, standing stones, museums, galleries, battlefields and nature reserves.

These are the focal points of Scottish culture where eyes are persuaded to see and ears to hear. They form a network for instruction and delight throughout the land.

NATURE RESERVES

Biggest nature reserve – Cairngorms National Nature Reserve (250 sq km/*97 sq miles*)
Only nature reserve in Scotland with 90 000 visitors a year – Loch Garten
First forest park in Britain – Argyll Forest Park (1935)
Britain's first nature reserve – Ben Eighe (1951)
Most visited part of Scotland – Spey Valley

Reserves to Which Access is Not Restricted and Permits Not Required

(Recommended visiting times given in brackets)

BORDERS
Duns Castle – (April–July) woodland, grassland and an artificial loch: tench, badger, red squirrel, otter
Lindean Reservoir – (April–August) reservoir, island, woodland: 200 flowering plants
Plora Wood – (spring/summer) ancient site, mixed woodland
St Abbs Head – (May–July) grassland, sea-cliffs: sea-bird colony – guillemot, kittiwake, razorbill, fulmar. Mire loch
Whitlaw Wood – (spring/summer) woodland valley: woodpecker, woodcock, sparrowhawk
Yetholm Loch – (no access in breeding season) marshland/loch: swan, geese, duck in winter

CENTRAL
Ben Lomond – (spring/summer) woodland, heathland, mountains: grouse, deer, wild goats
Ben Lui – (June–July) mountain (1200 m/ *3937 ft*) cliffs
Dollar Glen – (April–June) woodland glen: woodland birds
Gartmore Dam – (all year) reservoir, island, hide, visitor centre: wildfowl
Inversnaid – (spring/summer) heather moorland, woodland: black grouse
Loch Lomond – (May–July/October/ December) islands, marsh (largest freshwater lake in Britain: powan, salmon, sea and brown trout)

Mugdock Country Park – (all year) lake, grassland, moorland, woodland
Queen Elizabeth Forest Park – (April–October) six sites, David Marshall Lodge
Skinflats – (September–March) mudflats, foreshore: shelduck
West Highland Way – (all year) woodland, moor, mountain

DUMFRIES AND GALLOWAY
Caerlaverock – (October–March) saltmarsh (merse), foreshore: geese, toads
Carstramon Wood – (spring/summer/autumn) ancient woodland
Castle and Hightae Lochs – (January–March) reedbeds, woodland, lochs
Eastgate – (October–March) farmland, saltmarsh: wildfowl (hides)
Fountainbleau and Ladypark – damp woodland: fungi, mosses, water vole
Galloway Forest Park – (all year) eight sites, museum, trail guides
Grey Mare's Tail – (April–August) heath, cliffs, loch, waterfall
Mull of Galloway – (May–July) sea-cliffs (87 m/*285 ft*): sea-bird colony
Plantain Loch – (July–September) dragonflies
Southwick Coast – (all year) fen, woodland: geese in winter
Stenhouse Wood – (spring/summer/autumn)
Threave Wildfowl Refuge – (November–March) wildfowl (hide)
Wood of Cree – (spring/summer) woodland, marsh, moor: owls, buzzards

FIFE
Eden Estuary – (April–June/August–May) sandbanks, mudflats: waders, eider
Firth of Tay – (April–June/August–May) sandbanks, mudflats: geese, seals
Isle of May – (April–October) island with cliffs: bird colony
Kilminning Coast – (spring/summer/autumn) raised beach, scrub
Lochore Meadows – (all year) deer, otters, coot, mallard
Long Craig Island – (spring/summer) nesting terns
Morton Lochs – (April–June/August–January) lochs, marsh, woodland

GRAMPIAN

Den Country Park – (all year) woodland, river, lake

Balmedie Country Park – (all year) beach, dunes, grassland

Bennachie – (all year) forest, moorland: ferns, lichens, fungi

Crathes – (all year) woodland

Culbin Forest – (April–August) plantation: capercailzie, owl, woodpecker

Darnaway – (summer) deciduous and conifer trees

Dinnet Oakwood – (May–June) jay, wood warbler

Drum – (April–July) forest: beech, oak, Scots pine, yew, rhododendron

Fowlsheugh – (May–July) cliff: sea-bird colony

Glenmuick and Lochnagar – (May–September/ November) mountainous, lochs: golden eagle, peregrine, deer (visitor centre)

Haddo Country Park – (spring/summer/ autumn) visitor centre

Leith Hall – (May–August) moor, farmland, woodland (hide)

Longhaven Cliffs – (May–July) cliffs by coast

Middle Deeside – (all year) 17 sites

Muir of Dinnet – (May–July/October– December) bog, moor, woodland, lochs

Speyside Way – (all year) walk by River Spey

White Cow and Loudon Wood – (all year) spruce trees; badgers, herons

HIGHLAND NORTH

Achmelvich – (spring/summer) beach, dunes, grassland

Allt nan Carnan – (April–June) 1.6 km/*1 mile* gorge, (to 30 m/*98 ft* in depth); rich flora

Ben Mor Coigach – (May–July) islets, coast, moorland, mountain: ptarmigan

Clachtoll – (spring/summer) beach, dunes, grassland

Corrieshalloch Gorge – (April–September) 1.6 km/*1 mile* gorge 60 m/*197 ft* at deepest

Creag Meagaidh – (all year) loch, mountain: osprey, golden eagle, falcons

Handa – (May–July) island: vertical cliffs, lochans, underground streams

Inveraver – (May–July) seashore, dunes, moorland

Rassal Ashwood – (April–June) heath, grassland: woodland flowers

Raven Rock – (all year) steep gorge

Tollie Path – (all year) conifers and hill

HIGHLAND SOUTH

Abernethy Forest – (all year) moorland, mountain, pine forest

Balmacaan Woods – (spring/summer) woodland, high above Loch Ness

Balmacara – (all year) islands, lochs, woodland, visitor centre

Cairn Gorm – (all year) mountains

Cairngorms – (April–August) forest, moors, mountains (largest reserve in Britain, 25 949 ha/*100 sq miles*)

Craigellachie – (May–August) cliff, moors, woods: insects

Culbin Sands – (September–March/May– August) saltmarsh, shingle

Falls of Glomach – (all year) 120 m/*394 ft* drop

Glen Affric – (April–October) pinewood

Glencoe – (all year) mountains, visitor centre

Glenmore Forest Park – (April–September) loch, heather, woodland

Glen Nevis – (all year) golden eagle

Glen Roy – (all year) 'parallel roads'

Insh Marshes – (April–July) marsh, woodland, flood-plain of River Spey

Kintail – (all year)

Loch Garten – (April–August) forest, lochs, moors: wildfowl (hide)

Pass of Ryvoan – (April–July) narrow pass: pinewood, loose scree

Rock Wood Ponds – (all year) bog, lochans, forest

Rothiemurchus – (all year), pinewood, lochs, visitor centre

Spey Valley – nine sites (most visited part of Scotland)

LOTHIAN

Aberlady Bay – (April–July/September– March) mudflats, saltings, dunes

Addiewell Bing – (spring/summer/autumn) former oil-shale spoil bing

Bass Rock – (May–July) island with high cliffs: 9000 pairs of gannets

Duddingston Loch – (October–March) wintering pochard

continued

East Lothian Coast – (all year) 11 sites
Erraid Wood – (spring/summer) used for educational purposes
Forth Islands (Fidra/ Eyebroughty) – (May–July) island flowers, birds, sea life
John Muir Country Park – (May–June/ September–March) dunes, beach, cliffs
Woodhall Dean – (spring/summer/autumn) woodland

ORKNEY
Birsay Moors and Cottasgarth – (May–August) moors: kestrels, voles
The Loons – (spring/summer) peat-cutting holes: ducks
Marwick Head – (May–July) cliffs
North Hoy – moor, cliffs, lochs
Noup Cliffs, Westray – (May–July) cliffs: sea-birds

SHETLAND
Fair Isle – May/September/October) migration station
Foula – (May–July) island with high cliffs: skuas
Haaf Gruney – (May–July) seals
Keen of Hamar – (May–June) mountain and maritime plants
Loch Spiggie – (October–November/March–April) loch, mountain
Lumbister (Island of Yell) – (May–July) moors, lochans, cliffs
Mousa – (May–July) island with Pictish broch and breeding birds
Noss – (May–July) sea-birds

SKYE
Canna – (spring/summer) island, cliffs, beaches
Corry Walk – (all year) along shore
Eigg – (May–July) woodland, lochans, ravines
Tokavaig Wood – (May–June) mixed woodland

STRATHCLYDE NORTH
Ardmore Point – (April–July/September–March) mudflats, moorland, foreshore
Argyll Forest Park – (all year) recreational facilities
Burg, Mull – (all year) 50-million-year-old fossil tree (McCulloch's tree)

Carradale Forest – (all year) sika and fallow deer
Fairy Isles – (spring/summer) six islands in Loch Sween, woodland
Inverliever – (all year) heather and hill
Loch Gruinart, Islay – (autumn/winter/spring) saltmarsh, moor, farmland

STRATHCLYDE SOUTH
Ayr Gorge Woodland – (spring/summer) woodland, valley: insects
Barons Haugh – (all year) marshes, woodland, parkland
Braehead Moss – (all year) very wet bogland
Brodick Country Park, Arran – (April–August) guided walks, nature trail
Clyde Islands – (all year) 16 sites
Clyde Valley Woodlands – (April–July) woodland cover
Culzean Country Park – (May–September) visitor centre, guided walks
Falls of Clyde – (April–July) gorge, woodland, visitor centre
Goatfell, Arran – (all year) woodland, mountains, guided walks
Lochwinnoch – (April–June/October–March) marsh, woodland, loch
Nethan Gorge – (spring/summer) woodland gorge
Possil Park – (all year) loch, marsh
Shewalton Sandpits – (spring/summer/ autumn) lagoon, marsh
Upper Nethan Gorge – (spring/summer/ autumn) woodland

TAYSIDE
Atholl – (all year) 12 sites
Ballinluig Shingle Islands – (spring/summer) islands, river
Brighty Wood – (spring/summer) woodland
Caenlochan – (April–May) plateaux, corries
Clatto Country Park – (summer) reservoir
Crombie Country Park – (summer/winter) woodland, reservoir
Hermitage – (April–October) falls, woodland, gorge
Linn of Tummel – (April–October) river banks, woods
Loch of Kinnordy – (April–June/October–November) loch, marsh: birds (hide)
Loch Leven – (September–March/April–August) loch: wildfowl

Monikie Country Park – reservoirs, woodland, grassland

Pass of Killiekrankie – (April–October) woods, gorge, visitor centre

Rannoch Moor – (April–July) moor, lochs, bog

Seaton Cliffs – (May–August) cliffs, nature trail

Stormont Loch – (autumn/winter/spring) two lochs, fen, scrub

Tummel Forest – (all year) lochs, woods, visitor centre, guided walks

WESTERN ISLES

Balranald, North Uist – (April–September) marsh, coast: butterflies

Forestry Commission Public Recreational Facilities (1989)

Forest walks/nature trails	246
Picnic places	185
Forest cabins/holiday houses	71
Camping and caravan sites	10
Visitor centres	8
Arboreta	4
Forest drives	2

Land of the National Trust

Balmacara Estate, Lochalsh – 2246 ha/ *5616 acres* of Kyle/Plockton peninsula

Ben Lawers, near Killin – 1214 m/*3984 ft*, national nature reserve

Ben Lomond, near Drymen – 973 m/*3194 ft*

Blackhill, Lanark – cairn, Iron Age fort looking over Clyde Valley

Branklyn Garden, Perth – finest 8000 sq m/ *2 acres* of private garden in Scotland

Goatfell, Isle of Arran – 873 m/*2866 ft* mountain with 2641 ha/*6603 acres*

Burg, Island of Mull – 464 m/*1525ft* with high cliffs: 'The Wilderness'

Castlehill, Dumbarton – 1.6 ha/*4 acres*

Corrieshalloch Gorge, Braemore – national nature reserve 1.6 km/*1 mile*-long gorge 61 m/*200 ft* deep

Craigower, Pitlochry – 4 ha/*11 acre* beacon hill

Culloden, Inverness – site of defeat of Jacobites in 1746

Dollar Glen, Dollar – 24 ha/*60 acres* of wooded glen

Falls of Glomach, near Kyle of Lochalsh – 120 m/*394 ft* waterfall

Glencoe and Dalness, Lochaber – 5680 ha/ *14 200 acres* of mountain

Greenbank Garden, Glasgow – 1 ha/*2.5 acres* of walled garden and 5 ha/*13 acres* of policies

Grey Mare's Tail, near Moffat – 61 m/*200 ft* waterfall

Hermitage, near Dunkeld – mixed conifer and deciduous woods with 1758 folly

Inveresk Lodge Garden, near Musselburgh – 17th-century house garden

Inverewe Garden, Poolewe – exotic plants

Killiecrankie, near Pitlochry – site of battle of 1689

Kintail and Morvich, near Kyle of Lochalsh – 6969 ha/*17 422 acres* with Five Sisters of Kintail

Linn of Tummel, near Pitlochry – 19 ha/ *47 acres* beside Rivers Tummel and Garry

Malleny Garden, Balerno – 17th-century house/garden

Parklea Farm, near Port Glasgow – 27 ha/ *68 acres* of recreation ground

Pitmedden Garden, near Pitmedden – Great Garden of 1675

Rockcliffe, near Dalbeattie – two 8 ha/*20 acre* sites, one a bird sanctuary

St Abb's Head, near Coldingham – 77 ha/ *192 acres* national nature reserve

St Kilda, Western Isles – national nature reserve 177 km/**110 miles** into the Atlantic

Shieldaig Island, Loch Torridon – 13 ha/ *32 acres*, largely pinewoods

Staffa, Argyll – island 0.8 km/*0.5 mile* long by 0.4 km/*0.25 mile* wide

Threave Garden, near Castle Douglas – 200 varieties of daffodil

Torridon, near Kinlochewe – 6440 ha/ *16 100 acre* estate with fine mountain scenery

Venniehill, Gatehouse-of-Fleet – 1.4 ha/*3.5 acre* field with viewpoint

GARDENS

Gardens Open to the Public With Over 10 000 Visitors (1988)

Royal Botanic Garden, Edinburgh	756 405
Glasgow Botanic Garden	300 000
Inverewe, Gairloch	132 745
Threave, Castle Douglas	51 983
Younger Botanic Garden, Dunoon	44 539
Logan Botanic Garden, Stranraer	35 366
Priorwood, Melrose	34 440
Pitmedden, Pitmedden	25 548
Greenbank, Glasgow	16 615
The Hirsel, Coldstream	16 456
Castle Kennedy, Stranraer	15 000
Branklyn, Perth	14 872
Crarae, Argyll	12 687

OBSERVATORIES

Airdrie Library Observatory
Coats Observatory – Paisley: seismic equipment; satellite weather receiver
Dumfries Museum Observatory
Eskdalemuir Observatory – atmospheric pollution
Glasgow University Observatory
Mills Observatory – Dundee: 10 inch Cooke refracting telescope
Robert Gordon's College Observatory – Aberdeen
Royal Observatory – Blackford Hill, Edinburgh: visitor centre
Royal Observatory – Calton Hill, Edinburgh: The Edinburgh Experience (seasonal)
St Andrews University Observatory
Stirling High School Observatory

Planetaria

Aberdeen Technical College Planetarium
Glasgow Nautical College Planetarium
Jewel and Esk Valley College Planetarium, Edinburgh
Paisley College of Technology Planetarium

ZOO

Edinburgh Zoo – Scotland's largest animal collection (2000): biggest penguin colony in Europe; only gorillas in Scotland; only successful polar bear (1988) and cheetah (1990) births in captivity in Britain

AQUARIA

Loch Faskally Dam (Pitlochry) – fish ladder with observation point
Millport Marine Biology Station
Oban Sea Life Centre – octopus, conger eels
Robertson Aquarium (Millport)
St Andrews Sea Life Centre – sharks, seals

LISTED and HISTORIC BUILDINGS

BORDERS
Edin's Hall Broch – Iron Age
Foulden Tithe Barn – two-storeyed barn

NATIONAL TRUST PROPERTIES
Priorwood Garden, Melrose – specializes in flowers grown for drying
Robert Smail's Printing Works, Innerleithen – Victorian printing works in working order
Turret House, Kelso – houses Kelso Museum

PRIVATE PROPERTIES
Abbotsford House, Melrose – home of Sir Walter Scott and largely designed by him (1817–24)
Bowhill, near Selkirk – seat of the Dukes of Buccleuch (1795)
Manderston, Duns – built by Sir James Miller, a wealthy merchant
Mellerstain, Gordon – begun by William Adam, completed by Robert Adam (1770–8)
Traquair House, Innerleithen – one of oldest inhabited houses

PRIVATE PROPERTIES SEEN BY APPOINTMENT ONLY
Old Gala House, Galashiels
Sir Walter Scott's Courtroom, Selkirk
Wedderlie House, Gordon

CENTRAL
Menteil House – 15th-century tower
Stirling: Argyll Lodging – 17th-century
mansion
　King's Knot – remains of formal garden
　Mar's Wark – 16th-century mansion
　Old Bridge – 15th century
Westquarter Dovecot – 17th-century
rectangular structure

NATIONAL TRUST PROPERTIES
The Pineapple, near Stirling – 14 m/*45 ft* high
garden retreat (1761)
Cunninghame Graham Memorial, near Aberfoyle
– cairn in memory of author R.B.
Cunninghame Graham (1937)
PRIVATE PROPERTIES SEEN BY APPOINTMENT ONLY
Gargunnock House by Stirling
Old Tolbooth Building, Stirling
Touch House by Stirling

DUMFRIES and GALLOWAY
New Abbey Corn Mill – water-powered
Wanlockhead Beam Engine – 19th-century lead
mining pump

NATIONAL TRUST PROPERTIES
Carlyle's Birthplace, Ecclefechan, Annandale –
birthplace of Thomas Carlyle, historian
and essayist (1795–1881)

PRIVATE PROPERTIES
Barnsalloch House, Kirton
Craigdarroch House, Moniaive – built by
William Adam (1729)
Kirkconnell House, near Dumfries
Tolbooth, Sanquhar

FIFE
Scotstarvit Tower – 16th-century home of Sir
John Scot
West Port, St Andrews – 16th-century city
gate

NATIONAL TRUST PROPERTIES
Culross – royal burgh 16th–17th centuries
Culross Palace – 16th-century mansion
Falkland Palace, Garden and Old Burgh –
country residence of the Stewart kings
and queens (1501–41)
Hill of Tarvit Mansionhouse, near Cupar – 200
ha/*500 acres* of garden and grounds

GRAMPIAN
Culsh Earth-House – Iron Age underground
passage
Dallas Dhu Distillery – 1899 malt whisky
supplier
Duff House – Georgian mansion
Peel Ring of Lumphanan – 13th-century
fortification

NATIONAL TRUST PROPERTIES
Haddo House, near Pitmedden – by William
Adam for the 2nd Earl of Aberdeen
Leith Hall, near Kennethmont – Leith family
house and estate
Provost Ross's House, Aberdeen – home of
Aberdeen Maritime Museum

PRIVATE PROPERTIES
Fasque, Fettercairn
James Dun's House, 61 Schoolhill

PRIVATE PROPERTIES SEEN BY APPOINTMENT ONLY
Balbithan House, Kintore
Corsindae House, Sauchen
Gordonstoun School, Elgin
Grandhome House, near Aberdeen
Kintore Town House, Kintore
Phesdo House, Laurencekirk

HIGHLAND
Carn Liath, Golspie – broch
Dun Beag Broch, Skye – occupied to 18th
century
Dun Dornaigil Broch – 7 m/*22 ft* high
Glenelg Brochs – two broch towers

NATIONAL TRUST PROPERTIES
Abertarff House, Inverness – 16th century;
Trust's Highland HQ
Boath Doocot, Nairn – 17th century

continued

Hugh Miller's Cottage, Cromarty – birthplace
of geologist and writer (1802–56) (built c
1711)

PRIVATE PROPERTIES
Ardtorinsh, Lochaline, Morvern

PRIVATE PROPERTIES SEEN BY APPOINTMENT ONLY
Embo House, Dornock

LOTHIAN
Doonhill Homestead – Anglian chief's
wooden hall site
Dunglass Collegiate Church – 15th century
Corstorphine Dovecot, Edinburgh – beehive
'doocot' with nesting-boxes
Linlithgow Palace – famous royal palace,
birthplace of James V and Mary, Queen
of Scots
Ormiston Market Cross – 15th century
Preston Market Cross – 17th century with
unicorn

NATIONAL TRUST PROPERTIES
Georgian House and Charlotte Square, Edinburgh
– finest example of New Town
architecture by Robert Adam
Gladstone's Land, Edinburgh – typical 17th-
century tenement
Hamilton House, Prestonpans – built by John
Hamilton
House of the Binns, West Lothian – home of
the Dalyell family
Lamb's House, Leith – late 16th-century
house and warehouse
Preston Mill and Phantassie Doocot, East Linton
– 16th-century water-mill

PRIVATE PROPERTIES
Amisfield Mains, near Haddington
Beanston, near Haddington
Dalmeny House, South Queensferry – home of
the Earls of Rosebery, designed by
William Wilkins
Gosford House, East Lothian – 18th-century
house partly by Robert Adam
Holyrood Palace – Scotland's premier royal
palace (c 1500)

Hopetoun House, South Queensferry – mansion
begun by Sir William Bruce and
completed by William and Robert Adam
Lennoxlove, Haddington – seat of the Duke of
Hamilton
Stevenson House, Haddington – dating from
16th and 18th centuries
Winton House, Pencaitland – 15th century
with 19th-century additions

PRIVATE PROPERTIES SEEN BY APPOINTMENT ONLY
Arniston House, Gorebridge
Cakemuir, Tynehead
Ford House, Ford
108–110 Grassmarket, Edinburgh
Linn House, near Livingston
Newbattle Abbey College, Dalkeith
Peffermill House, Edinburgh
Penicuik House, Penicuik
Preston Hall, Pathhead
Tolbooth, South Queensferry
Town House, Haddington

ORKNEY
Birsay, Brough of – 12th-century Norse
village and church
Bishop's and Earl's Palaces – 12th-century
hall-house
Click Mill, Dounby – horizontal water mill
Earl's Palace, Birsay – 16th century with
courtyard
Grain Earth-House – Iron Age
Gurness, broch of – with many Iron Age
buildings
Knap of Howar – one of oldest remaining
stone houses in Europe
Maes Howe Chambered Cairn – finest
megalithic tomb in Britain
Martello Tower, Hackness – built 1813–15
with 24-pounder canon
Midhowe Broch – in good condition
Orphir: Earl's Bu – perhaps Viking Earl's
palace
Rennibister Earth-House
Skara Brae Settlement – Stone Age village

SHETLAND
Clickhimin Broch – tower with Iron Age
outbuildings
Jarlshof Settlement – 12 000 sq m/*3 acre* site
with Bronze Age village, Iron Age broch

Mousa Broch – 12 m/*40 ft* broch tower
Ness of Burgi – Iron Age stone blockhouse

PRIVATE PROPERTIES
The Lodberrie, Lerwick

STRATHCLYDE
Biggar Gas Works – oldest surviving coal-gas
  works (1839)
Kilpatrick, dun – drystone homestead

NATIONAL TRUST PROPERTIES
Bachelors' Club, Tarbolton – 17th-century
  thatched house where Burns debated
Hill House, Helensburgh – designed by
  Charles Rennie Mackintosh (1902-4)
Hutchesons' Hall, Glasgow – designed by
  David Hamilton (1802-5)
Provan Hall, Easterhouse – 15th century; most
  perfect pre-Reformation mansion in
  Scotland
Souter Johnnie's Cottage, Kirkoswald – home
  of character from Burns's 'Tam o'
  Shanter'
Tenement House, Glasgow – turn-of-the-
  century tenement living (1892)
Weaver's Cottage, Kilbarchan – 18th-century
  handloom weaver's cottage

PRIVATE PROPERTIES
Finlayson House, Langbank
Pollok House, Glasgow – mansion built by
  William Adam (1752)

PRIVATE PROPERTIES SEEN BY APPOINTMENT ONLY
New Lanark, Caithness Row
Place of Paisley, Paisley
Langy Mill, near Campbeltown
Tannahill's Cottage, Paisley

TAYSIDE
Ardestie Earth-House – 24 m/*80 ft* Iron Age
  underground gallery
Carlungie Earth-House – 46 m/*150 ft*
  underground Iron Age structure
Tealing Dovecot – 16th century
Tealing Earth-House – Iron Age underground
  passage

NATIONAL TRUST PROPERTIES
Angus Folk Museum, Kirkwynd Cottages –
  farming implements, Bothy Exhibition
Barrie's Birthplace, Kirriemuir, Angus –
  birthplace of J.M. Barrie, author of **Peter
  Pan**
Branklyn Garden, Perth – finest 8000 sq m/*2
  acres* of private garden in Scotland
Dunkeld – 20 houses in Cathedral and High
  Streets
House of Dun, near Montrose – Palladian villa
  by William Adam
Killiecrankie, near Pitlochry – near site of
  battle, Soldier's Leap (1689)

PRIVATE PROPERTIES
Scone Palace, Perth – where all the early
  Scottish kings were crowned

PRIVATE PROPERTIES SEEN BY APPOINTMENT ONLY
Craig House, Montrose
Michael Bruce's Cottage, Kinnesswood

WESTERN ISLES
Black House, Arnol – Lewis thatched cottage
Dun Carloway Broch – well-preserved broch
  tower

Listed Buildings – 36 635
    Category A Building of national interest
                or importance   2 661
             B Building primarily of local
                importance   22 978
             C Good buildings which retain
                elements of interest 10 823
Historic Scotland – monuments in the care
  of, 330

MUSEUMS, GALLERIES and VISITOR CENTRES

General Local Museums

BORDERS
Castle Jail, Jedburgh – 19th-century prison
  exhibition
Coldstream Museum, Coldstream – local
  history

continued

General Local Museums – continued

BORDERS – continued
Galashiels Museum, Galashiels – history of the woollen mill industry
Halliwell's House Museum, Selkirk – ironmongery and local history
Hawick Museum, Hawick – history of knitwear and hosiery and local life
Kelso Museum, Kelso – Kelso and district displays
Tweeddale Museum, Peebles – local history

CENTRAL
Alloa Museum, Alloa – local history
Bannockburn Heritage Centre, Stirling – battlefield (1314) interpretation
Bo'ness Heritage Area, Bo'ness – industrial heritage: maritime/mining
Dollar Museum, Dollar – Provost's regalia
Dunblane Cathedral Museum, Dunblane – local history
Falkirk Museum, Falkirk – local history
Grangemouth Museum, Grangemouth – history of canal and petro-chemical
Kinneil Museum, Bo'ness – pottery and local history from Roman times
Smith Museum, Stirling – local history

DUMFRIES AND GALLOWAY
Castle of St John, Stranraer – history of the castle
Dalbeattie Museum, Dalbeattie – local history
Dumfries Museum, Dumfries – minerals, birds, pre-history, carved stones
Moffat Museum, Moffat – local history of spa town
Museum, Newton Stewart – local history, Victorian nursery
Old Bridge House, Dumfries – 19th-century kitchen, nursery and dental laboratory
Sanquhar Museum, Sanquhar – local history
Stewarty Museum, Kirkcudbright – fire-arms, uniforms, natural history
Stranraer Museum, Stranraer – local history
Wigtown Museum, Wigtown – local history

FIFE
Burntisland Museum, Burntisland – walk through an Edwardian fair
Crail Museum, Crail – local history
Dunfermline District Museum, Dunfermline – linen damask and local history
Fife Folk Museum, Ceres – trades, costumes and cottar's living-room
Inverkeithing Museum, Inverkeithing – naval/nautical displays
Kirkcaldy Museum, Kirkcaldy – local history
Leven Museum, Leven – local history
Laing Museum, Newburgh – Victorian Scotland
Pittencrieff House Museum, Dunfermline – costume collection
St Andrews Preservation Trust Museum, St Andrews – 19th-century shops
Town House, Culross – 17th-century architecture
Wemyss Environmental Education Centre, East Wemyss

GRAMPIAN
Alford-Donside Heritage Centre, Alford – local history
Arbuthnot Museum, Peterhead – local history
Banchory Museum, Banchory – local history
Banff Museum, Banff – local history, scientific instruments
Blairs College Museum, Aberdeen – Mary Queen of Scots, vestments
Brander Museum, Huntly – local history
Dufftown Museum, Dufftown – local history
Elgin Museum, Elgin – local history
Falconer Museum, Forres – local history
Natural History Museum, Aberdeen – vertebrates, invertebrates
Tolbooth Museum, Stonehaven – local history
Tomintoul Visitor Centre, Tomintoul – farm-house kitchen, peat-cutting, wildlife

HIGHLAND
Cnoc an T-Sithein Museum, Staffin, Isle of Skye – fossils, arrowheads
Colbost Folk Musuem, Colbost, Isle of Skye – black house museum
Cromarty Courthouse, Cromarty – local history
Culloden Visitor Centre, Culloden Moor – relics, audiovisual display
Dingwall Museum, Dingwall – local history
Dunnet Pavilion, Dunnet Bay – natural history and geology

Gairloch Heritage Museum, Gairloch – folk museum

Groam House Museum, Rosemarkie – Pictish Centre

Highland Folk Museum, Kingussie – click mill, black house, kailyard

Inverness Museum, Inverness – local history, Highland silver, taxidermist's workshop

Landmark, Carrbridge – audiovisual exhibition, pine woods walk

Lochbroom Highland Museum, Ullapool – Wester Ross local history

Loch Ness Monster Exhibition, Drumnadrochit – multi-media display

Luib Folk Museum, Luib, Isle of Skye – 20th-century Skye life

Nairn Literary Institute Museum, Nairn – ethnographic collection

Skye Museum of Island Life, Portree, Isle of Skye – crofting life

Timespan, Helmsdale – audiovisual Highland experience

Thurso Heritage Museum, Thurso – carved stones, fossils, flagstone

West Highland Museum, Fort William – local history, Jacobite relics

Wick Heritage Centre, Wick – local history, fish-kiln, lighthouse

LOTHIAN

Almond Valley Heritage Centre, Livingston – 18th-century farm steading

Edinburgh
Royal Museum of Scotland
Chambers Street – ethnography, decorative arts, natural sciences, technology
Queen Street – Scottish pre-history, Romans, medieval, 18th century
Holyrood Park Visitor Centre – flora, fauna, history of the park
Huntly House Museum – local history collections including Field Marshall Earl Haig
Lady Stair's House – important collections on R.L. Stevenson, Sir Walter Scott and Robert Burns
Museum of Childhood – the history of childhood paraphernalia
People's Story – popular life recreated with sounds and smells

Queensferry Museum, South Queensferry – Forth Bridges and civic life

ORKNEY

Stromness Museum, Stromness – local history

SHETLAND

George Waterson Memorial Centre, Fair Isle – local history

Old Haa, Yell – local history

Shetland Museum, Lerwick – ship models, textiles, archaelogy

Scalloway Museum, Scalloway – the 'Shetland Bus', fishing

STRATHCLYDE

Auchindrain Museum of Country Life, Inveraray – life in the Highlands

Auld Kirk Museum, Kirkintilloch – local history

Baird Institute Museum, Cumnock – local history, pottery

Barony Chambers Museum, Kirkintilloch – local history, ('single end' life)

Burgh of Irvine Museum, Irvine – local history

Campbeltown Museum, Campbeltown – local history

Cathcart Visitor Centre, Dalmellington – 18th-century weaving

Clydebank District Museum, Clydebank – shipbuilders and sewing machines

Colzium Museum, Kilsyth – Battle of Kilsyth and local history

Dick Institute, Kilmarnock – shells, guns, archaeology

Gladstone Court Museum, Biggar – a 19th-century street with shops

Glenfinnan Visitor Centre, Glenfinnan – Jacobite memorial

Greenhill Covenanters House, Biggar – the Covenanters

Haggs Castle, Glasgow – Victorian nursery, 16th-century kitchen, 17th-century bedroom

Hamilton District Museum, Hamilton – local history and local crafts

Hunterian Museum, Glasgow – pre-history, Roman, Pacific ethnography

Inveraray Jail, Inveraray – 19th-century prison with smells and sounds

Iona Abbey Museum, Iona – Celtic stone crosses

Isle of Arran Heritage Museum, Brodick – local history, rural crafts

John Hastie Museum, Strathaven – local history with porcelain and pottery

continued

General Local Museums – continued

STRATHCLYDE – continued
Kelvingrove Museum, Glasgow – armour, geology, wildlife
Kilmaurs Historical Society Museum, Kilmaurs – local history
Kilsyth's Heritage Museum, Kilsyth – local history
Lochwinnoch Community Museum, Lochwinnoch – local history
McCaig Museum, Oban – local history
McKechnie Institute, Girvan – local history, underwater archaeology
McLean Museum, Greenock – local history
Moat Park Heritage Centre, Biggar – geology, embroidery, the Albion Motors Archive
Mull Museum, Tobermory, Isle of Mull – local history
Museum of Islay Life, Isle of Islay – whisky-making, Victorian life
Museum of the Cumbraes, Millport – local history
North Ayrshire Museum, Saltcoats – local history
People's Palace Museum, Glasgow – social history and public art
Provand's Lordship, Glasgow – period rooms (16th to 20th centuries)
Roberton Museum, Millport – fisheries and science
Rutherglen Museum, Rutherglen – history of the burgh
Springburn Museum, Glasgow – community life past and present
Stewarton and District Museum, Stewarton – local history
Summerlee Heritage Park, Coatbridge – electric tram, canal, ironworks
The Old Byre Heritage/Visitor Centre, Isle of Mull – local history
Weaver's Cottage, Kilbarchan – 18th-century life with weaving equipment
Winter Garden, Rothesay, Isle of Bute – holiday resort life

TAYSIDE
Alyth Museum, Alyth – local history
Arbroath Museum, Arbroath – Bell Rock lighthouse, fishing
Atholl Country Collection, Blair Atholl – village life with crafts

Barrack Street Museum, Dundee – wildlife and geology
Brechin Museum, Brechin – local history
Broughty Castle Museum, Broughty Ferry – fishing, armour
Dunkeld Cathedral Chapter House Museum, Dunkeld – local history
Highland Tryst Museum, Crieff – tartan weaving, local history
Kinross Museum, Kinross – local history
Meigle Museum, Meigle – fine collection of Christian crosses, outstanding display in Europe
Montrose Museum, Montrose – sword of the Marquis of Montrose, local history
Perth Museum, Perth – archaeology, natural history, ethnography

WESTERN ISLES
Museum Nan Eilean, Lionacleit – local history
Museum Nan Eilean, Stornaway, Isle of Lewis – local history
Ness Historical Society, Port-of-Ness, Isle of Lewis – crofting
Shawbost School, Shawbost – local history
Uig Historical Sociey, Uig, Isle of Lewis – crofting

Agricultural Museums

Galloway Deer Museum, Clatteringshaws
Hirsel Homestead Museum, Coldstream
Orkney Farm and Folk Museum, Corrigal
Scottish Deer Centre, Cupar, Fife
Lhaidhay Croft Museum, Dunbeath
Shetland Croft House Museum, Dunrossness
Scottish Agricultural Museum, Ingliston, Edinburgh
Pitmedden Museum, Ellon
Angus Folk Museum, Glamis
Tingwall Agricultural Museum, Gott
Orkney Farm & Folk Museum, Kirbuster
North-East of Scotland Agricultural Heritage Centre, Mintlaw
Maxwelton Museum, Moniaive
Ruskie Farm and Landscape Museum, Ruskie
Session Cottage Museum, Turriff

Art Galleries with Permanent Collections

Rozelle Galleries, Alloway
Arbroath Art Gallery, Arbroath
Peter Anson Gallery, Buckie
McManus Galleries, Dundee
Dunfermline District Small Gallery, Dunfermline
Gracefield Arts Centre, Dumfries
City Art Centre, Edinburgh
Richard Demarco Gallery, Edinburgh
National Gallery of Scotland, Edinburgh
Scottish National Portrait Gallery, Edinburgh
Scottish National Gallery of Modern Art, Edinburgh
Talbot Rice Gallery, Edinburgh
Art Gallery, Kelvingrove, Glasgow
Burrell Collection, Glasgow
Glasgow School of Art, Glasgow
Hunterian Art Gallery, Glasgow
Corridor Gallery, Glenrothes
McLean Art Gallery, Greenock
Inverness Art Gallery, Inverness
Kirkcaldy Art Gallery, Kirkcaldy
Lillie Art Gallery, Milngavie
Montrose Art Gallery, Montrose
Paisley Art Gallery, Paisley
Perth Art Gallery, Perth
Smith Art Gallery, Stirling
Pier Arts Centre, Stromness

Clan Museums

Clan Cameron Museum, Achnacarry
Clan Donald Centre. Museum of the Isles, Sleat, Isle of Skye
Clan Donald and crowning the Lord of the Isles, Finlaggan, Isle of Islay
Clan Donnachaidh, Robertson Museum, Blair Atholl
Clan Gunn Heritage Centre and Museum, Latheron
Clan MacDonald, Glencoe and North Lorn Folk Museum, Glencoe Village
Clan Mackay and Clearances, Strathnaver Museum, Bettyhill
Clan MacPherson House and Museum, Newtonmore
Clan MacRae, Eilean Donan Castle Museum, Dornie
Tain Museum and Clan Ross Centre, Tain

Museums Dedicated to Individuals

Baird Institue Museum, Cumnock
Barrie's Birthplace, Kirriemuir
James Boswell Museum, Auchinleck
Michael Bruce Cottage Museum, Kinnesswood
John Buchan Centre, Broughton, Borders
Robert Burns:
    Robert Burns Centre, Dumfries
    Burns House, Dumfries
    Burns Cottage and Museum, Alloway
    Land o' Burns Centre
    Irvine Burns Club Museum, Irvine
    Souter Johnnie's Cottage, Kirkoswald
    Burns House Museum, Mauchline
    Bachelors Club, Tarbolton
    Ellisland Farm, Holywood
    Lady Stair's Museum, Edinburgh
    Glasgow Vennel Museum and Burns Heckling Shop, Irvine
Carlyle's Birthplace, Ecclefechan
Jane Welsh Carlyle Museum, Haddington
Andrew Carnegie Birthplace Museum, Dunfermline
Carnegie Museum, Inverurie
Jim Clark Memorial Room, Duns
E.A. Hornel, Broughton House, Kirkcudbright
John Knox House, Edinburgh
William Lamb Memorial Studio, Montrose
David Livingstone Centre, Blantyre
Giant Macaskill Museum, Dunvegan, Isle of Skye
McDougall Stuart Museum, Dysart
Mary Queen of Scots House, Jedburgh
Huge Miller's Cottage, Cromarty
John Muir House, Dunbar
Thomas Muir Museum, Bishopbriggs

Museums of Fisheries and the Sea

Aberdeen Maritime Museum, Aberdeen
North Carr Light Vessel, Anstruther
Scottish Fisheries Museum, Anstruther
Buckhaven Museum, Buckhaven
Buckie Maritime Museum, Buckie
Denny Ship Model Experiment Tank Building, Dumbarton
HM Frigate 'Unicorn', Dundee

continued

Museums of Fisheries and the Sea – continued

Royal Research Ship 'Discovery', Dundee
Eyemouth Museum, Eyemouth
Sherryvore Museum, Hynish
Scottish Maritime Museum, Irvine
Lossiemouth Fisheries and Community
    Museum, Lossiemouth
Nairn Fishertown Museum, Nairn
Pier House, Whalsay

Regimental Museums

Argyll and Sutherland Highlanders
    Regimental Museum, Stirling
Black Watch Museum, Perth
Cameronians (Scottish Rifles) Regimental
    Museum, Hamilton
Coldstream Guards Museum, Coldstream
Gordon Highlanders Regimental Museum,
    Aberdeen
Queen's Own Highlanders Regimental
    Museum, Fort George
Royal Highland Fusiliers Regimental
    Museum, Glasgow
Royal Scots Museum, Edinburgh Castle
Scottish Horse Museum, Dunkeld
Scottish United Services Museum,
    Edinburgh Castle

Specialized Technological Museums

Building
    The Cornice, Peebles
Cloth
    Scottish Tartans Museum, Comrie
    Shambellie House Museum of
        Costume, New Abbey
    New Lanark, New Lanark
    Paisley Museum, Paisley
    Scottish Museum of Textiles,
        Walkerburn
Communication
    Museum of Communication,
        Edinburgh
    Orkney Wireless Museum, St
        Margaret's Hope
Crime
    Black Museum, Strathclyde Police HQ,
        Glasgow
    Police Museum, Leith

Drink
    Glenfarclas Distillery, Ballindalloch
    Tugnet Ice House, Tugnet
Education
    History of Education Centre,
        Edinburgh
    Scotland Street School Museum of
        Education, Glasgow
Fire and Heat
    Biggar Gasworks, Biggar
    Museum of Fire, Edinburgh
    Famous Old Blacksmith's Shop,
        Gretna
    Bonawe Iron Works, Taynuilt
Medicine
    Bennie Museum, Bathgate
    Royal College of Physicians, Edinburgh
    Royal College of Surgeons, Edinburgh
    Victorian Pharmacy, Edinburgh
    Sunnyside Royal Hospital Museum,
        Montrose
    Heatherbank Museum of Social Work
    Strathpeffer Spa Exhibition,
        Strathpeffer
Mining
    Scottish Mining Museum
        Lady Victoria, Newtongrange
        Prestongrange, Prestonpans
    Museum of Scottish Lead Mining,
        Wanlockhead
Money
    Bank of Scotland Museum, Edinburgh
    Savings Bank Museum, Ruthwell
Music
    Piping Heritage Centre, Dunvegan, Isle
        of Skye
    Reid Collection, Edinburgh
    Russell Collection of Early Keyboard
        Instruments, Edinburgh
Rocks
    Creetown Gem-Rock Museum,
        Creetown
    Fossil Visitors Centre, Spittal
Sport
    Spalding Golf Museum, Dundee
    Scottish Rugby Union Museum,
        Murrayfield, Edinburgh
    British Golf Museum, St Andrews
Transport
    Grampian Museum of Transport,
        Alford
    Bo'ness and Kinneil Railway, Bo'ness
    Doune Motor Museum, Doune

Museum of Flight, East Fortune
Myreton Motor Museum, East Lothian
Errol Station Railway Heritage Centre,
Errol
Museum of Transport, Glasgow
Glenluce Motor Museum, Glenluce

CASTLES and MILITARY BUILDINGS

There are approximately 2000 castles and
towers in Scotland
Oldest castle – Cubbie Row's Castle,
Orkney (Island of Wyre) built in 1145 by
Norseman Kolbein Hruga
Oldest inhabited castle – Dunvegan Castle,
Isle of Skye
Most photographed castle in Britain – Eilean
Donan Castle, Dornie
Most northerly castle in Britain – Muness
Castle, Shetland
Kilravock Castle, Inverness – continuously
occupied since 1640 by the Rose family
Britain's only triangular castle – Caerlaverock
Castle, Nithsdale
Only two remaining round towers in Scotland –
Brechin and Abernethy

Top Paid-Entry Castles (1990)

Edinburgh Castle	1 078 120
Culzean Castle/Country Park, Ayrshire	365 679
Stirling Castle	264 734

Largest castle – Edinburgh Castle, 1025 m/
3360 ft along perimeter wall including
the Esplanade
Largest fort in Britain – Fort George (1748–
69) 640 m/*2100 ft* long and covering an
area of 17 ha/*42 acres*
Longest Roman wall in Britain – Hadrian's
Wall, (AD122–126), 5 m/*15 ft* tall and
118 km/*73 miles* long, designed to keep
the tribes of Scotland out of England
NOTE: *at no point does Hadrian's Wall touch
Scotland*

Castles and Forts Open to Visitors

BORDERS
Greenknowe Tower – 16th-century tower
Hermitage Castle, Hawick – massive ruin
Smailholm Tower, Smailholm – rectangular
tower now used as museum

PRIVATE PROPERTIES
Ayton Castle, Ayton – red sandstone building
(1851)
Floors Castle, Kelso – 18th century by
Vanbrugh, remodelled by Playfair
(1838–49)
Neidpath Castle, Peebles – L-plan tower-
house
Thirlestane Castle, Lauder – red sandstone
(c 1590)

PRIVATE PROPERTIES SEEN ONLY BY APPOINTMENT
Darnick Tower, Melrose

CENTRAL
Antonine Wall
    Castlecary – earthworks of a fort
    Rough Castle – well-preserved rampart
    and ditch
    Seabegs Wood – rampart and ditch
    Watling Lodge – well-preserved ditch
Blackness Castle, Blackness – 15th-century,
reinforced in 16th century
Castle Campbell, Dollar – 15th-century 'Castle
of Gloom'
Clackmannan Tower – 14th-century tower-
house
Doune Castle, Doune – 14th century with
keep, gatehouse and hall
Stirling Castle, Stirling – most impressive of
all Scottish castles

NATIONAL TRUST PROPERTIES
Bannockburn, near Stirling – victory of Bruce
over Edward II (1314)

PRIVATE PROPERTIES
Menstrie Castle, Menstrie – 16th-century
fortified house

PRIVATE PROPERTIES SEEN BY APPOINTMENT ONLY
Bardowie Castle, by Milngavie
Castlecary Castle, by Bonnybridge

continued

CASTLES AND FORTS OPEN TO VISITORS –
continued

DUMFRIES AND GALLOWAY
Barsalloch Fort – Iron Age hill fort
Caerlaverock Castle, Bankend – surrounded by
moat with 17th-century range
Cardoness Castle, Gatehouse-of-Fleet – 15th-
century tower-house
Carsluith Castle, Creetown – 16th-century
tower-house
Castle of Park, Glenluce – 16th-century tower-
house
Druchtag Motte – earth mound round castle
Drumcoltran Tower – 16th-century tower
Lochmaben Castle, Lochmaben – 15th-century
ruins
MacLellan's Castle, Kirkcudbright – 16th-
century town house
Morton Castle, Thornhill – 13th-century hall-
house
Orchardton Tower – 15th-century tower-house
Rispain Camp – AD100 bank and ditch
settlement
Threave Castle, Threave – 14th-century tower

NATIONAL TRUST PROPERTIES
Bruce's Stone, near New Galloway – Moss
Raploch boulder where Bruce defeated
the English, 1307

PRIVATE PROPERTIES
Drumlanrig Castle, near Thornhill – 17th-
century red sandstone castle
Bonshaw Tower, Kirtlebridge, near Annan

FIFE
Aberdour Castle, Aberdour – 14th-century
tower
Ravenscraig Castle, Kirkcaldy – 15th-century
artillery fort
St Andrews Castle, St Andrews – 13th-century
ruins

NATIONAL TRUST PROPERTIES
Kellie Castle and Garden, near Pittenweem –
mainly 16th century, restored by Lorimer
family (1878)

PRIVATE PROPERTIES
Balgonie Castle, by Markinch – 15th century
Earlshall Castle, Leuchars – 16th-century
mansion, restored by Sir Robert Lorimer

PRIVATE PROPERTIES SEEN ONLY BY APPOINTMENT
The Castle, Elie

GRAMPIAN
Balvenie Castle, Dufftown – 13th century,
owned by Comyns
Corgaff Castle, The Lecht – 16th-century
tower-house
Duffus Castle, Duffus – motte and bailey
castle
Glenbuchat Castle, Glenbuchat – 16th-century
Z-plan tower
Huntly Castle, Huntly – ruin of 16th-century
hall
Kildrummy Castle, Kildrummy – 13th-century
ruin, seat of the Earls of Mar
Tolquhon Castle, Tarves – 15th-century tower
and 16th-century mansion

NATIONAL TRUST PROPERTIES
Castle Fraser, near Dunecht – one of the
Castles of Mar (1575)
Craigievar Castle, near Alford – Scottish
baronial castle with magnificent plaster
ceilings (1626)
Crathes Castle, Garden and Estate, near Banchory
– mid-16th-century castle with large
walled garden and yew hedges from
1702
Drum Castle, near Peterculter – with 13th-
century square tower
Fyvie Castle, near Turriff – oldest part dates
from 13th century

PRIVATE PROPERTIES
Balmoral Castle, Crathie – private residence of
the Queen
Braemar Castle, Braemar – five-storey, L-plan
tower-house (1628)
Muchalls Castle, Stonehaven – L-plan house
overlooking the sea (1619–27)

PRIVATE PROPERTIES SEEN BY APPOINTMENT ONLY
Balfluig Castle, Alford
Barra Castle, Old Meldrum
Castle of Fiddes, Stonehaven
Craig Castle, Lumsden
Craigston Castle, Turriff
Drumminor Castle, Rhynie

HIGHLAND
Castle of Old Wick – early Norse tower
Fort George – huge 18th-century artillery
fort with barracks

Inverlochy Castle, Inverlochy – 13th-century
   square castle with towers
Ruthven Barracks – 18th-century infantry
   barracks
Urquhart Castle, Drumnadrochit – large 16th-
   century building with tower

NATIONAL TRUST PROPERTIES
Brodie Castle, near Forres – 16th-century with
   17th- and 19th-century additions, home
   of the Thanes of Brodie
Glenfinnan Monument, Loch Shiel – Raising of
   Prince Charles's Standard, 19 August 1745
Strome Castle, near Lochcarron – destroyed
   1602

PRIVATE PROPERTIES
Cawdor Castle, near Inverness – mainly 17th
   century
Dunrobin Castle, Golspie – seat of Dukes of
   Sutherland, with some restoration by Sir
   Robert Lorimer
Dunvegan Castle, Isle of Skye – home of the
   chiefs of Clan MacLeod
Eilean Donan Castle, Dornie – picturesque
   tower-house castle on shores of Loch Duich

LOTHIAN
Castlelaw Fort and Earthwork – Iron Age
Chesters, the – Iron Age fort with ramparts
   and ditches
Craigmillar Castle, Edinburgh – 15th-century L-
   plan tower-house
Crichton Castle, Crichton – 16th century with
   faceted stonework
Dirleton Castle, Dirleton – 13th-century castle
   with 16th-century gardens
Eagle Rock, Cramond – said to have been
   carved by Roman garrison
Edinburgh Castle, Edinburgh – Norman, 15th
   and 16th centuries on Bronze Age site
Hailes Castle, East Linton – 13th-century
   manor with pit-prison
Tantallon Castle, North Berwick – great 14th-
   century wall with towers

PRIVATE PROPERTIES
Luffness Castle, Aberlady – late 16th century
   with circular dovecot
Niddry Castle, Winchburgh – early 16th-
   century L-plan tower-house

PRIVATE PROPERTIES SEEN ONLY BY APPOINTMENT
Castle Gogar, Edinburgh
Fa'side Castle, near Tranent

ORKNEY
Cubbie Row's Castle – probably earliest stone
   castle left in Scotland
Links of Noltland – 16th-century Z-plan tower
Noltland Castle, Kirkwall – ruined 16th-
   century Z-plan tower

SHETLAND
Fort Charlotte – 17th-century artillery fort
Muness Castle, Unst – 16th-century tower-
   house
Scalloway Castle, Scalloway – 17th-century
   mansion

STRATHCLYDE
Antonine Wall
   Barhill – highest fort with headquarters
      and bathhouse
   Bearsden – 2nd-century bathhouse
   Croyhill – two beacon platforms
   Dullatur – section of ditch
   Tollpark and Garnhall – section of ditch
Bothwell Castle, Bothwell – largest and best
   13th-century stone castle in Scotland
Coulter Motte Hill – Norman castle mound
Craignethan Castle, Crossford – 16th-century
   with gun ports, wide ditch
Crookston Castle, Crookston – 15th-century
   central tower with four square towers
   (ruin)
Dumbarton Castle, Dumbarton – 18th-century
   fortifications
Dunadd Fort – Dark Age hill-fort, part of
   kingdom of Dalriada
Dunstaffnage Castle, Oban – 13th-century with
   ruined chapel
Kilchurn Castle, Dalmally – 16th-century
   square tower
Loch Doon Castle, Dalmellington – 15th-
   century wall moved from island in Loch
   Doon in 1930s
Lochranza Castle, Isle of Arran – 16th-century
   tower house
Newark Castle, Inverclyde – 15th-century
   tower
Rothesay Castle, Isle of Bute – 13th century
   (residence of Stewart kings)
Skipness Castle – 13th century
Torr a'Chaisteal – Iron Age fort

continued

CASTLES AND FORTS OPEN TO VISITORS –
Strathclyde – continued

NATIONAL TRUST PROPERTIES
Brodick Castle, Garden and Country Park, Isle of Arran – from 13th century; seat of Dukes of Hamilton
Culzean Castle and Country Park, Maybole – Robert Adam (1772–92)

PRIVATE PROPERTIES
Blairquhan Castle, Straiton, Maybole, Ayrshire
Inveraray Castle, Inveraray – seat of Clan Campbell, Dukes of Argyll
Penkill Castle, Girvan – typical 16th-century tower-keep
Torosay Castle, Craignure, Isle of Mull

PRIVATE PROPERTIES SEEN BY APPOINTMENT ONLY
Barcaldine Castle, Benderloch
Craufurdland Castle, Kilmarnock
Duntrune Castle, Lochgilphead
Kelburn Castle, Fairlie
Saddell Castle, near Campbeltown

TAYSIDE
Abernethy – one of two surviving Irish round towers in Scotland from 11th century
Ardunie Signal Station, – Roman watch-tower of 1st century
Balvaird Castle, Strathmiglo – 15th-century tower extended 1581
Blackhall – parts of two Roman camps (probably 3rd century)
Broughty Castle, Dundee – 16th-century tower, now part of Dundee Museums
Burleigh Castle, Milnathort – roofless tower house of c 1500 often visited by James IV
Caterthuns, Brown and White, Bridgend – two very large hill forts
Claypotts Castle, Broughty Ferry – complete tower-house owned by John Graham of Claverhouse
Edzell Castle, Edzell – late medieval tower-house and 16th-century mansion
Elcho Castle, Rhynd – 16th-century fortified mansion
Huntingtower Castle, Perth – two towers, (15th century and 16th century), painted ceilings

Loch Leven Castle, Loch Leven – on an island, (Mary Queen of Scots imprisoned 1567–8)
Muir o' Fauld – Roman watch-tower

PRIVATE PROPERTIES
Blair Castle, Blair Atholl – original castle built 1269, renovated and restored by David Bryce (1872)
Castle Menzies, Weem – built in 16th century
Glamis Castle, Glamis – 17th century, French château-style, childhood home of the Queen Mother
Kelly Castle, Arbroath

PRIVATE PROPERTIES SEEN BY APPOINTMENT ONLY
Ardblair Castle, Blairgowrie
Tulliebole Castle, Crook of Devon

STANDING STONES and CAIRNS

DUMFRIES and GALLOWAY
Cairn Holy Chambered Cairns – Neolithic
Drumtroddan, Cup and Ring marked rocks – Bronze Age Standing Stones – three stones
Torhouse Stone Circle – 19-stone Bronze Age circle
Wren's Egg – large stone deposited by glacier

FIFE
Dogton Stone – cross slab

GRAMPIAN
Brandsbutt Symbol Stone – Pictish with ogham inscription
Cullerie Stone Circle – Bronze Age eight-stone circle
Dyce Symbol Stones – two Pictish stones
Easter Aquhorthies Stone Circle – stones lying on ground
Loanhead Stone Circle – pre-2000 BC
Maiden Stone, Garioch – Celtic cross with Pictish symbols on reverse
Memsie Cairn – Bronze Age
Picardy Symbol Stone, Insch – Pictish
Sueno's Stone – 6 m/*20 ft* sculptured Pictish monument
Tomnarvie Stone Circle – stones on ground

HIGHLAND
Caim o' Get – burial cairn
Clava Cairns – two early Bronze Age
  chambered cairns
Cnoc Freiceadain Long Cairns – Neolithic
Corrimony Chambered Cairn – burial cairn with
  11 standing stones
Hill o' Many Stanes – over 22 rows of low slabs
Knocknagael Boar Stone – Pictish symbols
Dunchraigaig Cairn – Bronze Age burial cists

LOTHIAN
Caimpapple Hill – burial site from 3000 to
  1400 BC
Cat Stane – inscribed pillar
Hully Hill

NATIONAL TRUST PROPERTIES
Caiy Stone, Edinburgh – 3 m/*9 ft* sandstone
  monolith on site of Pictish battle

ORKNEY
Brodgar, Ring of – stone circle and henge
Cuween Hill Cairn – Neolithic chambered tomb
Dwarfie Stone – Neolithic burial chamber
Knowe of Yarso, Cairn – Neolithic
Midhowe Cairn – megalithic tomb
Quoyness Cairn – megalithic tomb
Taversoe Tuick Cairn – megalithic
Unstan Cairn – Neolithic

STRATHCLYDE
Achnabreck Cup and Ring Marks – rocky ridge
Ballygowan Cup and Ring Marks – Bronze Age
Baluachraig Cup and Ring Marks – Bronze Age
Caimbaan Cup and Ring Marks – on rock
Kilmartin: Glebe Cairn – early Bronze Age
  burial cairn
Kilmichael Glassary Inscribed Rock – Bronze
  Age cup and ring carvings
Machrie Moor Stone Circles – five Bronze Age
  stone circles
Moss Farm Road Stone Circle – Bronze Age
  cairn with stone circle
Nether Largie Cairns – two Bronze Age, one
  Neolithic
Ri Cruin Cairn – Bronze Age cairn with three
  cists
Temple Wood Stone Circles – 3000 BC circle of
  stones
Torrylin Cairn – Neolithic chambered cairn

TAYSIDE
Dunfallandy Stone – Pictish sculptured stone

Eassie Sculptured Stones – richly decorated
  Celtic cross and Pictish symbols
Fowlis Wester – sculptured Pictish symbol
  stone

WESTERN ISLES
Callanish Standing Stones – 3000 BC in cross
  formation and chambered cairn
'Steinacleit' Cairn and Stone Circle – prehistoric

RELIGIOUS BUILDINGS

There are approximately 1000 old parish
  churches in Scotland
Oldest ecclesiastical building in Britain – 6th-
  century cell erected by St Brendan on
  Eileachan Naoimh, Garvelloch Islands,
  Argyll
Earliest Scottish church excavated – Candida
  Casa, Whithorn (c AD 790)
Most complete Romanesque parish church –
  Dalmeny Kirk (mid 12th century)
Best preserved monastic building – Inchcolm
  Abbey (12th century)
**Only surviving pre-Reformation stained glass in
  situ** – Magdalen Chapel, Cowgate,
  Edinburgh (mid 16th century)
Smallest cathedral in Britain – Cathedral of
  the Isles, Millport, Cumbrae, built in
  1849–51 (12 × 6 m/*40 × 20 ft*)
Smallest chapel – St Margaret's Chapel,
  Edinburgh Castle (floor area of 16 sq m/
  173 sq ft)
Most complete mainland medieval cathedral –
  Glasgow Cathedral
Smallest parish in Britain – the Scares, Luce
  Bay, Wigtown (4450 sq m/*1.1 acres*)
**Oldest Norwegian seamen's church outside
  Norway** – Old Norwegian Church, Leith
  (1868)

Religious Monuments (in the care of
  Historic Scotland)

BORDERS
Cross Kirk, Peebles – ruins of 13th-century
  friary
Dryburgh Abbey – romantic 12th-century ruin
Edrom Church – Romanesque doorway

continued

Religious Buildings – continued

Jedburgh Abbey – Romanesque and Gothic, 12th century, part-ruined
Kelso Abbey – magnificent 12th-century ruin
Melrose Abbey – 12th century, most famous ruin in Scotland

CENTRAL
Cambuskenneth Abbey – Bruce's parliament (1326), burial place of James III
Dunblane Cathedral – Romanesque and 13th century building
Inchmahome Priory – 13th-century monastery

DUMFRIES AND GALLOWAY
Chapel Finian – foundation of AD 1000 chapel
Dundrennan Abbey – 12th-century ruins
Glenluce Abbey – 12th-century ruins with 15th-century chapter house
Kirkmadrine: Early Christian Stones – three 5th-century stones
Laggangairn Standing Stones – two Christian stones with crosses
Lincluden Collegiate Church – built by Duke of Touraine
Merkland Cross – 15th-century carved wayside cross
Ruthwell Cross – 7th-century Anglian Cross
St Ninian's Cave – crosses once carved on wall
St Ninian's Chapel – 13th-century ruins now restored
Sweetheart Abbey – ruins of 13th-century abbey
Whithorn Priory – 5th-century site of St Ninian's 'Candida Casa'

FIFE
Balmerino Abbey, near Newport – ruins of Cistercian monastery of 1229
Blackfriars Chapel, St Andrews – rebuilt in 16th century
Culross Abbey – 13th-century remains
Dunfermline Abbey Nave – 11th-century church founded by Queen Margaret
Inchcolm Abbey – 12th-century, best preserved monastic building in Scotland
St Andrews Cathedral – ruins of largest cathedral in Scotland
St Bridget's Church, Dalgety – medieval shell
St Mary's Church, St Andrews – ruined pre-Reformation church

GRAMPIAN
Burghead Well – early Christian baptistry
Deer Abbey – 13th-century remains of monastery
Deskford Church – ruined medieval building with sacrament house
Elgin Cathedral – ruin of 13th-century church with chapter house
Kinkell House – ruined 16th-century parish church
Pluscarden Abbey, Elgin – remains of 13th-century Priory
St Machar's Cathedral, Aberdeen – 14th-century nave, towers and ruined transept
St Mary's Cathedral, Auchindoir – roofless medieval parish church
Tarves Medieval Tomb – finely carved altar-tomb

HIGHLAND
Ardclach Bell Tower – 17th-century fortified bell tower
Beauly Priory – 13th-century ruined priory church
Hilton of Cadboll Chapel – small rectangular ruins
Fortrose Cathedral – 13th-century undercroft of chapter house

LOTHIAN
Dalmeny Kirk – oldest complete Romanesque building in Scotland
Haddington: Lauderdale Aisle, St Mary's Church – 14th-century parish church
Holyrood Abbey – 12th century, romantic ruins
St Martin's Kirk – ruined nave of Romanesque church
St Triduana's Chapel – shrine to Pictish saint built by James III
Torphichen Preceptory – 13th-century home of Knights Hospitaller of St John

ORKNEY
Eynhallow Church – ruins of 12th-century church
Orphir Church – 12th century
Pierowall Church – medieval church ruins
St Magnus's Church – 12th-century roofless church and tower
Westside Tuquoy Church – 12th-century roofless church

STRATHCLYDE

Barochan Cross – Celtic cross in Paisley Abbey

Crossraguel Abbey – early 13th century (church, cloister, chapter and domestic)

Eileach an Naoimh – ruins of beehive cells, chapel, graveyard

Eiliean Mor, St Cormac's Chapel – vaulted chancel, 12th-century figure

Glasgow Cathedral – only Scottish medieval cathedral to have survived the Reformation unscathed

Inchkenneth Chapel – medieval monuments

Iona: MacLean's Cross – 15th century

Keills Cross and Chapel – grave slabs

Kilberry Sculptured Stones – late medieval

Kildalton High Cross – 9th century, very fine

Kilmartin Crosses and Sculptured Stones – over 24 grave slabs

Kilmodan Burial Ground – grave slabs

Kilmory Knap Chapel – grave slabs; medieval Macmillan's Cross

Kilwinning Abbey – 13th-century fragments

Largs Old Kirk – 17th century with carved tomb and painted ceiling

Rothesay: St Mary's Chapel – late medieval with fine tombs

St Blane's Church – 12th-century chapel on site of Celtic monastery

St Bride's Church, Douglas – 14th-century parish church

Skipness Chapel – 14th century, very fine

TAYSIDE

Aberlemno – Pictish cross-slab in church; three symbol stones by the road

Arbroath Abbey – (ruins) founded 1178 William the Lion (1320 Declaration of Arbroath)

Brechin Cathedral – second of two surviving Irish round towers built 11th century

Dunkeld Cathedral – 15th-century nave and tower (rest is parish church)

Innerpeffray Chapel – collegiate church with altar, founded 1508

Maison Dieu Chapel, Brechin – part of medieval hospital founded c 1260

Meigle Museum – 25 Celtic Christian sculptured stones (one of best collections in Europe)

Muthill: Old Church and Tower – tall Romanesque tower of medieval church

Restenneth Priory – chancel and tower

St Mary's, Grandtully – 16th-century parish church with painted wooden ceiling

St Orland's Stone – early Christian sculptured slab

St Serf's Church, Dunning – square Romanesque tower and arch

St Vigean's Museum – 32 early Christian Pictish sculptured stones

Tullibardine Chapel – founded 1446 (one of most complete small medieval churches)

WESTERN ISLES

Rodel: St Clement's Church – 16th-century church with decorated tomb

BATTLES

84 Mons Graupius – 30 000 Picts and Britons under Calgacus v Agricola; 10 000 Caledonians killed and 340 Romans

600 Catterick – 300 horsemen from Edinburgh annihilated by the English

685 Nechtansmere (Dunnichen), Forfarshire (20 May) – Saxons of Northumbria defeated by Picts under King Brude. Pictish King Nechtan rejected Celtic Church 685

937 Brananburgh – Athelstane King of Saxons defeats Danes and Britons on 300 m/*1000 ft* flat-topped hill near Solway

973 Luncarty (near Perth) – Danes walked onto thistles (Wha dare meddle wi me? Nemo me impune lacessit). Defeated by Kenneth III

1014 Mortlach, Banffshire – Malcolm II of Scotland defeats Danes

1018 Carham – Malcolm II and Owen King of Strathclyde defeat Northumbrian army on the Tweed

1057 Lumphanan (Aberdeenshire) (15 Aug) – Macbeth defeated and killed by Malcolm Canmore

1093 Alnwick (13 Nov) – Malcolm III killed

1138 Northallerton (22 Aug) 6.00 am – 'Battle of the Standard' (ship's mast topped with a silver 'pyx' containing a consecrated wafer hung with English banners): David I (12 000 men) v Normans under Archbishop Thurstan of York. Scots defeated (10 000 dead)

continued

BATTLES – continued

1263 Largs (2 Oct) – Scots defeat Norwegian fleet under King Haakon

1296 Dunbar (27 April) – Edward I with 30 000 and 5000 cavalry defeats Scots

1297 Stirling (11 Sept) – Wallace defeats English

1298 Falkirk (22 July) – Edward I with 87 500 men defeats Wallace (c 29 100 men)

1308 Inverurie (22 May) – Bruce's army defeats Comyn of Buchan and the English

1314 Bannockburn (24th June) – England, 3000 heavy cavalry and 15 000 foot (total 22 000); Scotland, c 500 mounted men; 5000 spearmen (total 8000). Scottish victory

1332 Dupplin (Strathearn) (12 Aug) – Edward Balliol defeats Scots under the Earl of Mar and is crowned at Scone

1333 Halidon Hill (19 July) – Edward III defeats Scots who are cut down by English archers. Scots: 70 lords, 500 knights, several thousand foot soldiers dead; English – one knight, one man-at-arms and Newcastle contingent dead

1338 Otterburn (Chevy Chase) (5 Aug) – Douglas with 300 lances and 2000 foot defeated English under Henry Percy (Hotspur)

1346 Neville's Cross (17 Oct) – David II defeated and captured by English (15 000); Scots (larger force)

1388 Otterburn (19 Aug) – English defeated. Harry Percy and his son Ralph captured

1402 Homildon Hill (Northumberland) (14 Sept) – Douglas with 10 000 men v Percy. Scots were defeated

1411 Harlaw (Aberdeen) (24 July) – Donald Lord of the Isles defeated by Lowlanders

1513 Flodden (9 Sept) – James IV defeated by English. Scots, 40 000; English, 26 000. Scots lost a king, two prelates, 25 lords and 10 000 men

1547 Pinkie (10 Sept) – Duke of Somerset with 15 000 defeated Scots

1568 Langside (13 May) – Moray with 45 000 troops defeated Mary with 4500

1645 Inverlochie (2 Feb) – Montrose v Argyll: 1500 Campbells killed (only four of Montrose's men killed)

  Auldearn (9 May) – Montrose defeats Covenanters

  Alford (2 July) – Montrose defeats Covenanters

  Kilsyth (15 Aug) – Montrose defeats Covenanters

  Philiphaugh (13 Sept) – Leslie defeats Montrose

1650 Invercharron (27 April) – Strachan defeats Montrose

  Dunbar (3 Sept) – Cromwell with 16 000 defeats Scots under Leslie (3000 killed or wounded; 10 000 prisoners)

1666 Rullion Green (28 Nov) – General Dalyell defeats Covenanters

1679 Drumclog (1 June) – Covenanters defeat Graham of Claverhouse leaving 36 dead and losing only three men

  Bothwell Brig (22 June) – Duke of Monmouth defeats Covenanters: 300 killed; 1200 prisoners

1689 Killiecrankie (27 July) – Viscount Dundee defeats General MacKay but is mortally wounded

  Perth – MacKay defeated Jacobites

  Dunkeld (21 Aug) – 4000 Jacobites defeated by Cameronians

1745 Prestonpans (20 Sept) – Prince Charles (2400) defeats Cope (3000). 500 Royal infantry and dragoons killed; 1000 captured

1746 Falkirk (17 Jan) – Jacobites defeat government troops

  Culloden (18 April) – Jacobites (4900); Hanoverians under Cumberland (10 000) destroy Jacobites (2000 dead); Hanoverians (364 dead)

1882 'The Battle of the Braes' (17 April) – on the Island of Skye (the last battle fought on British soil) Glasgow police v crofters who were protesting over the introduction of sheep and the destruction of their communities. It forced Gladstone to set up a Royal Commission on crofters' grievances

Calendar

The Scots are a quirky breed at the best of times. They enjoy
enjoying themselves, contrary to the image entertainingly
projected by the likes of Sir Harry Lauder.

Today the Scottish heritage spawns festival after festival as a
showcase for native talent and overseas ebullience.

FOLK MUSIC FESTIVALS

Note: the exact dates of festivals are
subject to change.

MARCH
Celtic Festival of Film and TV
Glenfarg Folk Feast

APRIL
Edinburgh Harp Festival
Edinburgh International Folk Festival
Girvan Traditional Folk Festival
Glencoe and Loch Leven Music Festival
Inverness Folk Festival
Orkney Folk Festival
Shetland Folk Festival

JUNE
Arran Festival of Folk
Dumfries Folk Weekend
Glasgow Folk Festival
Highland Traditional Music Festival,
    Dingwall
Keith Traditional Festival
Newcastleton Traditional Folk Festival
Strathaven Folk Festival

JULY
Blairgowrie Folk and Blues Festival
Dundee Folk Festival
Rhinns of Islay, Argyll
Skye Folk Festival
Stonehaven Folk Festival

AUGUST
Acoustic Music Centre, Edinburgh
Auchtermuchty Festival, Fife
Kincardine and Deeside Pipe Band
    Championship

SEPTEMBER
Dunbar Traditional Music
Kirriemuir Festival
Melrose

OCTOBER
Gaelic MOD

NOVEMBER
Glasgow Tryst

TRADITIONAL FESTIVALS

Note: the exact dates of festivals are
subject to change.

JANUARY
Burns Supper, Strathclyde Regional
Council, Glasgow – charity night
New Year's Day Boys and Men's Ba'
Games, Kirkwall – almost 200-year-old
game of mass street football
Scalloway Fire Festival, Shetland – galley
burning and squad acts
Up-Helly-Aa, Lerwick, Shetland – Viking
Fire Festival

MARCH
Badenoch and Strathspey Music Festival,
    Kingussie
Lossiemouth Spring Flower Show,
    Lossiemouth
Whuppity Scourie, Lanark – banishing
    winter

APRIL
Torcher Parade, Aberdeen – Aberdeen
    Students Charities

MAY
Atholl Highlanders Parade, Blair Atholl
Banchory Strathspey and Reel Festival of
    Music, Banchory
Bo'ness Victorian Street Fair, Bo'ness
Buchan Heritage Doric Drama Festival,
    New Pitsligo
Buchan Heritage Festival, Strichen
Feis Ile Islay Festival, Islay
Girvan Traditional Folk Festival, Girvan
Glencoe and Loch Leven Music Festival,
    Glencoe and district

Highlands and Islands Music and Dance
  Festival, Oban
Livingston Spring Festival, Livingston
New Lanark Steam Fair, New Lanark
  Conservation Village
Orkney Traditional Folk Festival,
  Stromness
Shetland Folk Festival, Lerwick

JUNE
Arran Festival of Folk, Isle of Arran
Aviemore Midsummer Music Festival,
  Aviemore
Ayrshire Arts Festival, Ayrshire
Bon Accord Festival, Aberdeen
Robert Burns Festival, Alloway, Ayr
Coronation Pageant, Scone Palace, Perth
Dundee City Festival, Dundee
Fiddle Festival, Elgin
Guid Nychburris Week, Dumfries
Highland Traditional Music Festival,
  Dingwall
International Festival of Music and Dance,
  Highlands
Lanimer Day Celebrations, Lanark
Linlithgow Riding of the Marches,
  Linlithgow
Melrose Festival Week, Melrose
Newcastleton Traditional Music Festival,
  Newcastleton
Peebles March Riding and Beltane Queen
  Festival, Peebles
St Magnus Festival, Kirkwall and
  Stromness
Selkirk Common Riding, Selkirk
Yetholm Festival Week, Yetholm

JULY
Annan Riding of the Marches, Annan
Boat of Garten Gala Day, Boat of Garten
Herring Queen Festival, Eyemouth
International Glasgow Folk Festival,
  Glasgow
Inverness Country Music Festival,
  Inverness
Rhinns of Islay Celtic Festival, Isle of Islay
Stirling Tartan Festival, Stirling
Stonehaven Folk Festival, Stonehaven
Strathclyde Irish Festival, Strathclyde
Upper Donside Annual Ceilidh

AUGUST
Ferry Fair, South Queensferry (with Burry
  Man)
Lammas Fair, St Andrews
Lonach Games, Bellabeg, Aberdeenshire –
  March of the Clansmen for six miles
  carrying pikes, halberds and
  broadswords
Medieval Banquets and Pageants in
  Linlithgow, Linlithgow

SEPTEMBER
Carrbridge Ceilidh Week, Carrbridge
Fisherman's Walk, Musselburgh
Kirriemuir Festival, Kirriemuir

OCTOBER
Glorious Tweed Festival, Tweed Valley
Scottish Storytelling Festival, Edinburgh

NOVEMBER
Firework Display and Bonfire, Forres
Scotland's Whisky Festival, Aviemore

DECEMBER
Biggar Ne'erday Bonfire, Biggar
Christmas Day Boys and Mens Ba'
  Games, Kirkwall
Flambeaux Procession, Comrie
Stonehaven Fireball Ceremony,
  Stonehaven – traditional ceremony of
  swinging fireballs to welcome the New
  Year

CALENDAR of UNUSUAL SPORTS

Note: the exact dates of festivals are
subject to change.

JANUARY
Scottish Cross-Country Ski Championships

FEBRUARY
Aviemore Nordic Skiing Festival,
  Aviemore

continued

CALENDAR OF UNUSUAL SPORTS – continued

FEBRUARY continued
North of Scotland Cross-Country Ski
    Championships

MAY
Bruichladdich Islands Peaks Race
Comrie to Crieff Raft Race
Goatfell Hill Race
Great Oban Raft Race
Great Tweed Raft Race

JUNE
Bridge Inn Canal Jumping Competition
Highland Balloon Festival
Highland Cross Biathlon, Kintail to
    Beauly
Kenmore to Aberfeldy Raft Race
North of Scotland Inflatable Boats Race
Scottish Hang Gliding Championships
Scottish Horse Driving Trials

JULY
Clan Donald Archery Tournaments,
    Armadale, Isle of Skye
Great Oban Bed Race, Oban

AUGUST
Edinburgh Croquet Tournament
Edinburgh Military Tattoo, Edinburgh
    Castle
Glen Nevis River Race
Highland Field Sports Fair
Inverleith Petanque Club Open Triples
    Tournament
Scottish Country and Game Fair

SEPTEMBER
Ben Nevis Race
Clydesdale Horseshoeing Competition,
    Closeburn, Dumfriesshire
Crossford Raft Race, River Clyde
Viking Boat Festival, Shetland

CONTEMPORARY ARTS and TECHNOLOGY FESTIVALS

Note: the exact dates of festivals are
subject to change.

MARCH
International Festival of Food and Wine,
    St Andrews

APRIL
International Festival of Science and
    Technology, Edinburgh

MAY
Isle of Bute Jazz Festival, Rothesay
Mayfest, Glasgow
Scottish International Children's Festival,
    Edinburgh

JUNE
Dumfries Jazz Festival, Dumfries
Glasgow International Jazz Festival,
    Glasgow

AUGUST
Craigmillar Festival, Edinburgh
Edinburgh Book Festival (biennial)
Edinburgh Festival Fringe
Edinburgh International Festival of Music
    and Drama
Edinburgh Jazz Festival
Edinburgh International Film Festival
International Youth Festival of Music and
    the Arts, Aberdeen
Television Festival

People

At the heart of a country is its people. In the case of Scotland they are stubborn ('thrawn'), cautious ('canny') and schizophrenic (the 'Caledonian antisyzygy' in the words of the poet Hugh MacDiarmid). They swing from hilarity to despair in a permanent struggle between optimism and pessimism perhaps generated by the Union of the Crowns (1603) and the Union of the Parliaments (1707) which left a large vacuum in Scottish political and social life.

Then there were the Highland Clearances and also the celebrated Protestant work-ethic which are said partly to explain the great desire of the Scots to get out of their own country and achieve greatness abroad.

Fortunately, enough Scots stayed at home and put their minds to innovation and invention, as the following pages show.

THE ROYAL LINE

All dates are AD
Key: m = married
*   (1) = one child*

Kenneth MacAlpin – King of Dalriada, king c 840

Malcolm II (954–1034), King of Picts and Scots, 1005–1034

Duncan I (1010–40) – king 1034–40; m cousin of Siward, Earl of Northumbria (2). Killed (probably in battle) near Elgin by Macbeth

Macbeth (1005–57) – king 1040–57, m Gruoch (0); killed in battle at Lumphanan, 40 km/*25 miles* west of Aberdeen

Lulach (Macbeth's stepson) – simpleton, king 1057–8; killed at Essie

Malcolm III (Canmore) (1031–93) – king 1058–93; m Ingebjorg of Orkney (3); m Margaret (8). Invaded England five times. Killed in battle at Alnwick

Donald Bane (1031–1100) – king 1093–4, 1094–7; m unknown (1); eyes put out; died in prison

Duncan II (1060–94) – king 1094; hostage of William the Conqueror (1072). Granted first existing Scottish charter

Edgar (1074–1107) – king 1097–1107; placed on throne by an English army; unmarried

Alexander I 'The Fierce' (1077–1124) – king 1107–24; m Sibylla, illegitimate d of Henry I of England (0), illegitimate son. Died at Stirling

David I (1084–1153) – king 1124–53; m Matilda of Huntingdon. Founded many religious houses. Defeated at the Battle of the Standard. Died at Carlisle

Malcolm IV ('The Maiden' unmarried) (1141–65) – king 1153–65. Gave up northern English counties to Henry II. Died at Jedburgh

William I (The Lion) (1143–1214) – king 1165–1214; m Ermengarde de Beaumont (4). Died at Stirling

Alexander II (1198–1249) – king 1214–49; m Joan, d of John of England; m Marie de Couci (1). Died from fever on Island of Kerrera (Oban); buried in Melrose

Alexander III (1241–86) – king 1249–86; m Margaret, d of Henry III of England (3). Died when his horse stumbled over cliff near Pettycur Bay, Fife

Margaret ('The Maid of Norway') (1283–90) – queen 1286–90; died aged eight in Orkney on her way to marry Prince Edward of England. Buried in Bergen

First interregnum – 1290–2

John Balliol (1250–1313) – king 1292–6; resigned kingdom. Known as 'Toom Tabard' (empty coat); m Isabella de Warenne, d of Earl of Surrey. Allowed to retire to France

Second interregnum – 1296–1306

Robert I (The Bruce) (1274–1329) – king 1306–29; m Isabella of Mar (1); m Elizabeth de Burgh (1). Died of leprosy at Cardross

David II (1324–71) – king 1329–71; m Joanna, d of Edward II of England; m Margaret Logie. Died in Edinburgh Castle

Robert II (Stewart) (1316–90) – king 1371–90; m Elizabeth Mure (9); m Euphemia of Ross (4). Died at Dundonald Castle, west of Kilmarnock

Robert III (1340–1406) – king 1390–1406; m Annabella Drummond (7). Died at Dundonald

James I (1394–1437) – king 1406–37; m Joan Beaufort (8). Assassinated in a privy in Perth

James II (1430–60) – king 1437–60; m Mary of Guelders (8). Killed by an exploding cannon at Floors Castle near Kelso.

James III (1451–88) – king 1460–88; m Margaret of Denmark (3). Murdered after the battle of Sauchieburn by a man disguised as a priest

James IV (1472–1513) – king 1488–1513; m Margaret Tudor (6). Killed at battle of Flodden

James V (1512–42) – king 1513–42; m Madeleine, d of Francis I of France (0); m Mary of Lorraine (3). Died at Falkland Palace

Mary Queen of Scots (1512–87) – queen 1542–87; m Francis, Dauphin of France (0); m Lord Darnley (1); m Earl of

Bothwell (0). Executed at Fotheringay Castle

James VI (1566–1625) – king of Scotland, 1567–1603, and king of England (as James I) 1603–25; m Anne of Denmark (7)

Charles I (1600–49) – king 1625–49; m Henrietta Maria, d of Henri IV (8). Executed at Palace of Whitehall

Cromwell (1599–1658) Protector – the Commonwealth, 1649–60

Charles II (1630–85) – restored as king 1660–85; m Catherine of Braganza (0)

James VII and II (1633–1701) – king 1685–8; m Anne Hyde (2); m Mary of Modena (1). Fled the country at Revolution in 1688

(None of the six Kings of Scotland called James had a Scottish wife)

Scottish Coronations

Scone – Charles II last crowned there
Kelso – James II
Stirling – Mary Queen of Scots
James VI
Holyrood James II
Charles I

Other Royal Facts

James II – born, crowned, married and buried in Holyrood

First Scottish king to issue own coinage – David I

Earliest extant dated coin in Britain – James V gold 'bonnet' piece (1539)

Stone of Scone – the 'Stone of Destiny', red sandstone removed from Scone by Edward I of England in 1296

Iona – many of the earliest kings were buried on the island

Jacobite Pretenders

James Francis Edward, The Old Pretender (1688–1766) – 'James III' ('reign' 1701–66)

Charles Edward Stuart, The Young Pretender (1720–88) – 'Charles III' ('reign' 1766–88)

Henry Benedict, Cardinal York (1725– 1807) grandson of James II – 'Henry IX' last survivor in the male line of the House of Stuart ('reign' 1788–1807)

Titles of Prince Charles in Scotland

Great Steward of Scotland
Lord of the Isles
Duke of Rothesay
Earl of Carrick
Baron of Renfrew

Royal Household in Scotland

Hereditary Lord High Constable – Earl of Errol
Hereditary Master of the Household – Duke of Argyll
Lord Lyon, King of Arms
Hereditary Bearer of the Royal Banner of Scotland – Earl of Dundee
Hereditary Keepers
    Duke of Hamilton (Holyrood)
    N. Crichton-Stuart (Falkland)
    Earl of Mar and Kellie (Stirling)
    Earl of Argyll (Dunstaffnage)
Hereditary Carver;
Keeper of Dumbarton Castle;
Governor of Edinburgh Castle;
Dean of the Order of the Thistle;
Dean of the Chapel Royal;
Chaplains in Ordinary;
Extra Chaplains;
Domestic Chaplain, Balmoral;
Historiographer Royal;
Botanist;
Painter and Limner;
Sculptor in Ordinary;
Astronomer;
Physicians in Scotland;
Surgeons in Scotland;
Extra Surgeons in Scotland;
Apothecary to the Household at Balmoral;
Apothecary to the Household at Holyroodhouse;
Heralds and Pursuivants of Arms

ARISTOCRATS

Dukes
Argyll
Atholl
Buccleuch
Fife
Hamilton
Montrose
Roxburghe
Sutherland

Marquesses
Aberdeen
Ailsa
Bute
Ely
Huntly
Linlithgow
Lothian
Queensberry
Tweeddale
Zetland

Countesses in their own right
Countess of Dysart
Countess of Mar
Countess of Sutherland

Last instance of a Scottish nobleman seriously resisting the authority of the crown from within his own castle – 6th Earl of Angus who shut himself up in Tantallon Castle to resist a charge of treason from the 17-year-old James V (1528)

Greatest age to which a baronet has lived – 101 years: Sir Fitzroy Maclean (1835–1936), last survivor of the Crimean War (1853–6)

Oldest orders of chivalry
Most Ancient Order of the Thistle (said to date from AD 809)
Order of St John in Scotland (founded 1124; suppressed in 16th century; revived 1747)

Court of the Lord Lyon
Heralds: Albany, Rothesay, Ross
Pursuivants: Kintyre, Unicorn

Oldest existing peerage – premier Earldom of Scotland, held by Rt Hon Margaret of Mar (1940–), heir of Roderick 1st Earl 1114

Also –
Seventeen-year-old David Bolton (whose father was Scottish and who is director of a computer firm), recently succeeded to the throne in Ghana where he is now King Nana Akweku Kyemaanu VI and rules the 20 000-strong Abrazic tribe

PRECEDENCE IN SCOTLAND

The Sovereign;
The Duke of Edinburgh;
Lord High Commissioner to General Assembly;
Duke of Rothesay;
younger sons of the Sovereign;
Duke of Gloucester, Duke of Windsor, uncles of the Sovereign;
Lords Lieutenants of counties;
Lords Provost;
Sheriffs Principal;
Lord Chancellor;
Moderator of General Assembly;
Prime Minister;
Keeper of the Great Seal of Scotland;
Lord High Constable of Scotland;
Master of the Household in Scotland;
Dukes;
eldest sons of Royal Dukes;
Marquesses;
eldest sons of Dukes;
Earls;
younger sons of Royal Dukes;
eldest sons of Marquesses;
younger sons of Dukes;
Keeper of the Great Seal (Secretary for Scotland if not a peer);
Keeper of the Privy Purse;
Lord Justice General;
Lord Clerk-Register;
Lord Advocate;
Lord Justice Clerk;
Viscounts;
eldest sons of Earls;
younger sons of Marquesses;
Barons;
eldest sons of Viscounts;
younger sons of Earls;
eldest sons of Barons;

Knights of the Garter;
Privy Councillors;
Lords of Session;
younger sons of Viscounts;
sons of Life Peers;
Baronets;
Knights of the Thistle;
Knights of other Orders;
Solicitor-General;
Lord Lyon King of Arms;
Sheriffs Principal;
Knights Bachelor;
Sheriffs Substitute;
Companions of Orders;
Commanders of Royal Victorian Order;
Commanders of British Empire Order;
eldest sons of younger sons of peers;
Companions of Distinguished Service
    Order;
members of fourth class of Royal
    Victorian Order;
officers of British Empire Order;
eldest sons of Baronets;
eldest sons of Knights of the Garter and
    Thistle;
eldest sons of Knights;
members of fifth class of Royal Victorian
    Order;
members of British Empire Order;
younger sons of Baronets;
younger sons of Knights;
Queen's Counsel;
Barons-feudal;
Esquires;
Gentlemen

POLITICIANS

First woman Conservative minister – Duchess
    of Atholl (1874–1960)
**First woman adopted as a parliamentary
    candidate** – Mary McArthur
First Marxist in Britain – John MacLean
First Soviet consul in Britain – John MacLean
First Communist MP in parliament – J.T.
    Walton Newbold (1922) for Motherwell
First Socialist MP in Britain – R.B.
    Cunninghame Graham
First (and last) Prohibitionist MP in Britain –
    Edwin Scrimgeour (1922)

Britain's first Labour PM – James Ramsay
    MacDonald
First working-class MP in Britain – Alexander
    Macdonald
**First working-class person to be member of
    British cabinet** – John Burns
Founder of the Independent Labour Party –
    James Keir Hardie

Scottish Prime Ministers of Great Britain

**George Hamilton Gordon, 4th Earl of Aberdeen
    (1784–1860)** – PM 1852–5 (Conservative)
**Archibald Primrose, 5th Earl of Rosebery
    (1847–1929)** – PM 1894–5 (Liberal)
Arthur Balfour (1848–1930) – PM 1902–5
    (Conservative)
Sir Henry Campbell-Bannerman (1836–1908) –
    PM 1905–8 (Liberal)
Andrew Bonar Law (1858–1923) – PM 1922–3
    (Unionist)
James Ramsay MacDonald (1866–1937) – PM
    1924, 1929–35 (Labour)
**Maurice Harold Macmillan, 1st Earl of Stockton
    (1894–1986)** – PM 1957–63 (Conservative)
Baron Alec Douglas-Home (1903–) – PM
    1963–4 (Conservative)

TEN RICHEST MEN (1990)

	£m
Duke of Buccleuch	300
Duke of Atholl	143
Brian Thomson (D.C. Thomson)	127
James Miller (Miller Group)	111
Sir Hector Laing (United Biscuits)	96
Duke of Argyll	87
Capt Alwyn Farquharson	87
Duke of Roxburghe	70
Marquess of Bute	60
Earl of Cawdor	60

CAPTAINS of INDUSTRY

Highest Annual Salaries and Dividends
(1990)

	£
John Menzies (John Menzies plc)	669 000
Tom Farmer (KwikFit)	567 375
Andros Stakis (Stakis plc)	314 903
Angus Grossart (Noble Grossart)	297 715
Lewis Robertson (Havelock, Lilley)	250 000
Freddie Johnston (Johnston Press)	233 000
Nelson Robertson (General Accident)	201 640
Sir Matthew Goodwin (Hewden Stuart)	199 000
Peter Runciman (Shanks and McEwan)	198 312
James Miller (Miller Group)	197 378

CLANS

Today there are 118 clans (about 40 original clans, the rest being Victorian) and names covering the whole of Scotland (from the Lowlands to the Highlands), each with an established chief (this includes the Royal house whose chief is the Queen)

Oldest clan – MacDonald (1st MacDonald, son of Donald, grandson of the Norse adventurer Sommerled c 1100)
Clan physical characteristics
    Campbell: crooked mouth
    Cameron: bent nose
    Kennedy: ugly head
Clan badges
    rock ivy (Gordon)
    holly (Mackenzie)
    foxglove (Ferguson)
Fairy flag – Clan MacLeod (waving flag – help on only four occasions)
Clan traditionally Lords of the Isles – Macdonalds
Brodie – Brodie Castle, Moray

Buchanan – east side of Loch Lomond; 'Clar Island'
Cameron – Achnacarry, Lochaber; 'Sons of the hounds come here and get flesh'
Campbell:
    Argyll – Inveraray Castle, 'Cruachan' mountain, Argyll
    Breadalbane – Taymouth Castle, Tayside
    Cawdor – Cawdor Castle, Nairn
Chattan – Lochaber, Badenoch (17 tribes, 2nd largest clan)
Chisholm, Highland and Lowland – Erchless Castle, Strathglass
Colquhoun – Rossdhu House, Dumbarton
Cumming – Altyre, Gordonston
Davidson – Tulloch, Castle Ross
Drummond – Stobhall, Perthshire
Dunbar – Dunbar Castle, East Lothian
Erskine – Braemar Castle, Aberdeenshire
    Dirleton Castle, East Lothian
Farquharson – Aberdeenshire; 'Cairn of Remembrance'
Ferguson – Kilkerran, Ayrshire
Forbes – Braes of Forbes, Aberdeenshire, 'Lonach' mountain
Fraser – Touch-Fraser, Stirlingshire; 'The Great Field and Castle Downie'
Gordon – Haddo House, Huntly Castle; 'A Gordon'
Graham – Braco, Brodick, Kincardine Castles
Grant – Castle Grant, Speyside; 'Stand Fast'
Gunn – Castle Clyth, Caithness
Innes – Innes House, Moray
Lamont/Lamond – Toward Castle, near Dunoon
Lennox – Lennox Castle, Stirlingshire
Leslie – Balgonie Castle, Markinch
Lindsay – Edzell Castle, Brechin
Macallister – north of West Loch Tarbert
Macalpin – Dunstaffnage, Argyll
Macarthur – Strachur, Argyll; 'Listen! Listen'
Macaulay – Argyll/Island of Lewis
Macbain/Macbean – Kinchyle, Inverness
Macdonald – Duntulm Castle, Isle of Skye; 'The Heathery Isle', 'Gainsay who dare' (largest Highland clan)
Macdonnel – Glengary, Keppoch; 'The Raven's Rock', 'God and St Andrew'
Macdougall – Dunollie Castle, Oban; 'Victory or Death'

Macduff – 'Kings' of Fife with duty of crowning King of Scots

Macfarlane – Inveruglas, Loch Lomond; 'The Loch of the Host'

Macfie – Colonsay; Hereditary Keeper of Records of the Isles

Macgillivray – Dun-ma-glas, Strathnairn; 'Dunmaghlas'

Macgregor – Glenorchy; 'Height of the Wood'

Macinnes – Kinlochaline Castle, Morvern

Mackintosh – Moy Hall, Inverness; 'Loch Moy'

Macintyre – Glen Noe

Mackay – Drimholisten to Kylescow; 'The White Banner of the Mackay'

Mackenzie – Cromarty; 'The High Hillock'

Mackinnon – Griban, Isle of Mull; 'Remember the death of Alpin'

Maclachlan – Castle Lachlan, Loch Fyne

Maclaren/Maclaurin – Perthshire, Tiree

Maclean – Duart Castle, Mull; 'Death or Life', 'Another for Hector'

Maclennan/Logan – Drumderfit, Kintail; 'The Ridge of Tears'

Macleod – Dunvegan Castle, Skye

Macmillan – Finlayston House, Firth of Clyde

Macnab – Kinneil, Glen Dochart; 'Bovain' lands

Macnaughten – Dundarave Castle, Loch Fyne; 'Frechelen' castle

Macneil – Kisimull, Barra; 'Victory or death'

Macpherson – Cluny, Laggan; 'The black rock'

Macquarrie – Mull and Ulva; 'The Red Speckled Army'

Macqueen – Garfad, Island of Skye

Macrae – Eilean Donan Castle; 'Sgur Urain' mountain

Macthomas – Thom, Glenshee

Malcolm – Lochawe, Argyll

Matheson – Lochalsh; 'The field with two slopes'

Menzies – Castle Menzies, Aberfeldy; 'Up with the red and white'

Morrison – Lewis; 'Hugh's Castle'

Munro – Foulis, Ross-shire; 'Foulis Castle on fire'

Murray – Blair Castle, Perthshire

Nicholson – Scorrybreac, Skye

Ogilvy – Cortachy, Winton Castles

Robertson/Donnachie – Dunalastair, Kinloch Rannoch; 'Fierce when roused'

Rose – Kilravock Castle, Nairn

Ross – Balnagown Castle, Easter Ross

Sinclair – Orkney, Caithness

Skene – Skene, Aberdeenshire

Stewart/Stuart royal house – Atholl, Appin, Bute; 'The Cormorant's Rock'

Sutherland – Dunrobin Castle, Golspie; 'Dunrobin Bridge'

Urquhart – Craigston Castle, Banff

Septs – each clan has a number of dependant family groupings

ARCHITECTS

And a characteristic work

William Bruce (1630–1710) – Hopetoun House, South Queensferry (1696)

Robert Mylne (1633–1710) – rebuilt Holyrood Palace (1671–9)

William Adam (1689–1748) – Chatelherault, Hamilton, Lanark

Sir William Chambers (1723–96) – Royal Bank of Scotland HQ, St Andrew Square, Edinburgh (1772–4)

Robert Adam (1728–92) – Culzean Castle, Ayr (1777)

Charles Cameron (1740–1812) – Pavlovsky Palace, Pavlovsk (architect to Catherine the Great)

James Craig (1744–95) – planned Edinburgh's New Town (1766)

Thomas Telford (1757–1834) – Dean Bridge, Edinburgh (1831)

Robert Stevenson (1772–1850) – Bell Rock, (Lighthouse) off Fife coast

James Gillespie Graham (1776–1855) – St Andrew's RC Cathedral, Glasgow (1814)

Thomas Hamilton (1784–1858) – Royal High School, Edinburgh (1825)

William Burn (1789–1870) – Dupplin Castle, Perthshire (1828–32)

William Playfair (1790–1857) – Royal Scottish Academy, Edinburgh (1826)

George Meikle Kemp (1795–1844) – Scott Monument, Princes Street, Edinburgh (1840–6)

continued

ARCHITECTS – continued

David Bryce (1803–76) – Bank of Scotland HQ, The Mound, Edinburgh (1864–71)

Alan Stevenson (1807–65) – Skerryvore Lighthouse (1844) off Tiree

David Rhind (1808–83) – Commercial Bank, 8–16 Gordon Street, Glasgow (1854–5)

Alexander 'Greek' Thomson (1817–75) – Great Western Terrace, Glasgow (1867–69)

Hippolyte Blanc (1844–1917) – decorated Coats Memorial Church, Paisley

Sir Patrick Geddes (1854–1932) – father of British town planning

Sir Robert Lorimer (1864–1929) – Scottish National War Memorial, Edinburgh Castle (1927)

Charles Rennie Mackintosh (1868–1928) – Glasgow School of Art (1894)

Jack Coia (1898–1981) – Cardross College (1966)

Sir Robert Matthew (1906–) – Royal Festival Hall, London (1951)

Sir Basil Spence (1907–69) – Coventry Cathedral

POETS

And a characteristic work

Oldest known poem on a Scottish theme – The Goddodin by Aneirin (c AD 600)

John Barbour (1316–95) – The Brus

James I (1394–1437) – The Kingis Quair

Robert Henryson (1430–1506) – The Testament of Cresseid

Blind Harry (1450–93) – Wallace

William Dunbar (1465–1530) – Lament for the Makeris

Gavin Douglas (1474–1522) – translated Virgil's Aeneid

Sir David Lindsay (1490–1555) – The Testament and Complaynt of the Papyngo

George Buchanan (1506–82) – Latin poems

Alexander Scott (1525–84) – A Rondel of Luve

Alexander Montgomerie (1556–1610) – The Cherry and the Slae

William Drummond of Hawthornden (1585–1649) – The Cypresse Grove

James Graham, Marquess of Montrose (1612–5?) – The World's a Tennis-Court

Allan Ramsay (1686–1758) – Tea-Table Miscellany

James Thomson (1700–48) – The Seasons

Duncan Ban Macintyre (1724–1812) – Oran da Cheile Nuadh Phosda (Song to his Bride)

James Macpherson (Ossian) (1736–96) – Finga

Robert Fergusson (1750–74) – The Tron-Kirk Bell

Robert Burns (1759–96) – Tam o' Shanter

Carolina Oliphant, Lady Nairne (1766–1845) – Will Ye No Come Back Again?

James Hogg, The Ettrick Shepherd (1770–1835) – Kilmeny

Walter Scott (1771–1832) – The Lady of the Lake

George Gordon, Lord Byron (1788–1824) – Don Juan

William McGonagall (1830–1902) – Railway Bridge of the Silvery Tay

Lewis Spence (1874–1955) – The Prows o' Reekie

Edwin Muir (1887–1959) – The Horses

Hugh MacDiarmid (1892–1978) – A Drunk Man Looks at the Thistle

William Soutar (1898–1943) – The Tryst

J.K. Annand (1908–) – Two Voices

George Bruce (1909–) – My House

Robert Garioch (1909–81) – Two Men and a Blanket

Norman MacCaig (1910–) – Toad

Sorley Maclean (1911–) – Gaoir na h-Eorpa (The Cry of Europe)

Douglas Young (1913–73) – Auntran Blads

Tom Scott (1918–) – The Ship

Sydney Goodsir Smith (1915–75) – Under the Eildon Tree

G.S. Fraser (1915–80) – Home Town Elegy

W.S. Graham (1918–) – The Nightfishing

Maurice Lindsay (1918–) – Glasgow Nocturne

Hamish Henderson (1919–) – The Freedom Come-All-Ye

Edwin Morgan (1920–) – King Billy

Ian Hamilton Finlay (1925–) – The Clouds Anchor (concrete poem)

George Mackay Brown (1927–) – Hamnavoe

Iain Crichton Smith (1928–) – Thistles and Roses

James Burns Singer (1928–64) – Still and All

George MacBeth (1932–) – St Andrews
Duncan Glen (1933–) – My Faither
Stewart Conn (1936–) – Stoats in the Sunlight
Robin Fulton (1937–) – Fields of Focus
Giles Gordon (1940–) – Elegy
David Black (1941–) – Leith Docks
Douglas Dunn (1942–) – The Apple Tree
Alan Bold (1943–) – One Woman
Liz Lochhead (1947–) – Bawd

Largest poetry-reading in Scotland – Norman MacCaig's eightieth birthday party in the Queen's Hall, Edinburgh on 15 November 1990 (800 people)

DRAMATISTS

And a characteristic work

Sir David Lyndsay (1490–1555) – Ane Satyre of the Thrie Estaitis
Allan Ramsay (1686–1758) – The Gentle Shepherd
John Home (1722–1808) – Douglas
J M Barrie (1860–1937) – Mary Rose
James Bridie (1888–1951) – The Anatomist
Joe Corrie (1894–1968) – The Shillin' a Week Man
Robert McLellan (1907–) – Jamie the Saxt
Robert Kemp (1908–67) – The Other Dear Charmer
William Douglas Home (1912–) – The Chiltern Hundreds
Alexander Reid (1914–) – The Lass Wi the Muckle Mou
Sydney Goodsir Smith (1915–75) – The Wallace
Roddy McMillan (1923–79) – The Bevellers
R.D. Laing (1927–89) – Knots
W. Gordon Smith (1928–) – Cocky
Hector MacMillan (1929–) – The Sash
C.P. Taylor (1930–) – Bread and Butter
Tom Gallacher (1934–) – Revival
John McGrath (1935–) – The Cheviot, the Stag and the Black, Black Oil
Stewart Conn (1936–) – The Burning
John Byrne (1940–) – The Slab Boys
Donald Campbell (1940–) – The Widows of Clyth
Tom McGrath (1940–) – The Hardman
Bill Bryden (1942–) – Willie Rough

Liz Lochhead (1947–) – Silver Service
Peter MacDougall (1947–) – Another Bloody Sunday
Catherine Lucy Czerkawaska (1950–) – The Golden Man
Ann Marie Di Mambro (1950–) – Tally's Blood
Marcella Evaristi (1954–) – Eve Set the Balls of Corruption Rolling
Tony Roper (1957–) – The Steamie

THEATRE DIRECTORS

Stephen MacDonald (1933–) – (writer/director) Not About Heroes
Giles Havergal (1938–) – Citizens Theatre, Glasgow
Gordon McDougall (1941–) – Traverse Theatre, Edinburgh
Max Stafford Clark (1941–) – Royal Court Theatre, London

PHOTOGRAPHERS

Early Scottish Photographers

Sir David Brewster (1781–1868) – 'The Stereoscope' described principles of stereoscopic vision
Mungo Ponton (1801–80) – made the crucial discovery that the action of sunlight makes bichromate of potassium insoluble, thus allowing permanent prints to be produced.
John MacCosh (1805–85) – first war photographer: 2nd Sikh War (1848–9); 2nd Burma War (1852–3) calotype
James Valentine (1815–80) – Dundee romantic
Duncan Brown (1819–97) – Clydeside life
Charles Piazzi Smyth (1819–1900) – Astronomer Royal in Scotland; first man to photograph the interior of the Pyramids
Robert Adamson (1821–48) – opened his Rock House studio (1843) in Edinburgh with the painter David Octavius Hill (1802–70), the result of the partnership being the unique sequence of 'sun-pictures' (portraits mainly)

PHOTOGRAPHERS – continued

Alexander Gardner (1821–82) – American Civil War (more than 3000 negatives)
Lady Clementina Hawarden (1822–65) – London portraits of rich young ladies
George Washington Wilson (1823–93) – Aberdeen (Photographer Royal) romantic
George Loudon of Dundee (1825–1912) – fixed focus pocket camera
William Carrick (1827–78) – studio in St Petersburg (1860s)
Dr Thomas Keith (1827–95) – Old Town of Edinburgh (waxed paper negatives)
Thomas Annan (1829–87) – Glasgow views before demolition (1868–77)
Sir James Clerk Maxwell (1831–79) – takes first colour photo (of a tartan ribbon) in 1861
Matthew Morrison (1842–94) West Coast (1880s)
Alexander Wilson Hill (banker) – bromoil transfer process (1894–1930s)
James Craig Annan (1864–1956) – President of the International Society of Pictorial Photographers (1904)

World's first amateur Photographic Society – Calotype Club, Edinburgh (1842)

Contemporary Scottish Photographic Artists

Oscar Marzaroli (1933–88) – film cameraman, photographed Glasgow
Ron O'Donnell (1952–) – colour photographs of decaying domestic interiors
Colin Baxter (1954–) – atmospheric landscapes
Calum Colvin (1961–) – photographs of constructed narratives

FILM-MAKERS/ DIRECTORS/PRODUCERS

Margaret Tait – Aspects of Kirkwall (writer/ director)
Forsyth Hardy (1910–) – founder of Edinburgh Film Guild, Scottish Film Council and the Edinburgh International Film Festival (writer/ producer), (produced more than 150 films for Films of Scotland)
Sandy Mackendrick (1912–) – director Whisky Galore, The Maggie, The Ladykillers (animator/screenwriter)
Jack Gerson (1928–) – Running Blind (writer
John Mackenzie (1932–) – A Sense of Freedom (director)
John McGrath (1935–) – Blood Red Roses (writer/director)
Bill Douglas (1937–) – Trilogy (writer/ director)
Charles Gormley (1938–) – Heavenly Pursuits (writer/director)
Murray Grigor (1939–)/Barbara Grigor (1946–) – Mackintosh (writer/director)
Robin Crichton (1940–) – The Stamp of Greatness (director/producer)
Paddy Higson (1941–) – Silent Scream (producer)
Brian Crumlish (1944–) – Into Nicaragua (director/producer)
Mike Alexander (1945–) – Dreaming (director/producer)
Bill Forsyth (1946–) – Gregory's Girl (writer/ director)
Mark Littlewood (1946–) – Pelicula Films (cameraman)
Gareth Wardell (1946–) – Conquest of the South Pole (director/producer)
Peter McDougall (1947–) – Just Another Saturday (writer)

Animators

James Macdonald (1906–91) – voice of Mickey Mouse for nearly 40 years, of yodelling, whistling, sneezing dwarfs (Snow White) and of Dormouse (Alice in Wonderland)
Norman McLaren (1914–87) – pioneer of drawing directly on to celluloid (eg 'Boggie Doodle' 1940)

Donald Holwill (1948–) – Scotch Myths
Jessica Langford (1952–) – After the Rains
Lesley Keen (1953–) – Ra

Film Workshops

Only film workshop in Scotland – Edinburgh Film Workshop Trust

FILM ACTORS

And a characteristic work

Jimmy Finlayson (1877–1953) – Blockheads
Finlay Currie (1878–1968) – The Robe
Jean Cadell (1884–1967) – I Know Where I'm Going
John Laurie (1897–1980) – Dad's Army
Alastair Sim (1900–76) – The Belles of St Trinian's
Moultrie Kelsall (1901–80) – The Maggie
Dame Flora Robson (1902–84) – Fire Over England
Duncan Macrae (1905–67) – Whisky Galore
James Robertson Justice (1905–75) – Doctor in the House
Molly Urquhart (1906–72) – Geordie
Andrew Cruickshank (1907–88) – Dr Finlay's Casebook (TV)
Jameson Clark (1908–84) – Battle of the Sexes
Hugh McDermott (1908–72) – Trent's Last Case
Alex McCrindle (1912–90) – Star Wars
Ann Crawford (1920–56) – It's Hard to be Good
Molly Weir (1920–) – You're Only Young Twice
Deborah Kerr (1921–) – From Here to Eternity (1953)
Robert Urquhart (1922–) – Mosquito Squadron
Gordon Jackson (1923–90) – Tunes of Glory
Walter Carr (1925–) – The Great Mill Race
Russell Hunter (1925–) – Lonely (TV)
Andrew Keir (1926–) – Royal Hunt of the Sun
Fulton Mackay (1927–87) – Local Hero
Rona Anderson (1928–) – The Prime of Miss Jean Brodie
Ian Bannen (1928–) – Gandhi
Sean Connery (1930–) – Dr No

Ian Cuthbertson (1930–) – Sutherland's Law
Angus Lennie (1930–) – The Great Escape
John Fraser (1931–) – Tunes of Glory
Adrienne Corri (1932–) – The River
Ann Todd (1932–) – The Jolson Story
David McCallum (1933–) – The Man from UNCLE
Mary Ure (1933–75) – Look Back in Anger
Roy Kinnear (1934–89) – Willie Wonka and the Chocolate Factory
Tom Conti (1941–) – Reuben Reuben
Hannah Gordon (1941–) – The Elephant Man
Ian McShane (1942–) – Journey into Fear
Isobel Black (1944–) – Twins of Evil
Paul Young (1944–) – Lorna Doone
Brian Cox (1946–) – Nicholas and Alexander
Bill Paterson (1946–) – Gregory's Girl
Hilton McRae (1949–) – French Lieutenant's Woman
Ian Charleson (1950–90) – Chariots of Fire
John Gordon Sinclair (1962–) – Gregory's Girl

THEATRE and TV ACTORS

Sir Johnston Forbes-Robertson (1853–1937) – actor/manager
Alex Matheson Lang (1879–1948) – film and stage actor/ manager
John Laurie (1897–80) – comic character actor
Lennox Milne (1909–80) – character actress
Eliot Williams (1917–83) – The Last of the Barnstormers
Phil McCall (1925–) – character actor
Edith MacArthur (1926–) – leading lady of great authority
Tom Fleming (1927–) – senior leading–actor and commentator
John Cairney (1930–) – Robert Burns one-man show
Victor Carin (1934–81) – actor and translator

COMEDIANS

Sir Harry Lauder (1870–1950) – the original Scot, creator of an enduring image of boorish stinginess. Highest-earning recording artist of his time

continued

COMEDIANS – continued

Will Fyffe (1885–1947) – I belong to Glasgow
Tommy Lorne (1890–1935) – Fastest man in the Forty-Twa
Jack Buchanan (1890–1957) – revue and musical leading man
Stan Laurel (1890–1965) – thin half of Laurel and Hardy
Harry Gordon (1893–1957) – The Laird o' Inversnecky and panto Dame
Dave Willis (1895–1973) – The nicest-looking warden in the ARP
Tommy Morgan (1898–1958) – Big Beenie (the blonde GI Bride)
Jack Radcliffe (1901–67) – Scotland's William Powell
Renée Houston (1902–) – revue, variety, film and TV actress
Alec Finlay (1906–84) – pawky Scotland s Gentleman
Rikki Fulton (1924–) – Francie and Josie (with Jack Milroy)
Stanley Baxter (1927–) – mimic (If you waant me Thingummy, Ringmy)
Jimmy Logan (1928–) – most versatile of comedians
Fran and Anna – Scottish baroque comedian/singers
The Krankies (Janet and Ian Tough) – Fandabbydosie
Ronnie Corbett (1930–) – The Two Ronnies
Scotland the What? – satirical revue group (Buff Hardie, Stephen Robertson, George Donald on piano)
Andy Cameron (1940–) – presenter/ comedian
Billy Connolly (1942–) – anarchic king of comedy
Rory Bremner – TV impersonator
Alan Cumming and Forbes Masson – Victor and Barry
Jerry Sadowitz (1961–) – alternative comedian

AUTHORS and WRITERS

And a characteristic work

John Major (1467–1550) – History of Greater Britain Both England and Scotland
John Knox (1505–72) – First Blast of the Trumpet Against the Monstrous Regiment of Women
George Buchanan (1506–82) – History of Scotland (20 vols)
James VI (1566–1625) – A Counterblaste to Tobacco
Sir George Mackenzie (1636–91) – Aretina
Andrew Fletcher of Saltoun (1655–1716) – Two Discourses concerning the Affairs of Scotland
David Hume (1711–76) – A Treatise of Human Nature
Tobias Smollett (1721–71) – Humphrey Clinke
James Boswell (1740–95) – The Journal of the Tour of the Hebrides
Henry Mackenzie (1745–1831) – The Man of Feeling
James Hogg (The Ettrick Shepherd) (1770–1835) – The Private Memoirs and Confessions of a Justified Sinner
Sir Walter Scott (1771–1832) – Waverley
Mary Brunton (1778–1818) – Discipline

John Galt (1779–1839) – Annals of the Parish
Susan Ferrier (1782–1854) – Marriage, The Inheritance, Destiny
John Wilson (Christopher North) (1785–1854) – Noctes Ambrosianae
Thomas Carlyle (1795–1881) – On Heroes and Hero Worship
Hugh Miller (1802–56) – The Old Red Sandstone
R.M. Ballantyne (1825–94) – The Coral Island
Robert Louis Stevenson (1850–94) – The Strange Case of Dr Jekyll and Mr Hyde
R.B. Cunninghame Graham (1852–1936) – Scottish Stories
Sir Arthur Conan Doyle (1859–1930) – A Study in Scarlet
J.M. Barrie (1860–1937) – A Window in Thrums
Helen Bannerman (1862–1946) – The Story of Little Black Sambo
George Douglas Brown (1869–1902) – The House with the Green Shutters
Edwin Muir (1887–1959) – An Autobiography
Neil Gunn (1891–1974) – Highland River
Christopher M. Grieve (Hugh MacDiarmid) (1892–1978) – Annals of the Five Senses
S.R. Crockett (1860–1914) – The Stickit Minister
Neil Munro (1864–1930) – The Daft Days
John Buchan (1875–1940) – The Thirty-Nine Steps
Compton Mackenzie (1883–1972) – Whisky Galore

Rebecca West (1892–1983) – The Return of
the Soldier

A.J. Cronin (1896–1981) – Hatter's Castle

Naomi Mitchison (1897–) – The Bull Calves

Eric Linklater (1899–1974) – Laxdale Hall

Bruce Marshall (1899–) Teacup Terrace

Lewis Grassic Gibbon (1901–35) – A Scots
Quair

Fionn Mac Colla (1906–75) – The Albannach

Robert Garioch (1909–81) – Two Men and a
Blanket

Robin Jenkins (1912–) – The Cone-Gatherers

Fred Urquhart (1912–) – Palace of Green
Days

David Toulmin (1913–) – Blown Seed

Sydney Goodsir Smith (1915–70) – Under the
Eildon Tree

Jessie Kesson (1916–) – The White Bird
Passes

Mary Stewart (1916–) – The Gabriel Hounds

Muriel Spark (1918–) – The Prime of Miss
Jean Brodie

Elspeth Davie (1919–) – Creating a Scene

George Mackay Brown (1921–) – A Calendar
of Love

Alistair Maclean (1922–87) – HMS Ulysses

Dorothy Dunnett (1923–) – The Ringed Castle

Alexander Trocchi (1925–63) – Cain's Book

Archie Hind (1928–) – The Dear Green Place

James Kennaway (1928–) – Tunes of Glory

Joan Lingard (1932–) – The Prevailing Wind

Alasdair Gray (1934–) – Lanark

Alan Sharp (1934–) – A Green Tree in Gedde

William McIlvanney (1936–) – Docherty

Allan Massie (1938–) – Change and Decay in
All Around I See

Robert Nye (1939–) – Falstaff

Giles Gordon (1940–) – 100 Scenes from
Married Life

Non-Scottish Writers Living and
Working in Scotland

Oliver Goldsmith (1730–74) – medical student,
Edinburgh University

Peter Mark Roget (1779–1869) – Roget's
Thesaurus

Thomas de Quincey (1785–1859) – editor,
Edinburgh

Beatrix Potter (1866–1943) – writer and
illustrator of children's books

Siegfried Sassoon (1886–1967) – poet
recuperating at Craiglockart Hospital

Wilfred Owen (1893–1918) – poet recuperating
at Craiglockart Hospital

George Orwell (1903–50) – novelist: Nineteen
Eighty-Four

Rosamunde Pilcher (1924–) – novelist: The
Shell Seekers

Stanley Eveling (1925–) – playwright: Dear
Mr Kooning

PAINTERS and SCULPTORS

Earliest rock-carving – Lagalochan, Argyll (c
3000 BC)

Earliest painted portrait of an eminent Scot –
James II by Jorg von Ehingen (a
Swabian knight) in his diary (1458)

George Jamesone (1588–1644) – portrait
painter, pupil of Rubens

John Scougall (1610–30) – portrait of Henry,
Prince of Wales

Joseph Michael Wright (1625–1700) – portrait
painter in London

Sir John de Medina (1659–1710) – Spanish
portrait painter (the last Scottish knight
before the Union of the Parliaments)

William Aikman (1682–1731) – pupil of
Medina; trained in Italy

John Smibert (1684–1751) – portrait painter
who settled in USA where he was
prominent in the New England School

Allan Ramsay (1713–84) – portrait painter of
great naturalness and charm

Catherine Read (1723–78) – pastellist (one of
earliest women artists)

James Tassie (1735–99) – sculptor of portrait
medallions

Alexander Runciman (1736–85) – history
painter (especially murals)

David Martin (1737–97) – painter to the
Prince of Wales (George IV)

Jacob More (1740–93) – scene- and
landscape-painter

John Kay (1742–1826) – barber and caricaturist

David Allan (1744–96) – painter of street-
scenes and rural subjects ('the Scottish
Hogarth')

continued

PAINTERS and SCULPTORS – continued

Archibald Skirving (1749–1819) – exciseman turned portrait painter

David Deuchar (1743–1808) – seal and metal engraver and etcher

Henry Raeburn (1756–1823) – painter of stylish but direct portraits. One of the finest of his day

Alexander Nasmyth (1758–1840) – 'the father of Scottish landscape', also a builder and architect

Hugh William Williams ('Greek Williams') (1773–1829) – visited Greece; painted 'on the spot' (an innovation at the time)

James Skene (1775–1864) – townscape artist of Edinburgh

Rev John Thomson (1778–1840) – landscape painter

Patrick Nasmyth (1787–1831) – deaf landscape painter

Charles Kirkpatrick Sharpe (1781–1851) – Oxford graduate, archaeologist, antiquarian, caricaturist

Andrew Geddes (1783–1844) – sensitive portrait painter

David Wilkie (1785–1841) – painter of village life and domestic misfortune

John Watson Gordon (1788–1864) – succeeded Raeburn

Thomas Campbell (1790–1858) – sculptor

Walter Geikie (1795–1837) – deaf and dumb artist who excelled at humorous low life

David Roberts (1796–1864) – circus and operatic scene-painter who drew Near Eastern architectural landscapes

Robert Scott Lauder (1803–69) – painted scenes from Scott's novels

Sir John Steell (1804–91) – sculptor of most of the major statues in Edinburgh (Scott, Queen Victoria, Wellington, Prince Albert)

Horatio McCulloch (1805–67) – one of first to show grandeur of the Highlands

William Dyce (1806–64) – decorated House of Lords with murals

David Scott (1806–49) – painter with melancholic imagination

William Scott (1811–90) – Pre-Raphaelite

William Brodie (1815–81) – sculptor

Mrs D.O. Hill (Amelia Robertson Paton) (1820–1904) – sculptor

Sir John Noel Paton (1821–1901) – painter of fairies and mythology

William Quiller Orchardson (1832–1910) – artist with a facility for composition

William McTaggart (1835–1910) – painter of rural subjects full of light and air and of the sea

Phoebe Anna Traquair (1852–1936) – mural artist in Edinburgh and Glasgow who specialized in illumination, embroidery, book-binding, metalwork and enamelling

E.A. Hornel (1864–1933) – expressed the colour and harmony of nature

John Duncan (1866–1945) – decorator of the Celtic renaissance. Worked often for Patrick Geddes, the conservationist and town-planner

S.J. Peploe (1871–1935) – colourist, almost Cubist in style

J.D. Fergusson (1874–1961) – colourist fascinated by linear rhythm

Leslie Hunter (1877–1931) – colourist who used bright colours and energetic paint application

F.C.B. Cadell (1883–1937) – witty, brilliant painter with contrasting styles

William McCance (1894–1970) – vorticist/surrealist

Anne Redpath (1895–1965) – vibrant colourist

William Johnstone (1897–1981) – geometric/biomorphic painter

William Gillies (1898–1973) – vital observer of Lowland terrain

John Maxwell (1905–1962) – painter of the magic of dreams

William Wilson (1905–72) – stained glass artist and etcher

J McIntosh Patrick (1907–) – super-realist in colour and detail

Scottie Wilson (1907–76) – primitive and colourist

Robert MacBryde (1913–66) – caught the trauma of the still life

Robert Colquhoun (1914–62) – painter of tragic emotion

Sir Robin Philipson (1916–) – aggressive and colourful expressionist

Sax Shaw (1916–) – stained-glass artist

Alan Davie (1920–) – glider-pilot, jazz musician, abstract expressionist

Joan Eardley (1921–63) – Gorbals children and east coast village of Catterline

George Wylie (1923–) – provocative and entertaining sculptor

Eduardo Paolozzi (1924–) – pop artist incorporating mechanical parts

Ian Hamilton Finlay (1925–) – concrete artist who has transformed his home in the Pentland Hills into 'Little Sparta'

Emilio Coia (c 1910–) – veteran cartoonist

John Houston (1930–) – ex-footballer turned colourist landscape painter

Elizabeth Blackadder (1931–) – painter of delicate fragments and nuances

John Bellany (1942–) – preoccupied with the powerful symbolism of fishing life and the angst of modern times

Jake Harvey (1948–) – sculptor: Hugh MacDiarmid Memorial Sculpture

Steven Campbell (1953–) – former engineer obsessed with the absurd

David Mach (1956–) – sculptor using magazines, bottles, tyres and toys

Peter Howson (1958–) – painter of dynamic working-class urban landscapes

Adrian Wiszniewski (1958–) – painter of large-scale melancholy symbols

Ken Currie (1960–) – Scottish labour history

Stephen Conroy (1964–) – claustrophobic classical interiors

COMPOSERS of CLASSICAL MUSIC

Robert Carver (1487–1566) – motets and masses

James Lauder (1535–95) – My Lord of Marche pavan (The Golden Pavane)

John Clerk (1676–1755) – violin sonata and cantata (pupil of Corelli)

William McGibbon (1695–1756) – oboist, violinist; 30 sonatas; 128 folk tunes

James Oswald (1711–69) – instrumental music and songs for the theatre

John Riddell (1718–95) – composer of reels

John Reid (1721–1807) – 12 flute sonatas, regimental marches

Niel Gow (1727–1807) – fiddler composer

Thomas Erskine (1732–81) – 10 symphonies, 6 sonatas, 12 minuets

Nathaniel Gow (1763–1831) – reels and strathspeys, band leader

Robert Smith (1780–1829) – song-writer (Jessie the flow'r o' Dunblane)

Finlay Dun (1795–1853) – edited and arranged song collections

John Thomson (1805–41) – 1st Reid Professor of Music at Edinburgh; opera composer, friend of Mendelssohn and Schumann

Alexander Hume (1811–59) – song-writer (Afton Water)

William Jackson (1828–76) – song-writer (The Lass o' Ballochmyle)

Alexander Ewing (1830–95) – Scotland's greatest hymn composer (Jerusalem the Golden)

John Grieve (1842–1916) – song-writer (Bonnie Wells o' Wearie)

Sir Alexander Campbell Mackenzie (1847–1935) – greatest Scottish composer after the Reformation, Principal of Royal Academy of Music, London

William Wallace (1860–1940) – A Scots Fantasy

Learmont Drysdale (1866–1909) – overture Tam o' Shanter

Hamish McCunn (1868–1916) – The Land of the Mountain and Flood

Francis George Scott (1880–1958) – Scottish Lyrics (6 vols)

Ian Whyte (1901–60) – operas, ballets, symphonies

Erik Chisholm (1904–65) – The Edge of the Great World

Robin Orr (1909–) – symphonies, operas, song-cycles

Cedric Thorpe-Davie (1913–83) – film, theatre, radio music

Iain Hamilton (1922–) – Sinfonia for two orchestras

Robert Crawford (1925–) – string quartets

Thomas Wilson (1927–) – choral triptych

Thea Musgrave (1928–) – concertos, operas

Ronald Stevenson (1928–) – Passacaglia for piano on DSCH

David Dorward (1933–) – Weather Beasts

John McLeod (1934–) – The Gokstad Ship

Sebastian Forbes (1941–) – chamber music to opera

Martin Dalby (1942–) – Cantica (Head of Music, BBC Scotland))

John Purser (1942–) – Prometheus Island

Non-Scottish Classical Musicians Who Have Been Based in Scotland

David Riccio (1533–66) – bass singer and secretary for Mary Queen of Scots

Johann F. Lampe (1703–51) – Handel's favourite bassoonist (The Dragon of Wantley – opera)

Giusto Ferdinando Tenducci (1736–1800) – only castrato known to have fathered a child

Domenico Corri (1746–1825) – The Wives Revenged (opera)

Frederick Niecks (1845–1924) – violinist/organist

Donald Tovey (1875–1940) – The Bride of Dionysus (opera)

Hans Gal (1890–1987) – musicologist/composer

William Wordsworth (1908–88) – Conflicts

Gian Carlo Menotti (1911–) – Amahl and the Night Visitors

Kenneth Leighton (1929–88) – Columba (opera)

Sir Peter Maxwell Davies (1934–) – The Martyrdom of St Magnus

Haflidi Hallgrimsson (1941–) – Poemi

Edward Harper (1941–) – In memoriam Kenneth Leighton

Lyell Cresswell (1944–) – Salm

INSTRUMENTALISTS, CONDUCTORS, ARRANGERS and SONG COLLECTORS

Simon Tailler – 13th-century church music theorist

David Herd (1732–1810) – song ballad collector

George Thomson (1757–1851) – publisher/collector

Helen Hopekirk (1856–1941) – pianist

Marjorie Kennedy-Fraser (1857–1930) – collector/arranger of Gaelic island folk-songs

Fredrick Lamond (1868–1948) – pianist (pupil of Liszt and von Bulow)

Sir Hugh Roberton (1874–1952) – founder/conductor of Glasgow Orpheus Choir

Francis Collinson (1898–1985) – ethno-musicologist

Robert Kinloch Anderson (1911–84) – Artistic Director EMI Records (1960s)

Sir Alexander Gibson (1926–) – first native-born principal conductor of RSO, co-founder of Scottish Opera

Moray Welsh (1947–) – cellist: Ariensky Ensemble

Paul Coletti (1959–) – Professor of Viola, Peabody Institute, Baltimore, USA

Paul Galbraith (1964–) – concert guitarist

Evelyn Glennie (1965–) – tympani player and percussionist

OPERA COMPOSERS

Allan Ramsay (1685–1758) – The Gentle Shepherd (1725)

Christina Bogue – The Uhlans (1885), first opera by Scotswoman

Hamish McCunn (1868–1916) – Jeannie Deans (1894)

Donald Tovey (1875–1940) – The Bride of Dionysus (1912)

Robin Orr (1909–) – On the Razzle (1986)

Iain Hamilton (1922–) – Anna Karenina (1976)

Thomas Wilson (1927–) – The Confessions of a Justified Sinner (1976)

Thea Musgrave (1928–) – Mary Queen of Scots (1976)

Judith Weir (1953–) – The Vanishing Bridegroom (1990)

CLASSICAL, OPERA and CONCERT SINGERS

John Wilson (1800–49) – the first great Scottish tenor

John Templeton (1802–86) – tenor: embraced by Donizetti ('Malibran's tenor')

David Kennedy (1825–86) – much-travelled tenor. Father of Marjorie Kennedy-Fraser. Ancestor of violinist Nigel Kennedy

Mary Garden (1877–1967) – soprano (created role of Mélisande in Debussy's opera 'Pelléas et Mélisande' 1902); director of Chicago Opera

oseph Hislop (1884–1977) – tenor with unrivalled international reputation. Based in Sweden. Teacher of Birgit Nilsson and Jussi Björling

Canon Sydney McEwan (1909–) – concert tenor who became a priest

Robert Wilson (1909–64) – tenor ('The Voice of Scotland')

an Wallace (1919–) – buffo bass, quiz panellist and singer of Flanders and Swan 'Mud'

David Ward (1922–83) – Wagnerian bass of great authority

Murray Dickie (1924–) – tenor

William McAlpine (1925–) – tenor

Kenneth McKellar (1927–) – popular tenor

Bill McCue (1934–) – buffo (comic/character) bass

Moira Anderson (1938–) – perennial soprano with chart success: The Holy City (No 43, 2 wks, 1969)

Peter Morrison (1940–) – baritone (Scots and light opera)

Linda Esther Gray (1948–) – Wagnerian soprano

Donald Maxwell (1948–) – dramatic baritone

Linda Ormiston (1948–) – mezzo

Margaret Marshall (1949–) – soprano

Linda Finnie (1952–) – dramatic soprano

Marie Slorach (1952) – soprano

Isobel Buchanan (1954–) – soprano

Marie McLaughlin (1954–) – soprano

BALLET, DANCE and MIME

Kenneth MacMillan (1929–) – outstanding among Scottish choreographers. He has been one of the leaders in contemporary ballet

Lindsay Kemp (1939–) – descendant of Shakespeare's clown William Kemp, a mime artist who has produced distinguished work in cabaret and rock spectacles.

Michael Clark (1962–) – an arrestingly original dancer and choreographer of anarchic invention (I am Curious Orange, 1988)

Forerunners of Scottish Ballet
(founded 1969)

The Celtic Ballet (1940) – the work of the dancer and teacher Margaret Morris (1891–1980), wife of the painter J.D. Fergusson

Marjory Middleton's Edinburgh Ballet School (1915) – produced leading dancers such as Alexander Bennett (1930–) and Kenneth Bannerman

The Scottish National Ballet (1960)

TRADITIONAL MUSIC

Genres

Ceilidhs – informal concerts

Work songs – milking, weaving, spinning, rowing, reaping

Lullabies – O can ye sew cushions? (Lady Nairne)

Industrial songs – Jute Mill Song (Mary Brooksbank)

Sea-music – shanties, hornpipes, reels, dredging-songs

Love-songs – Ae Fond Kiss (Robert Burns)

Travelling songs – When the Yellow's on the Broom (Adam McNaughtan)

Military songs – Scots Wha Hae (Robert Burns)

Clarsach

The Caledonian harp had 30 strings struck by the fingers or a plectrum. James I and Mary Queen of Scots were fine harpists. Harpists performed at court and many Highland chiefs kept a harpist (eg Rory Dall, the legendary 17th-century harpist to the MacLeods). In the 1850s music on the harp almost died out. The Clarsach Society was founded in 1931.

Contemporary Clarsach Players

Alison Kinnaird – brilliant, traditional, technical musician

Isobel Mieras – singer/harpist

Sileas – clarsach duo

Savourna Stevenson – composer/Jazz innovator

Traditional Singers in Gaelic, Scots and English

Anne Lorne Gillies – television presenter and singer
Lizzie Higgins – Jeannie Robertson's daughter
Callum Kennedy – Gaelic tenor, entertainer and entrepreneur
Willie John MacAulay – popular Gaelic singer
Jimmy MacBeath (King of the Cornkisters)
Flora MacNeil – Gaelic singer
Jean Redpath – musical missionary
Jeannie Robertson – diva of the traditional ballad
Willie Scott – storyteller
Duncan Williamson – storyteller and traveller ('Living National Monument')

Traditional Music Institutions

First Chair of Gaelic in Scotland – Edinburgh University (1882)
MOD – annual gathering with competition in the arts of the Gael
Norman Buchan – one of prime movers behind Scots Folk Song Revival (1945)
School of Scottish Studies (founded 1951) – receptacle of traditional Scottish lore and language through the work of Francis Collinson, Hamish Henderson and many others
Scottish Ethnology (traditional lore of Scotland) – first university degree of its kind (Edinburgh University 1990)

The Bagpipe

An ancient instrument found in France, Greece, Italy and Asia. The traditional components of the bagpipe are: blowpipe, chanter, two tenor drones, bass drone, bag. The effects of the great Highland bagpipe in war continue to be stunning as in the exploits of Lieutenant-Colonel Campbell Mitchell ('Mad Mitch') of the Argylls who as recently as 1967 disarmed the rebels in Aden with its disorienting music.

Highland (Great Highland, Half-Set, Miniature or Parlour) bagpipe is blown by mouth
Lowland and Border pipes are blown by a bellows held under the arm.

Hereditary pipers
MacCrimmons (Clan Macleod) with a college at Boreraig, Skye
Macintyres (Menzies of Menzies)
Mackays (MacKenzies of Gairloch)
McArthurs (McDonalds of the Isles)
Rankins (Macleans of Duart)

The bagpipes were banned after the Reformation and again by the Whigs after Culloden. The piper James Reid was executed at York in 1746 as a rebel because the pipes were deemed to be an instrument of war. The tartan and the bagpipes were kept alive by the Highland regiments and by emigrants to America. During World War I, 500 pipers were killed.

Modern Bagpipe Music
Highland: Strathclyde Police Band (1885)
Lowland: Battlefield Band
Ossian
Whistlebinkies, original and traditional

Pipe Band World Championship (six times in a row: 1981-6) – Strathclyde Police Pipe Band
Most successful pipe band – Shotts and Dykehead Caledonian Pipe Band (10th world title, 1980)
Fastest bagpipe playing – Sergeant Mick Maitland, Pipe Major, No 111 RAF Fighter Squadron, played 'Scotland the Brave' at a speed of Mach 2.0 at a height of 12 190 m/*40 000 ft* in a Phantom XV574 piloted by his Squadron Commander 40 miles south of Akrotiri, Cyprus (1986)
Longest bagpipe playing – 120 hrs from 6 to 11 Aug 1988 (Jordan Anderson, William Scannell, Frederick Cote and Andrew Belson at the Old Fort on St Helen's Island, Quebec, Canada)

gpipes ruled not a musical instrument – by
Chicago judge in 1899 (they caused a
horse to bolt and throw its rider through
a shop window)

lix Mendelssohn – introduced bagpipe
music into his 'Hebrides' overture

oday the bagpipe is used in jazz, pop and
classical music

he Scots Fiddle

raditional fiddle styles include Highland,
orth East and Shetland – though these are
ow suffused with Lowland and Irish influ-
aces. Notable contemporary players include:
ngus Grant (1931–) – Highland
ill Hardie (1916–) – North East
am Anderson (1910–91) – Shetland

FOLK BANDS and ARTISTS

attlefield Band – dynamic and innovative
oys of the Lough – Scottish/Irish fusion
apercaillie – Lowland and Gaelic new-wave
auld Blast Orchestra – developed for Liz
Lochhead's 'Jock Tamson's Bairns'
(jazzed-up folk)
eolbeg – keyboards, clarsach, pipes
orries – 'Flower of Scotland' (disbanded
by the death of the much-lamented Roy
Williamson who composed the tune)
usy Club – Scottish swing
shers – Jean, Archie, Ray, Joyce, Cynthia,
Audrey, Cilla (one of the largest families
in the Scottish folk revival); traditional
and contemporary
aundry Bar Band – ceilidh fundamentalists
aberlunzie – roots with rock
ick Gaughan – Scotland's tune-fork
ue and Cry – rock with roots
amish Imlach – honky-tonk Falstaff of folk
credible String Band (disbanded) – Robin
Williamson and Mike Heron;
psychedelic pioneers
ert Jansch – Boroughmuir blues
cCalmans – perennial harmonizers
van MacColl (1915–89) – leading figure in
British folk revival. Wrote over 300
songs (eg Dirty Old Town)
astair McDonald – born-again Jacobite

Rory and Alex McEwen (disbanded)
Matt McGinn (1928-75) – pawky parodist of
political protest
Jimmy Macgregor and Robin Hall (now
disbanded)
Ian MacIntosh – gentle political persuader
Mike Maran – guitarist, composer
Mike Marra – solo keyboard with laconic
style (the Lochee Corncrake and musical
director for 'Your Cheatin' Heart')
Hamish Moore – author of 'The Pipes that
came in from the Cold' (he re-
established Border/Lowland folk)
Ossian – pan-Celtic interpreters
Run-Rig – Gaelic/rock fusion
Seannachie – broadbeat
Silly Wizard (disbanded) – Phil Cunningham
and Dougie Maclean
Singing Kettle – Cilla Fisher, Artie Tresize,
Gary Coupland (children's entertainers)
Tannahill Weavers – Celtic thunder-band
Whistlebinkies – Scottish/Irish folk with
classical overtones

Most recordings – Genesis P. Orridge with
Psychic TV released 14 live albums on
Temple Records (1987-9)

JAZZ BANDS and ARTISTS

ABERDEEN
Sandy West
AYRSHIRE
Jim Galloway – soprano sax
DUMFRIES
Riverside Jazz Band
DUNDEE
East Coast Jazzmen
EDINBURGH
Sandy Brown – hard-brush clarinettist
George Chisholm – trombone star
Jay Craig – baritone saxophonist with
Buddy Rich
Gordon Cruickshank – tenor sax
anchorman for BBC Radio
Scotland's 'Take the Jazz Train'
Jack Duff – tenor sax and clarinet in
Jersey Jazz Club
Al Fairweather – trumpet/arranger Stan
Greig – 'stride' piano

continued

JAZZ BANDS and ARTISTS – *continued*

Mike Hart – leader of Scottish Society Syncopators, banjo/guitar player, director of the Edinburgh Jazz Festival

Johnny Keating – ex-trombonist, chief arranger for Ted Heath (composed 'Z Cars' theme)

Charlie McNair – trumpet (Charlie McNair Jazzband)

Archie Semple – clarinet

Alex Shaw – piano (Alex Shaw Trio)

Tommy Smith – wonder-boy saxophonist

Symon Stungo (piano) – introduced jazz to the capital (5-piece Jazzmaniacs. 1919)

Alex Welsh – Dixieland trumpeter

An unofficial record is claimed for Edinburgh's Royal High School for having produced more than 50 jazz musicians

GALASHIELS
   Jackie Doule – tenor sax (Modernist)
   Robbie Richardson – tenor sax (Mainstream)
GLASGOW
   Back o' Town Syncopators –'Good Time' trad
   Clyde Valley Stompers – highly popular in 1950s and 60s
   Dean Kerr Dixielanders
   Carol Kidd and Trio
   George Ogilvie and his Dixielanders
   George Penman
   Annie Ross (Jimmy Logan's sister) – singer/actress
   Southside – New Orleans jazz
   Vernon Jazz Band – New Orleans jazz
   Bobby Wishart – sax
INVERNESS
   Rhythm Kings

Elizabeth Welch (1909–), whose mother was Scottish, popularized the Charleston in the 1920s and had songs written for her by Cole Porter and recently (1990) recorded on CD (Solomon by Cole Porter)

ROCK and POP MUSIC

Only Scot to have won Eurovision Song Contest Lulu (Boom Bang-a-Bang, 1969)

First British female pop singer to appear behind Iron Curtain – Lulu (1966)

Only Scottish politician to make a reggae record – Sir David Steel ('I feel Liberal')

No 1 Hits and Chart Records

Altered Images
   Happy Birthday (No 2, 17 wks, 1981)
   I Could be Happy (No 7, 12 wks, 1981)
   Don't Talk to me About Love (No 7, wks, 1983)
Associates
   Party Fears Two (No 9, 10 wks, 1982)
Average White Band
   Pick up the Pieces (No 6, 9 wks, 1975)
Aztec Camera
   Somewhere in My Heart (No 3, 14 wks, 1988)
Bay City Rollers
   Keep on Dancing (No 9, 13 wks, 1971
   Remember/Sha-la-la (No 6, 12 wks, 1974)
   Shang-a-lang (No 2, 10 wks, 1974)
   Summerlove Sensation (No 3, 10 wks, 1974)
   All of Me Loves All of You (No 4, 10 wks, 1974)
   Bye Bye Baby (No 1, 16 wks, 1975)
   Give a Little Love (No 1, 9 wks, 1975)
   Money Honey (No 3, 9 wks, 1975)
   Love Me Like I Love You (No 4, 6 wks, 1976)
   I Only Wanna Be With You (No 4, 9 wks, 1976)
   It's a Game (No 16, 6 wks, 1977)
   You Made Me Believe in Magic (No 34, 3 wks, 1977)
Maggie Bell
   Hazell (No 37, 5 wks, 1978)
Big Country
   Fields of Fire (No 10, 12 wks, 1983)
   Chance (No 9, 9 wks, 1983)
   Wonderland (No 8, 8 wks, 1984)
   Look Away (No 7, 8 wks, 1986)
Bronski Beat
   Smalltown Boy (No 3, 13 wks, 1984)

Why (No 6, 10 wks, 1984)

Hit That Perfect Beat (No 3, 14 wks, 1985)

ros (Craig Logan)

When Will I be Famous? (No 2, 13 wks, 1988)

Drop the Boy (No 2, 10 wks, 1988)

I Owe You Nothing (No 1, 11 wks, 1988)

I Quit (No 4, 8 wks, 1988)

Cat Among the Pigeons (No 2, 5 wks, 1988)

ndy Cameron

Ally's Tartan Army (No 6, 8 wks, 1978)

thna Campbell

The Old Rugged Cross (No 33, 11 wks, 1975)

unior Campbell

Hallelujah Freedom (No 10, 9 wks, 1972)

Sweet Illusion (No 15, 9 wks, 1973)

eil Christian

That's Nice (No 14, 10 wks, 1966)

octeau Twins

Pearly-Dewdrops' Drops (No 29, 5 wks, 1984)

loyd Cole and The Commotions

Lost Weekend (No 17, 7 wks, 1985)

ommunards

Don't Leave Me This Way (No 1, 14 wks, 1986)

So Cold the Night (No 8, 10 wks, 1986)

Never Can Say Goodbye (No 4, 11 wks, 1987)

illy Connolly

D.I.V.O.R.C.E. (No 1, 10 wks, 1975)

'Supergran' – Theme Music (Tyne Tees TV)

eacon Blue

Real Gone Kid (No 8, 12 wks, 1988)

ackie Dennis

La Dee Dah (No 4, 9 wks, 1958)

Purple People Eater (No 29, 1 wk 1958)

ydney Devine

Scotland For Ever (No 48, 1 wk, 1978)

im Diamond

I Should Have Known Better (No 1, 13 wks, 1984)

Hi Ho Silver (No 5, 11 wks, 1986)

arbara Dickson

Answer Me (No 9, 7 wks, 1976)

Another Suitcase in Another Hall (No 18, 7 wks, 1977)

Caravan Song (No 41, 7 wks, 1980)

January February (No 11, 10 wks, 1980)

In the Night (No 48, 2 wks, 1980)

Barbara Dickson/Elaine Paige

I know him so well (No 1, 16 wks, 1985)

Lonnie Donegan

Rock Island Line (No 8, 13 wks, 1956)

Lost John (No 2, 17 wks, 1956)

Bring a Little Water Sylvie (No 7, 12 wks, 1956)

Don't You Rock Me Daddy-o (No 4, 17 wks, 1957)

Cumberland Gap (No 1, 12 wks, 1957)

Putting on the Style (No 1, 19 wks, 1957)

My Dixie Darling (No 10, 15 wks, 1957)

Grand Coolie Dam (No 6, 15 wks, 1958)

Tom Dooley (No 3, 14 wks, 1958)

Battle of New Orleans (No 2, 16 wks, 1959)

My Old Man's A Dustman (No 1, 13 wks, 1960)

I Wanna Go Home (No 5, 17 wks, 1960)

Lorelei (No 10, 8 wks, 1960)

Have A Drink On Me (No 8, 15 wks, 1961)

Michael Row the Boat (No 6, 11 wks, 1961)

The Party's Over (No 9, 12 wks, 1962)

Donovan

Catch The Wind (No 4, 13 wks, 1965)

Colours (No 4, 12 wks, 1965)

Sunshine Superman (No 2, 11 wks, 1966)

Mellow Yellow (No 8, 8 wks, 1967)

There is a Mountain (No 8, 11 wks, 1967)

Jennifer Juniper (No 5, 11 wks, 1968)

Hurdy Gurdy Man (No 4, 10 wks, 1968)

Sheena Easton

Modern Girl (No 8, 12 wks, 1980)

9 to 5 (No 3, 15 wks, 1980)

One Man Woman (No 14, 6 wks, 1980)

Take My Time (No 44, 5 wks, 1981)

When He Shines (No 12, 8 wks, 1981)

continued

ROCK and POP MUSIC – continued

For Your Eyes Only (No 8, 13 wks, 1981)
Just Another Broken Heart (No 33, 8 wks, 1981)
You Could Have Been With Me (No 54, 3 wks, 1981)
Machinery (No 38, 5 wks, 1982)
Exploited
Dogs of War (No 63, 4 wks, 1981)
Dead Cities (No 31, 5 wks, 1982)
Attack (No 50, 3 wks, 1982)
Fairground Attraction
Perfect (No 1, 13 wks, 1988)
Find My Love (No 7, 10 wks, 1988)
Gallacher and Lyle
I Wanna Stay With You (No 6, 9 wks, 1976)
Heart On My Sleeve (N0 6, 10 wks, 1976)
Breakaway (No 35, 4 wks, 1976)
Every Little Teardrop (No 32, 4 wks, 1977)
Goodbye Mr Mackenzie
Goodbye Mr Mackenzie (No 62, 2 wks, 1988)
Hipsway
The Honeythief (No 17, 9 wks, 1986)
Hue and Cry
Labour of Love (No 6, 16 wks, 1987)
Jesus and Mary Chain
April Skies (No 8, 6 wks, 1987)
Jethro Tull (Ian Anderson)
Living in the Past (No 3, 14 wks, 1969)
Paul Jones
High Time (No 4, 15 wks, 1966)
I've Been A Bad Bad Boy (No 5, 9 wks, 1967)
Thinkin' Ain't For Me (No 32, 7 wks, 1967)
Aquarius (No 45, 2 wks, 1969)
Johnny Keating
Theme from Z Cars (No 8, 14 wks, 1962)
Annie Lennox (Eurythmics)
Sweet Dreams Are Made Of This (No 2, 14 wks, 1983)
Love Is A Stranger (No 6, 8 wks, 1983)
Who's That Girl (No 3, 10 wks, 1983)
Right By Your Side (No 10, 11 wks, 1983)

Here Comes The Rain Again (No 8, 8 wks, 1984)
Sexcrime (No 4, 13 wks, 1984)
There Must Be An Angel Playing (No 1, 13 wks, 1985)
Thorn In My Side (No 5, 11 wks, 1986)
Love and Money
Candybar Express (No 56, 4 wks, 1986)
Lulu
Shout (No 7, 13 wks, 1964)
Leave A Little Love (No 8, 11 wks, 1965)
The Boat That I Row (No 6, 11 wks, 1967)
Me The Peaceful Heart (No 9, 9 wks, 1968)
I'm A Tiger (No 9, 13 wks, 1968)
Boom Bang-a-bang (No2, 13 wks, 1968)
The Man Who Sold The World (No 3, 9 wks, 1974)
Shout (No 8, 10 wks, 1986)
McGuinness Flint
When I'm Dead and Gone (No 2, 14 wks, 1970)
Malt and Barley Blues (No 5, 12 wks, 1971)
Mad Jocks
Jock Mix (No 46, 5 wks, 1987)
Marillion
Market Square Heroes (No 60, 2 wks, 1982)
Kayleigh (No 2, 14 wks, 1985)
Lavender (No 5, 9 wks, 1985)
Incommunicado (No 6, 5 wks, 1987)
Marmalade
Lovin' Things (No 6, 13 wks, 1968)
Ob-la-di Ob-la-da (No 1, 20 wks, 1968)
Baby Make It Soon (No 9, 13 wks, 1969)
Reflections Of My Life (No 3, 12 wks, 1969)
Rainbow (No 3, 14 wks, 1970)
Cousin Norman (No 6, 11 wks, 1971)
Radancer (No 6, 12 wks, 1972)
Falling Apart At The Seams (No 9, 11 wks, 1976)
Lena Martell
One Day at a Time (No 1, 18 wks, 1979)

Middle of the Road
Chirpy Chirpy Cheep Cheep (No 1, 34 wks, 1971)
Tweedle Dee Tweedle Dum (No 2,17 wks, 1971)
Soley Soley (No 5, 12 wks, 1971)

Frankie Miller
Darlin' (No 6, 15 wks, 1978)

Nazareth
Broken Down Angel (No 9, 11 wks, 1973)
Bad Bad Boy (No 10, 9 wks, 1973)

Orange Juice
Rip It Up (No 8, 11 wks, 1983)

Elaine Paige
Don't Walk Away Til I Touch You (No 46, 5 wks, 1978)
Memory (No 6, 12 wks, 1981)
I Know Him So Well (No 1, 16 wks, 1985)

Pilot
January (No 1, 10 wks, 1975)

Proclaimers
Letter From America (No 3, 10 wks, 1987)
Sunshine on Leith (No 41, 5 wks, 1988)

Jesse Rae
Over the Sea (No 65, 2 wks, 1985)

Gerry Rafferty
Baker Street (No 3, 15 wks, 1978)
Night Owl (No 5, 13 wks, 1979)
Get It Right Next Time (No 30, 9 wks, 1979)
Bring It All Home (No 54, 4 wks, 1980)
Royal Mile (No 67, 2 wks, 1980)

Neil Reid
Mother of Mine (No 2, 20 wks,)

Rezillos
Top of the Pops (No 17, 9 wks, 1978)

B.A. Robertson
Bang Bang (No 2, 12 wks, 1979)
Knocked It Off (No 8, 12 wks, 1979)
Kool in the Kaftan (No 17, 12 wks, 1980)
To Be Or Not To Be (No 9, 11 wks, 1980)
Hold Me (No 11, 8 wks, 1981) with Maggie Bell

Royal Scots Dragoon Guards
Amazing Grace (No 1, 2 wks, 1972)
Heykens Serenade (No 30, 7 wks, 1972)
Little Drummer Boy (No 13, 9 wks, 1972)

Scotland World Cup Squad
Easy Easy (No 20, 4 wks, 1974)
We Have A Dream (No 5, 9 wks, 1982)

Sensational Alex Harvey Band
Delilah (No 7, 7 wks, 1975)
Gamblin' Bar Room Blues (No 38, 8 wks, 1975)
The Boston Tea Party (No 13, 10 wks, 1976)

Simple Minds
Don't You Forget About Me (No 7, 11 wks, 1985)
Alive And Kicking (No 7, 9 wks, 1985)
Sanctify Yourself (No 10, 7 wks, 1986)
All The Things She Said (No 9, 8 wks, 1986)

Skids
Into the Valley (No 10, 11 wks, 1979)

Andy Stewart
Donald Where's Your Troosers (No 37, 1 wk 1960)
A Scottish Soldier (No 19, 38 wks, 1961)
The Battle's O'er (No 28, 13 wks, 1961)
Dr Finlay (No 43, 4 wks, 1965)

Tourists
I Only Want To Be With You (No 4, 14 wks, 1979)
So Good To Be Back Home Again (No 8, 9 wks, 1980)

Midge Ure
Do They Know It's Christmas? (No 1, 13 wks 1984)
No Regrets (No 9, 10 wks, 1982)
If I Was (No 1, 11 wks, 1985)

Wet Wet Wet
Wishing I Was Lucky (No 6, 14 wks, 1987)
Sweet Little Mystery (No 5, 12 wks, 1987)
Angel Eyes (No 5, 12 wks, 1987)

Lena Zavaroni
Ma He's Making Eyes At Me (No 10, 11 wks, 1974)
Personality (No 33, 3 wks, 1974)

PIONEERS of SCIENCE and INVENTION

Scottish Nobel Prizewinners

Sir William Ramsay – discovery of inert gaseous element in air (1904)
John MacLeod – discovery of insulin (1923)
Charles Wilson – making paths of electrically charged particles visible (1927)
Sir Alexander Fleming – discovery of penicillin (1945)
John Orr – Peace Prize (eliminating world hunger and promoting global unity and peace (1949)
Alexander Robertus Todd – research on vitamins B and E (1957)
Sir James Black – physiology and medicine (beta-blockers and Tagamet) (1988)

Science

DISCOVERED, IDENTIFIED OR INVENTED BY SCOTS

Adenosine diphosphate/triphosphate (synthesis) – Alexander Robertus Todd (1907–)
Arch, correspondence with inverted chain (observation) – David Gregory (1659–1708)
Atmolysis (principle of separation of gases) – Thomas Graham (1805–69)
Binomial theorem – James Gregory (1638–75)
Brownian motion – Robert Brown (1773–1858)
Cannabis (active principle) – Alexander Robertus Todd (1907–)
Capillary action – John Leslie (1766–1832)
Carbohydrate molecules, constitution – James Irvine (1877–1953)
Carbon and chemically identical nature of diamonds – George Mackenzie (1780–1848)
Carbon, theory of quadrivalency – Archibald Couper (1831–92)
Carbon dioxide (identification) – Joseph Black (1728–99)
Chloroform (preparation) – William Gregory (1803–58)
Chlorophyll, fluorescence in – David Brewster (1781–1868)
Ciliary action – William Sharpey (1802–80)

Cloud chamber (providing subatomic detail) – Charles T.R. Wilson (1869–1959)
Cloud formation by ion condensation – Charle T.R. Wilson (1869–1959)
Colour–blindness theory – James Clerk Maxwell (1831–79)
Colour photograph, first – James Clerk Maxwell (1831–79)
Colour, three-colour reproduction – James Cle Maxwell (1831–79)
Colloid science (dialysis) – Thomas Graham (1805–69)
Combustion, theory of – Joseph Black (1728–99)
Cosmic radiation, first to investigate systematically – Charles T.R. Wilson (1869–1959)
Convergent series (algebra) – James Gregory (1638–75)
Cybernetics, concepts (proposed) – James Cle Maxwell (1831–79)
Decimal fraction point – John Napier (1550–1617)
Dynamics, development of molecular – William Thomson (1824–1907)
Earth's formation, plutonic theory of – James Hutton (1726–97)
Earth's formation, uniformitarian theory of – James Hutton (1726–97)
Earth's rotation, proof of – Edward Sang (1805–90)
Electromagnetism (identification) – James Cle Maxwell (1831–79)
Energy, doctrine of available – William Thomson (1824–1907)
Energy (kinetic) among molecules of a gas, law of equipartition – John Waterston (1811–8
Eocene geological era, first to name – Charles Lyell (1797–1875)
Ethylene, carbon double bond – Alexander Crum Brown (1838–1922)
Evolution, theory of (independent) – Alfred Russell Wallace (1823–1913)
Evolution from monkeys – James Burnett (1714–99)
Gas, argon – William Ramsay (1852–1916)
Gas, krypton – William Ramsay (1852–1916
Gas, helium – William Ramsay (1852–1916)
Gas, neon – William Ramsay (1852–1916)
Gases, differentiated from air – Joseph Black (1728–99)
Gases, kinetic theory – James Clerk Maxwel (1831–79)

...ses, law of diffusion (Graham's Law) – Thomas Graham (1805–69)

...ochemistry, founder – James Hall (1761–1832)

...ology, founder of modern – James Hutton (1726–97)

...egory's mixture (upset stomach cure: magnesia, rhubarb, ginger) – James Gregory (1753–1821)

...at, latent – Joseph Black (1728–99)

...at pump principle – William Thomson (1824–1907)

...at, specific – Joseph Black (1728–99)

...at, variable absorption of radiant – John Leslie (1766–1832)

...drochloric acid (preparation) – William Gregory (1803–58)

..., artificial congelation – William Cullen (1710–90)

...topes, existence of and origin – Frederick Soddy (1877–1956)

...ght, wave theory of – William Thomson (1824–1907)

...garithms – John Napier (1550–1617)

...echanics, statistical (founded) – James Clerk Maxwell (1831–79)

...olecules, layer on polished surface (forerunner of semi-conductors) – George Beilby (1850–1924)

...olecular structure, correlation with pharmacological effect – Alexander Crum Brown (1838–1922)

...orphia (preparation) – William Gregory (1803–58)

...trogen (in air) – Joseph Black (1728–99)

...ucleotide components of nucleic acids (synthesis) – Alexander Robertus Todd (1907–)

...ucleus of cells (identification) – Robert Brown (1773–1858)

...cillations, theory of electrical – William Thomson (1824–1907)

...raffin extraction (from Persian naptha) – William Gregory (1803–58)

...iocene geological era, first to name – Charles Lyell (1797–1875)

...utonium, atomic weight – William Dittmar (1833–92)

...lariser (Nicol prism) – William Nicol (1768–1851)

...olymerization, physical chemistry – Harry Melville (1908–)

Prism, theory of mechanics of – Edward Sang (1805–90)

Rainfall, modern theory – James Hutton (1726–97)

Refrigeration, open cycle – William Thomson (1824–1907) and William Rankine (1820–72)

Sal ammoniac manufacture by sublimation of soot – James Hutton (1726–97)

Sea, mean level determination – James Jardine (1776–1858)

Solar parallax determination – James Gregory (1638–75)

Soliton (solitary wave of translation) – John Scott Russell (1808–82)

Spectroscopy (metals give line spectra) – Thomas Melvil (1726–53)

Steam line flow theory – William Rankine (1820–72)

Telescope, reflecting (proposal) – James Gregory (1638–75)

Telescope, achromatic (proposal) – David Gregory (1659–1708)

Thermodynamics, second law development – William Thomson (1824–1907)

Thermos flask – James Dewar (1847–1932)

Thiamine (vitamin B) structure – Alexander Robertus Todd (1907–)

Water, lowering of freezing point by pressure – James Thomson (1822–92)

Water, maximum density at 4–6°C – John Hope (1725–86)

Water, steam from salt water produces fresh – James Lind (1716–94)

Zeno's paradox, solution – James Gregory (1638–75)

Medicine

MEDICAL AND SCIENTIFIC DYNASTIES

Hereditary Physicians to Macleans of Duart for 300 years – the Beatons

Physician to three Tsars of Russia – James Wylie

Munros – Chair of Anatomy at Edinburgh (1719–1846)

  Alexander Munro
    Primus (1697–1767)
    Secundus (1733–1817)
    Tertius (1773–1859)

Gregorys – John Gregory (Professor of Practice of Physic, Edinburgh 1766–73)

continued

His grandfather was first Professor of Mathematics, Edinburgh
His father was Professor of Medicine, King's College, Aberdeen
His son James was Professor of Medicine, Edinburgh
His cousin David was Savilian Proessor of Astronomy, Oxford (1962)

Darwins – who studied at Edinburgh University
Erasmus Darwin, Edinburgh Faculty of Medicine (1754)
His sons, Robert, Francis and Charles followed
A Charles Darwin (1758–78) is buried in the family vault of Dr Andrew Duncan in Edinburgh's Buccleuch Cemetery
Two sons of Robert Darwin – Francis and Charles (1825)
Charles's grandson, Charles Darwin, Tait Professor of Natural Philosophy (1923–36)

First dissection of an elephant in Britain – Patrick Blair (1666–1728)
First medical society in Britain – Society for Improvement of Medical Knowledge, Edinburgh (1737)
First company doctor – appointed at New Lanark Cotton Spinning Manufactory (1784)
First operation performed under antiseptic conditions – Joseph Lister amputated cancerous breast of sister Isabella using carbolic acid (1867)
First X-Ray in Britain – by Alan Campbell Swinton of contents of locked cash-box (1896)
First hospital X-Ray in Britain – Glasgow Royal Infirmary (1896)

MEDICAL DISCOVERIES AND APPLICATIONS

Anaemia, description of pernicious – James Combe (1796–1883)
Angina, amyl nitrate treatment – Thomas Brunton (1844–1916)
Ante-natal clinics – John Ballantyne (1861–1923)
Blood, a living substance (proposal) – John Hunter (1728–93)

Bone (new), formed from periosteum – James Young Simpson (1811–70)
Brain, functions of – Charles Bell (1774–184⬛
Brain, relationship with movement of the limbs David Ferrier (1843–1928)
Brucellosis, cause of – David Bruce (1855–1931)
Caesarian section, distorted pelvis – Murdoc⬛ Cameron (1880s)
Capillaries, linking veins and arteries – Archibald Pitcairne (1652–1713)
Cartilage, prolapsed intervertebral (slipped dis⬛ – George Middleton (1853–1923)
Childbirth, anaesthesia first used for – James Young Simpson (1811–70)
Chloroform, anaesthetic properties – James Young Simpson (1811–70)
Cod liver oil, medicinal use – John H. Benne⬛ (1812–75)
Cotton wool, in treatment of burns – Alexand⬛ Anderson (1794–1871)
Decompression, stage techniques – John Haldane (1860–1936)
Diabetes, treatment with insulin – John MacLeod (1876–1935)
Diptheria description – Robert Whytt (1714–66)
Dressings, sterilised by heat – Joseph Lister (1827–1912)
Dum–dum fever parasite – William B. Leishman (1865–1926)
Elephantiasis parasite – Patrick Manson (1844–1922)
Fingerprinting – Henry Faulds (1843–1930)
Foetal screening, tests for cystic fibrosis – David Brock (1936–)
Foetal screening, tests for spina bifida – Davi⬛ Brock (1936–)
Foramen of Monro – Alexander Monro (1733–1817)
Forceps, axis-traction for midwifery – Alexander Simpson (1835–1916)
Forceps, bone-cutting – Robert Liston (1794–1847)
Forceps, sinus – Joseph Lister (1827–1912)
Heart disease, systematic treatment – James MacKenzie (1853–1925)
Heart lung machine, first in Britain – Ian Air⬛
Hemlock, active principle – Robert Christiso⬛ (1797–1882)
Hospital ship – Gilbert Blane (1749–1834)
Hospital ships, establishment – James Lind (1716–94)

ypnosis, first use in successful operation – James Esdale

ypothermia, identification – James Lind (1716–94)

eas, association of – William Hamilton (1788–1856)

dia rubber, effective solvent – James Syme (1799–1870)

on lung, first in Britain – Robert Henderson (1933)

terferon, discovery of – Alick Isaacs (1921–67)

dney transplants, first in Britain – Ian Aird

ock knees, first corrective operation – William McEwen (1848–1924)

ucocythaemia (blood disease), description – John H. Bennett (1812–75)

mph glands, function – John Hunter (1728–93)

alaria parasite – Patrick Manson (1844–1922), Ronald Ross (1857–1932)

astoid, standard operation – William McEwen (1848–1924)

edicine, first chair in Britain – Aberdeen (15th century)

edicine (tropical), first authoritative text – James Lind (1716–94)

entally ill, first public lunatic asylum for the humane treatment of – Andrew Duncan (1744–1828)

ental outpatient clinic, first – Robert D. Gillespie (1897–1945)

urology, first school – James Crichton Browne (1840–1938)

tric acid to prevent contagion spread – James Smyth (1741–1821)

rsing staff, first systematic training – William McEwen (1848–1924)

stetric forceps – James Young Simpson (1811–70)

iarotomy – James Young Simpson (1811–70)

thology, experimental verification – John Hunter (1728–93)

nicillin, discovery of – Alexander Fleming (1881–1955)

ritoneum, fold of the – James Douglas (1675–1742)

acenta, structure – John Hunter (1728–93)

lygraph – James MacKenzie (1853–1925)

ychiatric nursing, first training scheme – Dumfries (1854)

Puerperal fever, transmission – D.N. Gordon (1795)

Pupil reaction, Argyll Robertson – Douglas Argyll Robertson (1837–1909)

Putrefactive process in spread of disease – John Pringle (1707–82)

Radiological department, first in world – John MacIntyre (1857–1928)

Reflex, seat of – Robert Whytt (1714–66)

Respiration process – John Cheyne (1777–1836)

Scissors, probe-pointed surgical – Joseph Lister (1827–1912)

Scurvy, treatment with lime/lemon juice – James Lind (1716–94)

Siamese twins, first successful separation in Britain – Ian Aird

Sick bays, cleanliness and ventilation in – James Lind (1716–94)

Snake venoms and antidotes – Thomas Fraser (1841–1920)

Splint, Liston – Robert Liston (1794–1847)

Staphylococcus bacteria – Alexander Oghton (1844–1929)

Strontium – discovered at village of Strontium (1764)

Sugar metabolism process – Edward Sharpey–Schaffer (1850–1935)

Surgery, first amputation using anaesthesia – William Scott (1846)

Surgery, first scapula removal – Robert Liston (1794–1847)

Surgery, first person to use anaesthesia in – William Morton (1819–68)

Surgery, first public use of anaesthesia (general) in – Robert Liston (1794–1847)

Surgery, bone graft – William McEwen (1848–1924)

Surgery, first textbook in the English language – Master Peter Lowe (Glasg)

Surgery (plastic), first operation using – James Syme (1799–1870)

Syringe, hypodermic in general practice – Alexander Wood (1817–84)

Tendon, repair – John Hunter (1728–93)

Thermometer, popularization of use – James Currie (1756–1801)

Tissue grafting – John Hunter (1728–93)

Tubercular joints, excision – James Syme (1799–1870)

Tuberculosis clinic, first – Robert Philip (1854–1939)

continued

MEDICINE – continued

Tuberculosis, 'Edinburgh System' – Robert Philip (1854–1939)
Tuberculous meningitis description – Robert Whytt (1714–66)
Typhoid, vaccine – William Boag Leishman (1865–1926)
Typhus/typhoid, distinction – Robert Perry (1783–1848)
Ultrasonic pregnancy scanner – Ian Donald (1910–)
Water, distilled on ships – James Lind (1716–94)
X–Ray unit, first in a hospital – Glasgow (1896)
X-Rays used for heart – John MacIntyre (1857-1928)
X-Rays used for lungs – John MacIntyre (1857-1928)
X-Rays used for skull – John MacIntyre (1857-1928)
X-Rays used for spine – John MacIntyre (1857-1928)

Astronomy, Engineeering, Electronics and Chemistry

First photograph with a magnesium flash – Charles Piazzi Smyth (1819–1900)
First high-speed rotative steam engine – James Watt (drive tilt hammer at Bradley Forge, England), (1783)
First textile machinery driven by steam power – Watt rotative engine in cotton factory at Papplewick, England (1785)
First manufacture of paraffin in Britain – James Young, Bathgate (1856)
First Electric fire-alarm system Britain – Glasgow (1878)
First rubber heels – Aberdeen Rubber Sole and Heel Co (1889)
First milking machine (pulsator) – Thistle Mechanical Milking Machine, invented by Alex Shields, Glasgow (1895)
First prototype fast breeder reactor – Dounreay
First successful cotton mill – Rothesay (1778)
First manufacture of rubber wellingtons – North British Rubber Co, Edinburgh (1865)

ENGINEERING AND TECHNOLOGY INVENTIONS

Air, compressed first in tunnelling – Earl of Dundonald (1775–1860)
Architect, first naval – John Scott Russell (1808–82)
Aurora borealis, reasons for – James Farquharson (1781–1843)
Automobile accident, originator of first – John Scott Russell (1808–82)
Balloon, first manned hot-air flight in Britain – James Tytler (1745–1804)
Bicycle, first pedal – Kirkpatrick MacMillan (1813–78)
Boiler, tubular marine – John Napier (1830)
Boiler, twin flues and furnaces – William Fairbairn (1789–1874)
Bovril (meat-extract drink) – James Johnston Lawson
Box-girder – Andrew Thomson (
Brougham carriage – Henry Lord Brougham (1778–1868)
Clock, electric – Alexander Bain (1810–77)
Condenser (separate) – James Watt (1736–1819)
Dew, reasons for – William Wells (1757–1817)
Dust in the atmosphere causes cloud, fog and sunsets – John Aitken (1839–1919)
Electric lighting – James Bowman Lindsay (1799–1862)
Engine, double-acting – James Watt (1736–1819)
Engine, heated air – Robert Stirling (1790–1878)
Engine, oscillating – Wiliam Murdoch (1754–1839)
Engine, steam – James Watt (1736–1819)
Engine, steeple – David Napier (1790–1869)
Engine, two-stroke – Dugald Clerk (1854–1932)
Engine, Z-crank – Morton and Hunt (1855)
Engineer, first structural – William Fairbairn (1789–1874)
Engineering (civil) pioneer – John Rennie (1761–1821)
Engineering (civil) pioneer – Thomas Telford (1757–1834)
Facsimile transmission – Alexander Bain (1810–77)
Flues, corrugated marine – John Scott (1830–1903)
Gas, first to use for domestic lighting – William Murdoch (1754–1839)

s, sulphur removal – James Neilson (1792–1865)

s-burner, fishtail – James Neilson (1792–1865)

vernor, centrifugal – James Watt (1736–1819)

and piano – John Broadwood (1732–1812)

ammer, steam – James Nasmyth (1808–90)

orsepower (68 kg/150 lb lifted nearly 1 m/4 ft per sec) – James Watt (1736–1819)

ot blast – James Neilson (1792–1865)

e-making (mechanical) machine – William Cullen (1710–90)

otherms and isobars, mapping – Alexander Buchan (1827–1907)

ule-Thomson effect – William Thomson (1824–1907)

aleidoscope – David Brewster (1781–1868)

elvin scale (temperature) – William Thomson, Lord Kelvin (1824–1907)

inetic energy – William Thomson (1824–1907)

tes used for meteorology – Alexander Wilson 1749

awnmower, first effective – Alexander Shanks 1841

tter-copier (duplicating Machine) – James Watt (1736–1819)

ght, wave theory (development) – William Thomson (1824–1907)

ghthouse pioneer – Robert Stevenson (1772–1850)

ghthouse, aseimatic (against earthquakes) – David Stevenson

ghthouses, aximurthal condensing system – Thomas Stevenson

ghthouse, paraffin lighting of – David Stevenson

acintosh waterproof – Charles Macintosh (1766–1843)

larmalade – James Keiller (1775–1839)

letal detector – Alexander Graham Bell (1847–1922)

lolecular dynamics (study of) – William Thomson (1824–1907)

bservatory, first magnetic astronomical – Thomas Brisbane near Kelso (1841)

il refinery, first – James 'Paraffin' Young (1811–83)

neumatic tyre – R.W. Thomson (1822–73)

ostage stamp, first adhesive – James Chalmers (1782–1853)

otential – William Thomson (1824–1907)

Printing machine (continuous rotary) – Thomas Nelson (1822–92)

Radar – Robert Watson–Watt (1892–1973)

Railway track, first all-steel – Robert Mushet (1811–91)

Revolution counter – James Watt (1736–1819)

Rivetting machine, first – William Fairbairn (1789–1874)

Rotary exhauster – Robert Thomson (1822–75)

Ship, first merchant ship powered by steam turbines – King Edward (1904)

Shipping vessel, first all steel (Clyde pleasure steamer) – William Denny and Brothers (1879)

Slipway (shipbuilding) – Thomas Morton (1781–1832)

Smelting, use of black band ironstone – David Mushet (1772–1847)

Soliton (single wave) – John Scott Russell (1808–82)

Speedometer – Keith Elphinstone (1864–1944)

Star (fixed), measurement of distance – Thomas Henderson (1798–1844)

Star, Nova Aurigae, discovery of the – T.D. Anderson (1780s)

Stars, observation of the Brisbane Catalogue of Stars in the southern hemisphere – James Dunlop (1795–1848)

Steam boat, first practical one in Britain – William Symington (1762–1831)

Steam tractor – R.W. Thomson (1822–73)

Steamer, first paddle-wheel (Charlotte Dundas) – William Symington (1762–1831) (1802)

Steel production, removal of excess oxygen – Robert Mushet (1811–91)

Stereotyping (printing) – Wiliam Ged (1690–1749)

Sun (solar parallax) – James Short (1710–68)

Sunshine recorder – John Campbell (1822–85)

Sunspots, their link with magnetic storms – John Brown (1817–79)

Sunspots, reasons for – Alexander Wilson (1714–86)

Tar, distilled from coal – Archibald Cochrane (1749–1831)

Tarmacdam road surface – John Loudon McAdam (1756–1836)

Telephone – Alexander Graham Bell (1847–1922)

continued

ENGINEERING and TECHNOLOGY INVENTIONS – continued

Teleprinter – Frederick George Creed (1871–1957)
Telescope (aplanatic) – Robert Blair (1752–1828)
Television – John Logie Baird (1888–1946)
Television, use of cathode ray tubes – Alan Campbell Swinton (1863–1930)
Transmission system, high-speed – William Fairbairn (1789–1874)
Turbine, Brown-Curtis marine – John Biles
Turbine (steam), first merchant ship powered by – King Edward (1904)
Tuyre (cooled or Scottish) – James Condie (1830s)
Valve (slide) – William Murdoch (1754–1839)
Water softening – Thomas Clark (1801–67)
Writing-paper, production of from bleaching rags – Joseph Black (1728–99)

Units of measurement named after Scots

the Henry	the degree Rankine
the degree Kelvin	the Watt
the Nicol	

Laws, Rules and Theories Formulated by Scots

Beilby Layer	Ivory Theory
Brewster's Law	Maxwell's Demon
Crum Brown's Rule	Newland's Law
	Purdie Reaction
Gordon-Rankine Formula	Rankine Cycle

Substances Discovered by Scots

Anthracene	Liquid Hydrogen
Collidene	Liquid Oxygen
Coniine	Lithopone
Dewar Benzene	Lutidene
Iridium	Lysozyme
Isotropic Diamonds	Morphine
	Nitroprussides

Osmium	Sodium
Phosgene	Pyrophosphate
Picolene	Strontium
Protactinium	Thyroxine
Pyridene	

Recent Hi-Tech Developments

Power from sea waves ('duck') – Dr Stephen Salter, Department of Mechanical Engineering, Edinburgh University
Fire brigade automatic distress system – Ellis Cohen (1982)
Glaucoma diagnosis eye-chart – Dr Bertil Damato (1985)
Testosterone male contraceptive – Dr Frederick Wu (1990)
Treatment of burned eyelids with thick pads of skin – Aberdeen Royal Infirmary Burns Unit
Tissue expanders for severe facial burns – Aberdeen Royal Infirmary Burns Unit
Dorsal column implants for back pain – Western General Hospital, Edinburgh
Only example in Britain of a brewery linked to distillery – International Centre for Brewing and Distilling, Heriot-Watt University
Only brewing school in Britain – Heriot-Watt University
Magnetic resonance imaging (early diagnosis of physical problems) – Professor John Mallard (1927–), University of Aberdeen
Amorphous silicon coatings – Professors Spear and LeComber, Dundee University
Urinary tract infection diagnostic kit – Dr H. McKenzie, Dundee University
Reagents for the diagnosis of auto-immune diseases – Dr M. Kerr, Dundee University

Engineering Feats

AUTOMOBILES
Up to the Depression of 1931 Scotland produced 43 makes of car
First motor car manufacturer in Scotland – Argyll Motor Co, Alexandra

BRIDGES

Forth Railway Bridge – completed in three years: 2.4 km/*1.5 miles* long with 54 000 tons of steel fastened with 6.5 million rivets (1890)

Forth Railway Bridge – took 20 men four years to paint the 58 ha/*145 acres* of steelwork (32 000 l/*7000 gal* of purpose-designed red paint)

Sydney Harbour Bridge – Dalbeattie granite used in construction

BUILDINGS

Russian Pavlosk Palace – built for Catherine the Great by Charles Cameron

London's St Katherine's Dock – Thomas Telford (1757–1834)

Versailles Palace – Portsoy Serpentine Marble used for finish

CANALS AND AQUEDUCTS

Swedish Gota Canal between Baltic and North Sea – Thomas Telford (1757–1834)

Caledonian Canal – 97 km/*60.5 miles* long

First passage of the Suez Canal – Captain Charles Mann (1832–1918), commander of the SS Danube of Leith who sailed through the canal in November 1869 before it was fully completed and when it was not open to general traffic

RAILWAYS

Britain's largest steam loco – 191-ton Garratt (built in North British loco works, Springburn, 1956)

Scotland's last time-served railway lockframe fitter – Bob Milligan of Inverness (1990)

SHIPS

Last sea-going paddle-steamer in world – Waverley

First practical passenger steamer in Europe – Comet

World's first train ferry – Granton to Burntisland (1849)

BANKING and COMMERCE

World's first savings bank – founded by Rev Henry Duncan in his parish of Ruthwell, Dumfries (1810)

World's first banking professional body – the Institute of Bankers (1875)

Biggest cheque issued in Britain – £1 088 524 128.30 issued by the Royal Bank of Scotland for the BP share offer (1988)

Scottish Clearing Banks with Headquarters in Scotland

	Total assets 1990 (£m)
Bank of Scotland (founded 1695)	18 394.5
Royal Bank of Scotland (founded 1727) Group	30 096.0

National Banks Founded by Scots

Bank of England – William Paterson (1658–1719)

Bank of France – John Law (1671–1729)

Some Companies Founded by Scots

Macmillan (publishers)
ICI (chemicals)
Bell Telephone Corporation
Dunlop
Cunard
Trust House Forte
Jardine Matheson (Far East trading Company)
Burmah Oil Co

World's oldest documented company still trading – The Shore Porters Society of Aberdeen (founded before 1498)

Oldest continuously used commercial premises in Britain – the Vaults, Leith (c1130)

Businesswoman of the Year (1990) – Ann Gloag, MD of Stagecoach (Holdings)

World's oldest independently-owned department store – Jenners, Edinburgh (1838)

AGRICULTURAL, HORTICULTURAL and ZOOLOGICAL INNOVATIONS

First swedes in Britain – introduced by Patrick Miller (1731–1815)

First modern reaping machine – Patrick Bell (1799–1867)

First use of steam power in agriculture – William Harley (b 1789)

First use of chemical principles in agriculture – Frances Home (1719–1813)

First successful threshing machine – Andrew Meikle (1719–1811)

First pulsating milking machine – Stewart Nicholson (1864–1960)

First subsoil plough – James Smith (1789–1850)

First practical threshing-machine – built Andrew Meikle, Haddington (1786)

First cotton sewing thread – manufactured by James and Patrick Clark (1812)

First agricultural society in Britain – Honourable Society of Improvers of the Knowledge of Agriculture in Scotland (1723)

First Chair of Agriculture in Britain – University of Edinburgh (1790)

First floral clock in the world – Edinburgh (1904)

First canned salmon – by John Moir, Aberdeen (1825)

Kew Botanical Gardens – founded by William Hooker (1841)

FLORA and FAUNA DISCOVERED by SCOTS

Douglas Spruce
Gardenia
Genus Hopea
Grant's Gazelle
Lechwe (named by David Livingstone)
Nu-Nu Mouse – first bred in Glasgow (used in medical research)
Sibbald's Rorqual (Blue Whale)
Thomson's Gazelle

SCOTS ABROAD

Africa

John Henderson of Fordell (d 1655) – a Zanzibar slave, married an Arab princess

James Bruce (1730–94) – discovered the source of the Blue Nile

Robert Gordon and William Paterson – discovered upper Orange River (1777)

John Campbell (1766–1840) – discovered the course of the Orange River and the source of the Limpopo

Mungo Park (1771–1806) – discovered most of the course of the Niger

Hugh Clapperton (1788–1827) – discovered Lake Chad (after crossing Sahara Desert)

Alexander Gordon Laing (1794–1826) – discovered the source of the Rokelle River; first white man to reach Timbuctoo (crossing 400 miles of the Sahara Desert with ten sabre cuts in his head, a bullet in his hip and two injured legs)

James Rose Innes – first Superintendant General of Education in Cape Colony (1821)

Robert Moffat (1795–1883) – missionary in Bechuanaland for 54 years

Robert, Lord Napier (1810–90) – led 1868 mission to Abyssinia

David Livingstone (1813–73) – discovered the Victoria Falls; crossed Kalahari Desert and discovered Lake Ngami; discovered Lake Nyasa; explored the Zambesi

William Mackinnon (1823–93) – founded British East Africa Company

James Augustus Grant – with John Speke the first European to cross Equatorial Africa (1860–63)

Charles George Gordon (1833–85) – Governor General of Sudan

Mary Slessor (1848–1915) – missionary in Nigeria ('Great Mother')

Walter Montagu Kerr (1852–88) – travelled alone from Cape Colony to the Lakes of Central Africa (1853–6)

Leander Starr Jameson (1853–1917) – instigated the Boer War by his Jameson Raid. Later Premier of Cape Colony

Verney Lovett-Cameron – made treaties with chiefs and gave the name Katanga to the inner basin of the Congo (1874)

Frederick Arnot and Daniel Crawford – Plymouth Brethren missionaries in Katanga (1886)

Joseph Thomson (1858–94) – explored Kenya and Tanganyika

Thomas Hyslop (1859–) – treasurer of Natal

Robert Jameson – Mayor of Durban (1895–7)

William Grant (1873–) – Professor of Gynaecology, Witwatersrand University

Arthur Falconer (1880–) – Principal of University of Cape Town

James Robertson (1901–83) – first Governor of Nigeria

Antarctic

Sir James Ross (1800–62) – discovered the world's most southerly volcanoes (Erebus and Terror)

C.W. Thomson (1830–82) – director of the Challenger Expedition to the Antarctic

Argentina, Chile and Peru

Thomas Lord Cochrane (1775–1860) – Vice-Admiral in Chilean navy. Fought for Chile and then Peru, defeating the Spaniards. Went into battle dressed in full dress of a Highland chief

Sir Gregor MacGregor – went to Venezuela in 1811. Rose to Colonel and then Commander. Captured Maracaibo and helped win indepedence for most of Venezuela at the Battle of Juncal (1816). Went into battle in full Highland dress with bagpipes playing

Captain Robertson – joined Chilean navy (1822). Fought against Spain in Peru and Chile. Granted the Island of Mocha

Mackay – privateer who captured the large Spanish ship 'Minerva' in early 1800s with 24 men in Valparaiso (Chile)

George Corbett – owned 741 000 acres of land in five provinces in Argentina (1840s)

First steamer to enter Latin American waters – 'Rising Star' (1818) under Lord Cochrane

First steamer on Lake Titicaca (Upper Andes, Peru) 400 miles from nearest coast over mountains – took nine years to arrive. In parts carried over Andes by mule. Launched 1871

COLONIES

Monte Grande Colony, Argentina (1825) – 220 Scots turned 16 000 acres of wasteland into full production

The Falklands (1840s) – one-third probably Scots (mainly shepherds)

Chile (1854) – 39 families of Clydeside miners

Arctic

James Ross (1800–62) – Discovered the North Magnetic Pole

Australia

Between 1788 and 1820 22 217 male and 3661 female convicts were transported

Scottish political martyrs – Thomas Muir (14 years); Thomas Palmer (7); William Skirving (14); Joseph Gerrald (14);

John McDowall Stuart (1815–66) – first person to cross Australia from north to south

John Hunter (1737–1821), magistrate, surveyor, Governor-in-chief of British colony (New South Wales) – introduced sheep to Australia

Lachlan Macquarie (1761–1824) – Governor of New South Wales, Australia

John Macarthur (1767–1834) – founded Australian wool industry, introduced Merino sheep and laid out the first Australian vineyard

Sir Thomas Brisbane (1773–1860) – second Governor of New South Wales

Alexander Thomson (1800–66) – Mayor of Geelong

Hugh Dixson (1810–80) – founded Australian tobacco industry

James Forbes (1813–51) – founded Melbourne Academy

James Service (1823–99) – Premier of Victoria

continued

AUSTRALIA – *continued*

Thomas McIlwraith (1835–1900) – Premier of Queensland

William Guthrie Spence (1846–1926) – leader of the Labour Party

David Syme (1827–1908) – Editor of the Age (Melbourne) (1852)

William Cresswell (1852–1933) – founded Australian navy

Robert Dickie Watt (1881–1965) – first Professor of Agriculture, University of Sydney

MOUNTAINS NAMED AFTER SCOTS

Lindsay	Dubsinane
Cunningham	Crawford
Fraser	Stuart
Aberdeen	Petrie
Greenock	

Belgium

Scots in Bruges had a chapel of St Ninian

Peter Wallace – buccaneer, previously Governor of the island of Tortuga ('the pirates' lair'), founded Belize, capital of British Honduras, in 1617 (from Wallace, pronounced 'Valeese' in Spanish)

Brazil

Rio Grande to Porto Alegre (Brazil) steamers – all Clyde-built

Canada

Alexander Mackenzie (1755–1820) – explored Great Slave Lake and down what is now the Mackenzie River

James Geddes (1763–1838) – Erie Canal chief engineer

Thomas Douglas (1771–1820) – founded Manitoba

Simon Fraser (1776–1862) – river flowing from Rockies to the sea

Sir John Ross (1777–1856) – charted coast of Davis Strait, extended whaling grounds to Baffin Island (1818); located the North Magnetic Pole (1829–33)

John Strachan (1778–1867) – first President of Canadian Board of Education

John Galt (1779–1839) – novelist and Secretary of the Canada Company

John McLoughlin (1784–1857) – Chief Factor of the Columbia Post (1821)

William Mackenzie (1795–1861) – Mayor of Toronto

James Douglas (1803–77) – first Governor of British Columbia

Robert McLure (1807–73) – discovered a North-West Passage (1850)

James Bruce, 8th Earl of Elgin (1811–63) – Governor-General of Canada (1847–54)

John Rae (1813–93) – surveyed route from Winnipeg to the Pacific (1865)

John A. McDonald (1815–91) – first Prime Minister of Canada

Alexander Mackenzie (1822–92) – second Prime Minister of Canada

Sandford Fleming (1827–1915) – railway engineer and designer of Canada's first stamp

George Stephen (1829–1921) – President of the Canadian Pacific Railway Co

Kicking Horse Pass – named after narrow escape by James Hector (1834–1907)

James Hector (1834–1907) – investigated Vancouver Island

James Naismith (1869–1931) – invented basketball

Reginald Stewart (1900–84) – founder of the Toronto Philharmonic Orchestra

PLACE-NAMES AFTER SCOTLAND

Paisley	Perth
Athol	Renfrew
Dunvegan	Arran
Dunrobin	Glencoe

China

George Boyle (1746–81) – first Briton in Tibet (to sign a commercial treaty)

Sir Robert Jardine (1825–1905) – 11 years in China from 1849

Melrose and Company – imported tea from Canton from 1833

William Keswick (1834–1912) – employed by Jardine Matheson in China; 27 years in Far East. Taipan from 1874

James Carnhill (1851–1926) – President of the Chinese Republic

Sir Reginald Johnston (1874–1938) – Tutor to Pu Yi (Emperor Kang Teh of Manchuria) 1919–25

Eric Liddell (1902–45) – 'The Flying Scotsman', Olympic gold medallist who became a missionary in China and died a prisoner of war

George Forest – plant-hunter for the Royal Botanic Garden, Edinburgh (1904–32)

Colonies (Scottish settlements)

1605 – Hugh Montgomerie and James Hamilton set up Plantation of Ulster (County Down)

1610 – the six Irish counties came into the control of the crown

1620 – some Scottish colonists at Couper's Cove, Newfoundland

1621 – Charter from James VI and I to Sir William Alexander of Menstrie giving sasine to baronets of Nova Scotia

1629 – Scots colony at Port Royal on the Bay of Fundy (Canada); Scots Covenanter colony on Cape Breton coast (New Galloway); Scots Quaker colony in East Jersey

1650 – c 50 000 Scots settled in Ulster

1684 – Scots Presbyterian colony at Stuart's Town, South Carolina

1695 – Company of Scotland Trading to Africa and the Indies established (to 1707)

1698 – First expedition to Darien peninsula (Panama) followed by two more. Destroyed by the Spanish and lack of support from England

1823 – Kingdom of Poyais (between Honduras and Nicaragua), a colony of 170 Scots employed by Sir Gregor McGregor

Denmark

John Machabeus (Macalpine) (d 1557) – Professor at University of Copenhagen

England

Michael Scott (1160–1235) – first Scot to study at Oxford. Known as the Wizard of the North, he was a scientist and astronomer

John Duns Scotus (1265–1308) – philosopher (originator of the word 'dunce'), Professor of Divinity at Oxford (1301)

Union of the Crowns (1603) – Scotland's King James VI became King James I of England. He left Edinburgh for London

William Smellie (1697–1763) – greatest obstetrician in England

James Thomson (1700–48) – author of 'Rule Britannia'

1705 – said to be 1000 Scots hawkers in England

William Murray, Earl of Mansfield (1709–93) – Lord Chief Justice (1756); succeeded by his nephew David (1727–96)

John Stuart, 3rd Earl of Bute (1713–92) – Prime Minister (1761–3)

William Hunter (1718–83) – president of Royal College of Physicians (1781)

John Hunter (1728–93) – (brother of former) physician extraordinary to the king

Sir Gilbert Bland (1749–1843) – Physician to the Fleet and to George IV

Thomas Campbell (1777–1844) – author of 'Ye Mariners of England' (buried in Westminster Abbey)

Thomas Graham (1805–69) – Professor of Chemistry at University College. He was also Master of the Mint (1837)

Thomas Alexander – Director-General of Army Medical Department (1855)

Sir William Dewar – Professor of Chemistry at the Royal Institution (1877)

Sir William Ramsay – Professor of Chemistry, University College, awarded Nobel Prize (1904)

ENGLISH MEDICAL INSTITUTIONS FOUNDED BY SCOTS

London Veterinary College – John Hunter
Royal Instituton of Liverpool – Thomas Traill
Manchester Infirmary – Charles White
Birmingham Medical School – Edward Johnstone
Sheffield Royal Infirmary – William Younger

ENGLISH BUILDINGS DESIGNED BY SCOTTISH ARCHITECTS

St Martin's-in-the-Fields church (1722–6) – James Gibb

Blackfriars Bridge (1760–9) – Robert Mylne

Tower Bridge (1760–9) – Sir William Arrol (engineer)

Landsdowne House, Berkeley Square (1762–68) – Robert and John Adam

Somerset House (1776–86) – Sir William Chambers

St Katherine's Dock (1828) – Thomas Telford

Original Waterloo Bridge – John Rennie

Original Southwark Bridge – John Rennie

LONDON – POLICE AND GUILDHALL

Sir Hugh Turnbull (1882–1973) – Commissioner of Police for the City of London (1925–50)

Sir David McNee (1925–) – Commissioner of the Metropolitan Police (1977–82)

Sir James Miller (19??–77) – Lord Provost of Edinburgh (1951–54) Lord Mayor of London (1964–5)

CONTEMPORARY SCOTS IN PROMINENT POSITIONS SOUTH OF THE BORDER

Earl of Airlie (1926–) – Chairman of General Accident Fire and Life Assurance Corporation (1987–)

Sir James Blyth (1940–) – Chairman of Boots (1987–)

Sir Alistair Burnet (1928–) – presenter ITN News (1976–91)

Alan Chisholm – Chairman of Bredero Properties (1980–)

Ian Clark (1939–) – Chairman of Costain Ventures (1987–)

William Cockburn (1943–) – Managing Director, Royal Mail Letters (1986–)

Sir James Duncan (1927–) – Chairman of Transport Development Group (1970–)

Sir Monty Finniston (1912–90) – Chairman of British Steel (1973–6)

Sir Charles Forte (1908–) – Chief Executive of Trusthouse Forte (1982–)

Sir Alastair Frame (1929–) – Chairman of Rio Tinto Zinc Corporation (1985–)

Sandy Gall (1927–) – Foreign Correspondent (1963–); newscaster ITN (1968–)

Alistair Grant (1937–) – Chairman, Argyll Group (1988–)

Sir Denys Henderson (1932–) – Chairman of ICI (1987–)

Sir Thomas Hetherington (1926–) – Director of Public Prosecutions (1977–87)

Jeremy Isaacs (1932–) – Director of the Royal Opera House, Covent Garden (1988–)

Sir John Junor (1919–) – editor of the *Sunday Express* (1954–86)

Gavin Laird (1933–) – General Secretary of Amalgamated Union of Engineering Workers (1982–)

Sir Robert MacAlpine – Director Sir Robert MacAlpine and Sons

Don McCrickard – Chief Executive of Trustee Savings Bank

Howard Macdonald – Chairman of County NatWest

Ian McGregor (1912–) – Chairman of British Steel Corporation (1980–3); Chairman of British Coal (1983–6)

Lord James Mackay of Clashfern (1927–) – Lord High Chancellor (1987–)

Lord Alexander Mackenzie Stuart (1924–) – President of European Court of Justice (1984–8)

Andrew Neil (1949–) – editor of the *Sunday Times* (1983–)

David Ogilvy (1911–) – founder (1948) of Ogilvy and Mather

Sir Bob Reid (1934–) – Chairman of Shell (1985–90); Chairman of British Rail (1990–)

Sir Norman Reid (1915–) – Director of Tate Gallery (1964–79)

Lord John Reith (1889–1971) – Director-General of the BBC (1927–38)

D. Smith – Chief Executive of Isosceles

Douglas Smith (1915–) – Commissioner of Inland Revenue (1968–75)

Robert Smith (1944–) – head of Morgan Grenfell's development capital arm

I. Steel – Chief Executive of BP Chemicals

Wilf Stevenson – Director of the British Film Institute

Norman Stone (1941–) – Professor of Modern History, Fellow of Worcester College, Oxford (1984–)

Lord George Thomson of Monifieth (1921–) – Chairman of the Independent Broadcasting Authority (1981–8)

Iain Vallance (1943–) – Chairman of British Telecom (1987–)

Viscount Weir (1933–) – Chairman of The Weir Group (1985–) Director of BICC (1977–)

Charles Wilson (1935–) – Editor of *The Times* (1985–90), *Sporting Life* (1990–)

1980s – 1300 Scots graduates per annum left for jobs south of the Border

France

Charles Martel (ruler of the Franks) – helped by Scots in defeat of the Saracens at the Battle of Poitiers (732)

Charlemagne – Scots fought for in Spain against the Moors (778)

Scots bodyguard for Charles III – 839–88

First French treaty with Scotland – 1060–1108

Louis IX – took Scottish knights on Crusade (1249 and 1268)

John Stewart, Earl of Buchan – later Constable of France, Duke of Touraine, commanded Scots force of 6000 men at siege of La Rochelle (1419)

Scottish officers hanged by English at capture of Melun – 1420

Sir John Stewart of Darnley – Lieutenant General of French armies and Duke of Touraine (1424)

Scots Guard – first mentioned 1425 (re-established 1445)

John Kirkmichael – Bishop of Orleans (1428), warrior chaplain to Earl of Douglas

James Power – painted personal standard of Joan of Arc (1429)

Scots Guard – numbered 120 men (1437)

University of Paris (1519–1615) – 400 names of Scottish students

William Davidson (1593–1669) – first Professor of Chemistry in France

Sir James Monypenny – made a lord by Charles VII

Bernard Stewart – Lord of Aubigny (twice held Calabria for France)

Sir John Hepburn (1598–1636) – Commander of Scots Brigade under Gustavus Adolphus; General and Maréchal of France. Died at siege of Saverne. Buried in Toul Cathedral

Lord James Douglas – colonel of Royal Scots, buried in Paris (1645)

John Law (1671–1729) – founded Bank of France (1716) and New Orleans with the West India Company. Comptroller-General of France (1720)

Lord George Douglas – colonel of Royal Scots, buried in St Germaine-en-Laye (1692)

Thomas Blaikie 'Father of the English Landscape' (1750–1838) – employed as a landscape gardener by Duc d'Orléans and by Empress Joséphine

Jacques Macdonald (1765–1840) – only one of Napoleon's generals to be made a Marshall on the battlefield (Wagram, 1809), first Commandeur and Grand-Officier of the Légion d'Honneur. Buried in Père Lachaise Cemetery, Paris

Scots Guard – disbanded 1787

Frederick Maitland of Lindores – captain of HMS Bellerophon, negotiated abdication with Napoleon (1815)

Admiral Sir George Cockburn – escorted Napoleon to St Helena on board his flagship HMS Northumberland (1815)

French versions of Scottish names – Quinemont (Kinninmond); Gohory (Gowrie); Dromont (Drummond); D'Oillenc on (Williamson)

Germany

Gustavus Adolphus – is believed to have made more than 60 Scots governors of German towns and castles in the 1620s

David de Berclay – applied for safe-conduct to Prussia with 12 knights (1362)

First Scottish settlement in Germany – at Danzig (suburb called Alt-Schottland) (1380)

Adam de Heburn – travelled to Prussia with 10 knights (1378)

Cologne University – 15th century: 2 Scots rectors; 2 Professors of Theology; 2 Professors of Law

Edict of town of Breslau – against pedlars, beggars, gipsies and Scots (1533)

Brandenburg – order against Scottish vagabonds (3000 Scots pedlars) (1558)

Robert Wedderburn – 1st hymn book of the Scottish Church published, Wittenburg (1567)

United Merchants Guild of Prussia –
complained that business spoiled by
travelling Scots (1569)

City of Danzig – hires 700 Scots to fight the
Poles (1577)

Ninian Winzet – elected Abbot of Monastery
of Ratisbon

Sir James Ramsay (1589 – Governor of
Hanau fortress (1634)

John Durie (1595–1680) – worked in Germany
to unite Lutheran and Calvinist
Reformers

William Ogilvie – Abbot of Monastery of
Würzburg (1609)

Scots Brotherhood of Merchants – 410
members in Brandenburg and Preussen
(1615)

John Mayor – founded chapel of St Rochus
at Arnsdorf (1617)

The Green (Hepburn's) – Scottish Brigade
formed (1630)

James Keith (1696–1758) – Marshall in army
of Frederick the Great

Gideon Ernest, Baron Loudon (1716–) – Field
Marshall to Frederick the Great

James Kabrun (Cockburn) (b 1759) – wealthy
merchant; financed Danzig Opera
House

John Gottfried Ross (b 1772) – first Bishop of
Evangelical Church in Berlin

Carl Aloysius Ramsay – pioneer of shorthand

Johann von Lamont (1805–79) – Professor of
Astronomy at Munich

Thirty Years War (1818–48) – 30 000 Scots
took part

Holland

Scots Brigade – in service of the United
Netherlands (1572–1782)

Scots church in Veere – 1612

Archibald Pitcairne (1652–1713) – Professor of
Physic at Leiden (1692) (in the 18th
century around 2000 Scots were trained
at Leiden University)

Scots community – in Amsterdam 80 (1699);
in Rotterdam 1000 (1700)

Hong Kong

Companies founded by Scots
Jardine Matheson
Butterfield and Swire

Sir Thomas Sutherland – first chairman of
Hong Kong and Whampoa Dockyard Co

Sir Robert Black – Hong Kong's last
Governor

India

Captain Alexander Hamilton – to Bombay for
the East India Company (1688)

William Hamilton (surgeon) – on mission to
Moghul court (1714–17)

Gilbert Elliott (1751–1814) – first Scot to be
Governor-General of India

David Baird (1757–1829) – conquered Mysore
and Tipu Sultan

John Malcolm (1769–1833) – East India
Company ambassador to Persia

Mountstuart Elphinstone (1779–1857) – founded
India's state education

Ewan Law – left India with £150 000 (1780)

Charles James Napier (1782–1853) – conqueror
of the state of Sind

Colin Campbell (1792–1863) – suppressed the
Indian Mutiny

Alexander Gardner (1801–77) – soldier of
fortune and artillery commander

James Outram (1803–63) – political agent,
military commander

John Wilson (1804–75) – Dean of Faculty of
Arts, University of Bombay

Alexander Duff (1806–78) – missionary and
architect of Indian education system

Hugh Falconer (1806–65) – botanist;
developed Indian tea plantations

James Hope Grant (1808–75) – commander of
the Madras army

James Ramsay (1812–60) – Governor-General
of India

Stephen Hislop (1817–63) – founder of Indian
schools

John Skinner (trader) – founder of Bombay
Chamber of Commerce (1836)

Robert Kyd – founded Calcutta Botanic
Garden

John Forbes Royle – botanist; developed
cotton and tea industries

Sir Colin Scott-Moncrieff (1836–1916) –
superintending engineer of Ganges
Canal; chief engineer in Burma

Gilbert Elliot – Viceroy of India (1905–10)

Victor Alexander John Hope – Viceroy of India
(1936–43)

Italy

Michael Scott (1160–1235) – tutor to the King of Sicily (c 1180)

Porta del Popolo – guarded by Scots during conclave which elected Pope Nicholas V (1447)

William Baillie – Rector of Faculty of Arts, Ferrara University (1486)

James Crichton (1560–85) – swordsman and scholar (The Admirable Crichton), murdered in Mantua

James Martin of Dunkeld – professor, Turin University (1569–86)

Robert Leslie – doctor preceptor in Casa Moro in the Giudecca (Jewish quarter) of Venice

Scots College, Rome (founded 1600) – centre of Jacobitism

Peter Grant (1708–84) – student at Scots College, Gaelic speaker and Scots Agent (1737)

Prince Charles Edward Stuart (1720–88) – born and died in Rome

Andrew Lumsden (1720–1801) – archaeologist; secretary to Prince Charles in the '45; under-secretary to Old Pretender (1750)

Gavin Hamilton (1723–98) – painter and archaeologist (Rome)

Prince Henry Benedict, Cardinal York (1725–1807) –

James Clarke (d 1799) – art connoisseur, dealer and guide (Naples)

Colin Morison (1732–1810) – collector of paintings (Rome)

James Byres (1734–1817) – artist/archaeologist expert on Etruscan antiquities

Japan

James Bruce, 8th Earl of Elgin (1811–63) – first diplomatic plenipotentiary sent to Japan

Richard Brunton (1838–1901) – lighthouse engineer to Japanese government (1868)

Thomas Blake Glover (1838–1911) – in Nagasaki (1859). Built up Takashima Coal Mine. Adviser to Iwasaki Yataro, founder of Mitsubishi

Alexander Shand (1844–1930) – acting manager of Mercantile Bank of India, London and China. Established school of banking administration in Japan

Henry Dyer (1848–1918) – principal of Imperial College of Engineering, Japan

Charles Meik (1853–1923) – Harbour Engineer with Japanese Government (1887)

Mexico

Thomas Blake – merchant in Mexico (1554–85)

New Zealand

William Cargill (1784–1860) – established Otago and Dunedin

Thomas Burns (1796–1871) – Free Church minister, founder of Otago

David Monro (1813–) – introduced sheep from Australia, House of Representatives (1853), Speaker (1861–70)

John Anderson (1820–97) – founded Canterbury ironworks

James Macandrew (1820–87) – MP and Minister

Charles Fraser – founded Christchurch Boys School

James Hector (1834–1907) – Director of Geological Survey for new Zealand; Director of the Colonial Museum of New Zealand; Manager of the Institute for the Advancement of Science and Art (New Zealand)

James Black (1835–1914) – Professor of Natural Science, Otago

Thomas Brydone (1837–1904) – pioneer of refrigeration and dairy industries

William Berry (1839–1903) – editor of the *New Zealand Herald*

James Bain (1841–99) – owner of the *Southland News* and *Southland Times*

Alexander Fleming (1843–73) – first headmaster, Invercargill Grammar School

Robert Stout (1844–1930) – Prime Minister (1884–7)

James Brown (1846–1935) – Professor of Classics, Canterbury College

David Fleming (1861–1938) – editor of the *Leader*

Peter Fraser (1884–) – Prime Minister (1940–9)

STREET NAMES OF EDINBURGH AND DUNEDIN

Princes Street	Cumberland Street
George Street	Great King Street
Moray Place	Canongate

Norway

Edvard Grieg (1843–1907) – composer of Scottish extraction (Aberdeen)

Poland

St John Isaiah de Bonar – canonized as saint (1483)

Peter Fergusson-Tepper (d 1794) – member of Warsaw legislative assembly

30 000 Scots in Poland – 17th century

Russia

Norman and Walter Leslie – soldiers for the Teutonic Knights (1356)

Peter Davidson – Danish Ambassador to Ivan III (1495)

David Gilbert – Captain in bodyguard of Tsar Boris

General Carmichael – Commander of 5000 men under Ivan the Terrible

Alexander Leslie (1582–1661) – Russian recruitment agent (1630)

Thomas Dalyell of the Binns (1599–1685) – General in army of the Tsar

Paul Menzie – Russian Ambassador to the Pope (1672)

Patrick Gordon (1635–99) – Russian General (serving the Tsar for 38 years)

Thomas Gordon (d 1741) – Admiral under Peter the Great

Robert Erskine – chief physician to Tsar Peter the Great (1706)

Thomas Garvine (b 1690) – on Russia's earliest medical mission to China

James Grieve – city physician to St Petersburg (1747)

Peter Anderson – Vice-Admiral in command of Baltic fleet (1769)

James Keith (1696–1758) – served in Russia. Later Field Marshall

James Mounsey (b 1710) – chief personal physician to Tsar Peter III

John Elphinston (1722–85) – Rear-Admiral (1769) (fought against Turks)

Samuel Greig (1735–88) – Rear-Admiral under Catherine the Great, reconstructed port of Kronstadt, founder of the Russian navy

Charles Cameron (1740–1812) – architect to Catherine the Great

John Rogerson (b 1741) – physician-general to the Russian fleet

Thomas Mackenzie (d 1786) – Rear-Admiral in Black Sea fleet, established harbour installations in Sevastopol

Matthew Guthrie (1743–1807) – chief physician to Imperial Land Cadet Corps of Nobles at St Petersburg

Adam Menelaws (1749–1831) – architect to Catherine the Great

John Grieve (1753–1805) – court physician to Tsars Paul and Alexander

William Hastie (1755–1832) – builder of cast-iron arched bridges in Russia

Charles Gascoigne – set up cannon foundries (1790s); director of textile mill at St Petersburg: Knight of St Vladimir and St Anna

Michael Barclay (1761–1818) – Field Marshal commanding 400 000 men for the Tsar against Napoleon (created Prince Barclay de Tolly)

Adam Armstrong (1762–1818) – director of the Petrozavodsk factories

Alexander Crichton (b 1763) – physician-in-prdinary to Tsar Alexander I

James Wylie (1768–1854) – Tsar's personal surgeon, head of Russia's military medical services

Charles Baird – constructed first Russian steamship (Elizaveta) (1815)

Alexander Wilson – Engineer-General, assistant director at Aleksandrovsk textile mill

William Carrick (1827–78) – portrait photographer, Kronstadt

Home, Daniel (1833–86) – magician to the Tsar of Russia and Napoleon

William Campbell (Villi the Clown) (1910–) – clown with Soviet State Circus

Spain

William Semple – soldier of fortune and political agent, founded Scots College (Roman Catholic seminary) in Madrid (1627). It later moved to Valladolid

Sir John Moore – mortally wounded at Corunna after defeating the French (1809)

Sweden

Gustavus Adolphus – employed 34 Scots colonels and 50 lieutenant colonels. He had a Scots bodyguard

Andreas Keith – Commandant of Vadstena Castle, Baron of Forsholm (1574)

Blasius Dundee – banker to King John III of Sweden (1577)

Jakob Roberston (1566–1652) – physician to Gustavus Adolphus

Jacob Neaf – Governor of Vastmanland and Dalecarlia (1583)

Samuel Cobron (Cockburn) (1574–1621) – Major-General in the Swedish army

Alexander Leslie (1582–1661) – Lt Colonel of Småland Regiment

Patrick Ruthven (1586–1651) – Colonel of the Kalmar Regiment

Hans Stuart – Swedish envoy to Russia (1611)

Sir James Spens – Swedish Ambassador to England (1613)

Simon Stewart – Admiral in Swedish navy (1616)

Anders Stuart – Rear-Admiral in Swedish navy (1621)

James King (1589–1634) – Lt General and Baron of Sanshult

Jacob MacDougall (1589–1634) – General of Swedish army in Silesia

David Drummond (1593–1638) – Major General in Swedish army

Robert Douglas (1611–61) – General, Baron Skålby, Count of Skånninge

Alexander Erskein – Baron (1655), diplomat and agent

Alexander Blackwell (1700–47) – physician to Frederick I

Charles Tottie (1703–66) – founded Stockholm's City Fire Insurance Office

Colin Campbell – founded Swedish East India Company (1731)

Immanuel Kant (1724–1804) (philosopher) – had two Scottish grandparents

Thomas Erskine (1746–1828) – founder of Gothenburg's 'Bachelors' Club' (1769)

William Chalmers (1748–1811) – founded Chalmers Institute of Technology, Gothenburg (1829)

George Carnegie – shipowner in Gothenburg (1764)

Rutger Maclean – 18th-century agricultural reformer

David Carnegie (1772–1873) – established D. Carnegie and Co (export/import)

William Gibson (1783–1857) – founder of Jonseredfabriken (Gothenburg)

Alexander Keiller (1804–74) – founder of Gøtaverken (Gothenburg shipyard)

Robert and James Dickson – founded James Dickson and Co (Gothenburg) 19th century

Joseph Hislop (1884–1977) – operatic tenor, Knight of the Vasa, naturalized Swede

Tibet

14th Duke of Hamilton – first over-flight of Mount Everest (1932)

United States

Nine of Washington's 22 brigadier generals were of Scots descent

Eleven out of the Congress of 56 who adopted the Declaration of Independence were of Scots descent

Two-thirds of the first 13 governors of states were of Scots descent

More than 30 Scots were governors of American colonies (1707-83)

From the Revolution more than 100 men of Scots descent were governors of states

15 judges of the Supreme Court (1789-1882) were of Scots descent

Log Colleges of Scottish foundation – Jefferson College, Mercer College, Wabash College, Dickinson College

Presidents with Scottish blood in their veins – James McCosh, Woodrow Wilson

Presidents of Scottish descent – Monroe, Grant, Hayes, Roosevelt, Polk, Buchanan, Arthur, McKinley, Jackson

UNITED STATES – continued

6 Vice-Presidents and 150 Cabinet members have been of Scottish descent

Scottish signatories of the Declaration of Independence – Edward Rutledge, William Hooper, George Ross, James Wilson

According to the 1920 Census – 254 570 US citizens had been born in Scotland

Investment in US – Scottish American Investment Company financed: Wyoming Cattle Ranch Company, Western Ranches Limited; Scottish American Mortgage Company financed: Matador Land and Cattle Company

In late 1870s – three-quarters of foreign investment in US ranching was from Scotland

James Blair (1656-1743) – founder of William and Mary College

Alexander Spotswood (1676-1749) – Governor of Virginia

William Keith (1680-1749) – Governor of Pennsylvania and and Delaware

John Smibert (1684-1751) – portrait painter

Peter Mackintosh (blacksmith) – ringleader in Boston riots (1765)

Gabriel Johnston (1699-1752) – Governor of North Carolina

Flora MacDonald (1722-90) – emigrated to America. Present at the Croos Creek Rising and Battle of Moore's Creek Bridge (27 Feb 1776) ('America's Culloden'); 850 Highlanders captured. Killed off the revival of Gaelic culture in Carolina

Robert Smith (1722-77) – architect of colonial buildings in Philadelphia

John Witherspoon (1723-94) – principal of the College of New Jersey (Princeton), 1768-94. The only clergyman to sign the Declaration of Independence

Daniel Malcolm (trader) – ringleader in Boston riots (1768)

Cosmo Alexander (1724-72) – portrait painter

William Smith (1727-1803) – Provost of College (later University) of Philadelphia

Alexander McDougall (1731-86) – member of Continental Congress

Samuel Johnston (1733-1816) – US Senator, member of Continental Congress

Robert Aitken (1734-1802) – printer and publisher in Philadelphia

Andrew St Clair (1734-1818) – Governor of North-West Territories

James Robertson (1742-1804) – founder of Nashville, Tennessee

James Wilson (1742-89) – signatory of the Declaration of Independence

Thomas Leiper (1745-1825) – director of the Bank of the US

John Paul Jones (1747-92) – founder of the American Navy

James McClurg (1747-1825) – Professor of Medicine, Williamsburg

William Small – Professor of Natural Philosophy, Williamsburg (1758-64)

Alexander McGillivray (1759-93) – Creek Indians tribal chief, Alabama

Alexander Cuming – lawgiver and spokesman for the Cherokee Indians

John McKenzie (1763-1823) – founder of Chicago

David B. Mitchell (1766-1837) – Governor of Georgia

Alexander Wilson (1766-1813) – ornithologist

Alexander Mackenzie (1767-1820) – first European to cross the American continent

Patrick Henry – five times Governor of Virginia. Largely behind adoption of Bill of Rights (1775)

George Bruce (1781-1866) – introduced the stereotype

Lawrie Walker (1784-1868) – Secretary of US Senate

James Gordon Bennett (1795-1892) – founded *New York Herald* (1835)

Charles Lockart (1818-1905) – President of Standard Oil

Allan Pinkerton (1819-84) – founder of the Pinkerton Detective Agency

Charles Burt (1823-92) – engraver in the Treasury Department

Alexander McGraw (1831-1905) – erected pedestal of the Statue of Liberty

Thomas Moonlight (1833-99) – Governor of Wyoming

James Hector (1834-1907) – investigated goldfields and mines, western America

Andrew Carnegie (1835-1919) – philanthropist

James Wilson (1836-1920) – Secretary of Agriculture

John Muir (1838-1914) – founder of Yellowstone Park

David Bremner Henderson (1840-1906) –
Speaker of House of Representatives
William Grant Laidlaw (b 1840) – Member of
Congress (1887-91) for New York
John McLaren (1846-1943) – created Golden
Gate Park, San Francisco
John Stuart Stuart Forbes (1849-76) – member
of 7th Regt US Cavalry, died with
General Custer at Little Bighorn,
Montana ('Custer's Last Stand')
John Sutherland Sinclair – North Dakota
farmer (1891)
Earl of Airlie – Chairman of the Prairie Land
and Cattle Company
William Wilson (1862-1934) – Secretary for
Labour (1913-21)

PLACE-NAMES AFTER SCOTS

Paterson town, Putman County, New York –
Matthew Paterson (18th-century stone-
mason
McDuffie County, Georgia – George McDuffie,
Governor of S Carolina (1838-40)
Crawford – 11 towns and villages
Leith – four villages (Alabama, Arkansas,
Nevada, N Dakota)

TRADITIONS

First Burns club in the USA – New York
(1847)
First Highland games in USA – New York
(1836)
Order of Scottish clans – St Louis (1878)
Scots who died at the Battle of the Alamo (1836)
– Richard Ballantine, John McGregor,
Isaac Robinson, David Wilson
Scots who died in the American Civil War (1861-5)
– Sgt-Major John McEwan, 65th Illinois
Vol Infantry; Lt Col William Duff, 2nd
Illinois Regt of Artillery; Robert
Steedman, 5th Regt Maine Infantry Vol;
James Wilkie, 1st Michigan Cavalry;
Robert Ferguson, 57th Regt New York
Infantry Vol
(all buried in Old Calton Cemetery,
Edinburgh)

SAINTS of SCOTLAND – A CALENDAR

It is said that in the Celtic Church 'Saint'
was the equivalent of 'Mr'. Formal
canonization by the Roman Church did
not begin until relatively late: Queen
Margaret was one of the earliest
canonizations of Scottish saints (AD 1250).
Of the 1848 formally canonized saints 271
are from Britain and Ireland.

Adamnan (23 Sept) – born Donegal c 627
Abbot of Iona
Adrian (4 Mar) – martyred on Isle of May,
Firth of Forth, in 9th century
Aidan (31 Aug) – founder of Lindisfarne,
died 651
Ailred (3 Feb/3 Mar) – (1109-66) Cistercian
abbot
Andrew (30 Nov) – one of the Apostles
Antony (17 Jan) – Egyptian hermit (died in
356 aged 105)
Athernaise (22 Dec) – probably did not have
the power of speech
Ayle (30 Aug) – Irish missionary in Europe
(died in 650 aged 66)
Baithene (9 June) – b 536, one of the 12
monks who crossed with Columba
Baldred (6 Mar) – a hermit who lived on the
Bass Rock (d 756)
Bega (31 Oct) – Irish nun who settled in St
Bee's, Cumbria
Blane (10/11 Aug) – Irish missionary on Bute
Boisil (23 Feb) – monk in Melrose (d c 664)
Bonach – 7th-century chaplain in Leuchars
Brendan (16 May) – Irish missionary who
founded churches on west coast
Bride/Bridget (1 Feb) – (c 452-524) Irish nun
Brioc (29/30 Apr) – missionary who came to
Britain c 429
Bryce (13 Nov) – 'the grumpy saint'
Cecilia (22 Nov) – patroness of music,
executed by the Romans
Colman (18 Feb) – Irish abbot at Lindisfarne
(661) (d 676)
Colmanella – monk at Iona (d 611)
Columba (9 June) – great Irish missionary
(d 597)
Comgan (13 Oct) – Irish missionary who
worked mainly east of the Great Glen

SAINTS OF SCOTLAND – continued

Constantine (11 Mar) – monk at Govan, martyred nearby

Convall (28 Sept) – Irish missionary in Renfrew (d 612)

Cuthbert (20 Mar) – (634-87) bishop of Lindisfarne

Cyrus (16 June) – Roman child martyr

David I (24 May) – founded many Scottish abbeys and cathedrals

Donan (16/17 Apr) – killed with 50 colleagues on island of Eigg (618)

Drostan (11 July) – a shadowy figure commemorated in Insch and Urquhart

Ebba of Northumbria (22 Aug) – daughter of King Aethelfrith of Bernicia

Ebba the Second (2 Apr) – abbess (d 683)

Edwin (12 Oct) – King of Northumbria (d 633)

Enoch (18 July) – mother of Kentigern

Fergus (15/27 Nov) – probably a Pictish bishop

Fillan of Loch Earn (22 June) – Irish missionary

Fillan of Strathfillan (9/19 Jan) – Irish 8th-century missionary

Finian (10 Sept) – Irish tutor at Whithorn

Fintan Munnu (21 Oct) – a leper and a missionary

George (23 Apr) – a martyr at Lydda, Palestine in 3rd or 4th century

Gerardine (8 Nov) – Irish monk who lived in a cave near Lossiemouth (d 934)

Germanus (31 July) – bishop of Auxerre, Gaul who came to Scotland to fight the Pelagian heresy in 429 or 447

Giles (1 Sept) – French Benedictine monk, friend of animals (d 725)

Godric (21 May) – ex-pedlar, the hermit of Finchale (d 1170)

Gordian (10 May) – Roman martyr of 2nd or 3rd century

Hilda (17 Nov) – outstanding abbess of Hartlepool and Whitby (614-80)

John the Baptist (24 June/29 Aug) – last of the Prophets on whose festival the battle of Bannockburn was fought

John the Evangelist (27 Dec) – author of the Book of Revelation

Katherine of Siena (29/30 Apr) – Italian nun and mystic (b 1347)

Kenneth (11 Oct) – Irish monk (525–600)

Kentigern (Mungo) (13 Jan) – born on Fife coast; lived as a monk at Culross (d 612)

Kentigerna (7 Jan) – 8th-century daughter of King of Leinster; missionary

Kessog (13 Jan) – Irish missionary in Scotland martyred abroad

Laurence (3 Feb) – bishop of Canterbury

Leonard (6 Nov) – French monk, patron of prisoners and midwives

Llolan (22 Sept) – 6th-century monk

Machar (12 Nov) – Irish missionary round the River Don

Maelrubha (21 Apr/22 Aug) – Irish monk in north-west Scotland (642–722)

Magnus (16 Apr) – Orcadian Viking earl, a pacifist who was murdered

Malachy (3 Nov) – Irish monk

Margaret (16 Nov) – Scottish queen who replaced Celtic by Roman Church

Marnock (18 Aug/25 Oct) – Irish monk and missionary in Scotland

Martin (11 Nov) – Hungarian-born Roman soldier turned monk (d 415)

Michael (29 Sept) – Prince and standard-bearer of the Angels of God

Mirren (15 Sept) – Irish missionary who died at end of 6th century

Mochaoi (23 June) – Irish missionary, follower of Patrick (d 496)

Modan (4 Feb) – 6th- or 7th-century Highland Gael, a contemplative at Loch Etive

Molios (18 Apr) – Irish missionary at Holy Island (off Lamlash)

Moluag (4 Aug) – Irish missionary who died at Rosemarkie in 592

Monirus (18 Dec) – missionary around Dee Valley (d 824)

Nathalan (8 Jan) – Aberdeenshire agricultural expert who found God (d 678)

Nicholas (6 Dec) – of Myra (Asia Minor), patron of detectives and architects

Ninian (16 Sept) – Irish missionary whose seaside cave is at Physgill, Whithorn

Ogilvie, John (10 Mar) – Banffshire Jesuit hanged in Glasgow

Olaf (29 July) – Haraldsson, king and patron of Norway

Oswald (28 Feb) – Anglo-Saxon king and warrior educated at Iona (d 642)

Palladius (7 July) – French priest, first bishop to the Scots (d 432)

Patrick (17 Mar) – British ex-slave converted in Gaul who worked in Ireland

Quivox (24 Feb) – 7th-century Irish monk (d 669)

Regulus (30 Mar/17 Oct) – early Celtic missionary in Fife

Ronan (7 Feb/1 June) – of Innerleithen, abbot and missionary

Roque (16 Aug) – French male nurse, vagrant and plague victim

Serf (1 July) – missionary who ordained Kentigern at Culross

Thomas (29 Dec) – a Becket, English bishop and martyr

Triduana (8 Oct/9 Nov) – missionary in Edinburgh and the Highlands who escaped marriage by gouging out her beautiful eyes

Vigean (Fechin) (20 Jan) – Irish monk (d 664)

Wilfred (12 Oct) – Northumbrian abbot of Ripon (b 633)

CHURCHMEN

David Beaton (1494–1546) – Cardinal, assassinated at St Andrews

George Buchanan (1506–82) – Principal of St Leonard's College, St Andrews (best Latin poet in Europe)

George Wishart (1513–46) – Reformer burned at St Andrews

Ninian Winzet (1518–92) – Abbot of Ratisbon

Andrew Melville (1545–1622) – Principal of St Andrews

John Ogilvie (1579–1615) – Jesuit priest executed for denying Royal Supremacy. Beatified by Roman Catholic Church

George Hay (1729–1811) – Roman Catholic Vicar apostolic of Lowland Scotland

Thomas Chalmers (1780–1847) – leading founder of the Free Church

Edward Irving (1792–1834) – Pentecostalist preacher

Hugh Miller (1802–56) – geologist and theologian

Thomas Guthrie (1803–73) – founder of Ragged Schools

Archibald Tait (1811–82) – Archbishop of Canterbury

Alexander Forbes (1817–75) – Bishop of Brechin

William Quarrier (1829–1903) – founded Quarriers Homes for children (1876)

Lord Macleod of Fuinary (1895–1991) – founded Iona Community

First Anglican bishop of overseas diocese – Samuel Seabury (US), consecrated Bishop of Connecticut at Aberdeen (1784)

Scottish-born Archbishops of Canterbury – Cosmo Gordon Lang (1864–1945), Archbishop 1928 (his brother Marshall Lang was Moderator of the General Assembly of the Church of Scotland in 1935); Archibald Campbell Tait (1811–82), Archbishop 1868–82

INVENTIONS for WAR

Aircraft carrier – Duke of Montrose (1878–1954)

Aircraft catapult system – Colin Mitchell

Anderson air-raid shelter – William Paterson (1874–1956)

Aircraft arresting gear – Colin Mitchell

Ballistics, as a science – Andrew Noble (1831–)

Breech-loading rifle – Colonel Patrick Fergusson (1744–80)

Carronade – General Robert Melville (1723-1809)

Cordite (explosive) – James Dewar (1842–1923)

Gas mask – John Stenhouse (1809–90)

Lee-Enfield rifle: bolt action and magazine – James Lee (1831–1904)

Percussion lock – Alexander Forsyth (1768–1843)

Ring bayonets – invented by General Mackay (1640–92). First used at Battle of Killiekrankie

Shrapnel – Lieutenant Henry Shrapnel RA (1761–1842) Tested Carron Ironworks, Stirling, 1784

Smokescreen – suggested by Archibald Cochrane (1749–1831)

First life-jacket (inflatable rubber) – ordered from Charles Mackintosh of Glasgow by Captain John Franklin (1824)

First rubber air-bed – ordered by Captain John Franklin from Charles Mackintosh (1824)

First dynamite factory opened – British Dynamite Co, Ardier (1873)

SCOTTISH REGIMENTS

Scottish Division

Argyll and Sutherland Highlanders (1881)
Black Watch (1739)
Gordon Highlanders (1794)
King's Own Scottish Borderers (1689)
Queen's Own Highlanders (late 18th
century)
Royal Highland Fusiliers (1678)
Royal Scots (1633)

Household Division

Scots Guards (1639)

Scottish Soldiers, Sailors, Airmen and Their Exploits

General Tam Dalyell of the Binns (c 1615–1685) – served Tsar of Russia against Poles and Turks

James Graham, Marquess of Montrose (1612–50) – defeated Covenanting army three times the size of his own

James Keith (1696–1758) – Marshall in the army of Frederick the Great of Prussia

General James Murray (1725–94) – commander of British army against French in Canada

Sir David Dundas (1735–1820) – wrote official British Army manual (1792)

General Simon Fraser (1726–82) – led General Wolfe up cliffs

Admiral Adam Duncan (1731–1804) – defeated Dutch at Camperdown (1797)

Sir Ralph Abercromby (1734–1801) – commander in West Indies, Ireland, Scotland and Mediterranean (1795–1801)

Major-General John Moore (1761–1809) –

Colonel William Inglis (1764–1835) – earned the 57th Regiment the title of the 'Die-Hards' at the Battle of Albuera in 1811 (out of 579 men, 23 officers and 415 rank and file dead or wounded)

Thomas Bruce, Earl of Elgin (1766–1841) – removed Elgin Marbles from the Parthenon (1803)

Jacques Law (1768–1828) – Napoleon's Aide-de-Camp and Maréchal of France

Charles James Napier (1782–1853) – annexed Indian Province of Sind; Governor of Karachi

Lieutenant-General William Crockat (20th Regiment of Foot) – last officer to be in charge of Napoleon at St Helena

General William Elliott (1792–1874) – saved Gibraltar

General Charles Gordon (1838–84) – 'Chinese Gordon'

Douglas, Earl Haig (1861–1928) – colour-blind Commander-in-Chief of the British forces in World War I

Lord Hugh Dowding (1882–1970) – leader of Fighter Command in World War II

Major General Robert Johnston (b Leith 1937) – Chief of Staff in the Gulf War, US Marine Corps

Scottish Regiments and NCOs

Scots Foot Guards and Archers (France) – established 1425

Garde Ecossaise – established c 1445

Scots Brigade – spearhead of army of Gustavus Adolphus at Battle of Leipzig (1631); after the battle many towns had Scots governors

Oldest royal personal bodyguard – Royal Company of Archers (dating from 15th century but formally established in 1676)

Sergeant (later Ensign) Charles Ewart (1769–1846) of Royal Scots Greys – captured Imperial Standard of 45th Invincibles at Waterloo

The Commandos (founded 1941) – trained at Inverailort and Achnacarry (Commando Memorial at Spean Bridge). Lord Lovat was a distinguished commando

Scottish Ships and Boats

One of earliest boats in Europe – dugout canoe found in buried forest bed at Friarton, Perth (8000 years old)

Largest and most powerful 16th-century warship – The Great Michael (73 m/240 ft long; 300 sailors; 120 gunners, built at Newhaven, 1511)

Oldest British warship still afloat – HMS Unicorn, Dundee (built 1824)

Miscellany

Last Covenanter martyr executed in Edinburgh – Rev John Renwick (1688)

Britain's only private army – the Atholl Highlanders (founded 1845) consists of 55 rank and file and a pipe band of 25 stationed at Blair Castle

Duke of Hamilton and Flight Lieutenant David McIntyre – first to fly over Mount Everest (1933)

Scottish Winners of the Victoria Cross

Since it was introduced (1856) – 108 Scots have been awarded the Victoria Cross

Longest lived of all Victoria Cross holders – Lieutenant Colonel Harcus Strachan (1884–1982) born in Bo'ness and lived to 97 yrs 175 days

Military Music

'Colonel Bogey' – the marching song, was inspired by a game of golf played by bandmaster Frederick J. Ricketts (1881–1945) of the 93rd Highlanders at Fort George golf course in 1913, during which another golfer signalled to him by whistling a musical interval of a descending minor third.

INFAMOUS SCOTS

Pontius Pilate – said to have been born in Fortingall, Perthshire where his father was on military service (Arezzo, Italy is also claimed as his birthplace)

The Royal Scots – known as 'Pontius Pilate's Bodyguard' because of an argument between the Scots and a French regiment, the Régiment de Picardie (founded 1562) who were envious of the fact that the Royal Scots had been founded earlier. An officer of the Picardie regiment boasted that the French were descendants of the Roman regiment on duty at the Crucifixion of Christ. The Scots replied, 'If we had been there we would not have slept at our post as you did. That night our ancestors were serving as Pontius Pilate's bodyguard!'

Pirate – Captain Kidd b Greenock (1645–1701)

The 109 voters (to 69) of the final Scottish parliament – they sold Scotland to England for £398 085 and 10 shillings (16 Jan 1707)

Most successful spy in Scotland – the author Daniel Defoe reporting on the Union to London (1707)

John Porteous (d 1736) – Captain of the Edinburgh Town Guard lynched by the mob

Pirate and American naval hero – John Paul Jones b Kirkcudbrightshire (1747–92)

Patrick Sellar (1780–1881) – factor on Sutherland estates who cruelly evicted tenants in Highland Clearances

William McGonagall (1825–1902) – worst poet in the world

Butch Cassidy of the Wild Bunch (he had a Scots mother) – gangster in the Wild West

Most notorious spy – the Soviet agent Donald Maclean (1913–83) who came from a Scottish family

Most dangerous spy captured in Scotland – Werner Wälti (arrested in Edinburgh's Waverley Station by Willie Merrilees dressed as a railway porter) (1938)

Most distinguished foreign spy in Britain – Rudolf Hess who landed in Scotland looking for the Duke of Hamilton (1941)

MURDER, THEFT, TREASON and MISCARRIAGE of JUSTICE

In earliest times serious cases were heard in the High Court of Justiciary, Edinburgh

Edward Simpson – dressed up as a 'guiser', stole money at New Year from a priest's bedroom. Fined 120 Scots merks (1507)

John Neilson – convicted of 'intercommuning with the English' (fire-raising, theft and horse-stealing). Hanged and drawn (1509)

Adam Scott – beheaded for extorting blackmail while a prisoner in Edinburgh Castle (1530)

Michael Scott – convicted of stealing 22 oxen and cows. Whipped through the streets, both his ears cut off. Banished for life (1531)

Janet Anderson – drowned for burning down a byre with 50 oxen and 11 cows inside it (1533)

John Master of Forbes – for conspiring to kill James V, dragged on a hurdle through the cobbled High Street of Edinburgh, hanged, quartered and dismembered (1537)

John Corry – ears cut off. Whipped through the streets for stealing wool from 7 live sheep (1538)

Isabella McFarlane – branded on the cheeks for burning down a house (1549)

Peter Chaplin – hanged for counterfeiting coin of the realm (1554)

John Hepburn, John Hay, William Powrie and George Dalglish – hanged, their heads, legs, arms cut off and hung on the city gates (their bodies burnt) for the murder of Henry Lord Darnley (1567)

Thomas Barry – Unicorn Pursuivant, had his right hand cut off for forging the Regent's signature (1570)

John Kello – the minister of Spott, convicted of murdering his wife. Hanged and body burnt to ashes (1570)

Andrew Thomson of Silverburn – burnt at the stake for fire-raising and burning corn (1577)

Archibald Croser – hanged for stealing 70 cattle (1584)

John Dickson – was broken on the wheel for killing his father (1591)

Janet Stewart – convicted of witchcraft, sorcery, incantation. Strangled and burnt to ashes (1597)

Robert Auchmowtie – surgeon and burgess, beheaded for killing James Wauchope in a duel at the Queen's Park (1600)

Earl of Gowrie's conspiracy to kill James VI – Earl of Gowrie killed in the incident. Later condemned to be hanged, drawn and quartered at the Cross of Edinburgh (1600)

Thomas (Johnnie) Armstrong – the Border reiver accused of the murder by shooting of Sir John Carmichael. His right hand was cut off, he was hanged and his body hung in chains. With him was executed Adam Scot King of the Borders (1601)

Archibald Cornwall – town officer, tried to nail a picture of James VI on the public gibbet in Edinburgh. He was condemned to be hanged and his body left up for 24 hours with a notice of his crime on his forehead (1601)

Sawney Bean – some time in the reign of James VI a notorious family of cannibals (45-strong) haunted Bennane Head three miles north of Ballantrae. After many strange tales of travellers disappearing never to be seen again, the authorities discovered the cave of the Beans by the shore. In it were piles of money, clothes, weapons and the pickled human limbs of their victims. The men of the family were executed by mutilation at Leith and the women were burnt

Francis Moubray (deceased) – convicted of high treason. He had tried to escape from Edinburgh Castle with knotted sheets but they broke and he fell to his death. His body was taken into the court and then hanged, quartered. His head and quarters were placed on the city gates (1603)

John and Alister Macgregor of Glenistra – were hanged and quartered for slaughtering 140 of the Laird of Luss's supporters (1604)

Robert Weir – convicted of the murder of the Laird of Warriston, was broken on a cart-wheel with the coulter of a plough (the first recorded instance of this punishment). His dead body, still on the wheel, was displayed in public in Scotland (1604)

Johnnie Jack – a servant in Roslin, convicted of bestiality (sodomy). Burnt at the Castle Hill (1605)

William Murdoch – a Catholic priest, convicted of saying Mass. Taken to the Mercat Cross wearing vestments. He was chained there from 10 am to 11.48 am. Then the vestments were burnt and he was banished (1607)

drew Crichton – for declining the authority of the king and Privy Council, hanged and dismembered (1610)

psies – for remaining within the kingdom – Moyses Fa, David Fa, Robert Fa, John Fa hanged at the Burgh Muir, Edinburgh (1611)

mes Middleton – (aged 14) beheaded at the Mercat Cross for the murder of Clement Mauchane (son of a burgess), stabbing a dirk 23 cm/9 in long under his ribs on the left side (1612)

hn Fleming – for making slanderous speeches against the king, hanged at the Cross (1615)

hn Ogilvie – a Jesuit priest, hanged in Glasgow for declining the king's authority, alleging the supremacy of the Pope and hearing and saying Mass (1615)

omas Rois – for maintaining that all Scots (except the king and his sons) should be debarred from the Court of England – his right hand cut off, then decapitated. The one stuck on the West Port, the other on the Netherbow Port (1618)

n Johnson (1572–1637) – after his visit to Scotland the poet was sentenced in absention to having his nose cut off for making fun of the Scots (1618)

hn Swyne – servant to the Laird of Randiefurd, beheaded at the Castlehill for the murder of John McArthur, a servant, by striking him with a dirk in the belly at a wedding (1619)

trick Roy Macgregor – accused of theft, fire-raising, robbery and murder with his band of 40 thieves. His right hand was cut off, he was hanged and his body hung in chains. The executioner so bungled the job that he lost his job the next day (1667)

nes Johnston – hanged in the Grassmarket for the murder of her grandson (1674)

drew Rutherford – beheaded for the murder of James Douglas (1674)

mes Gray – dyer and lieutenant in the Duke of Lauderdale's Regiment of Lothian Militia, for the murder of Archibald Murray, gentleman of His Majesty's Troop of Guards, beheaded in the Grassmarket (1678)

James Skene – hanged and decapitated for treasonable opinions (1680)

John Chieslie of Dalry – accused of the murder of Sir George Lockart, Lord President of the Court of Session, Privy Councillor, whom he shot in the back on his way home from church. His right hand was cut off, he was hanged with his pistol round his neck and his right hand was then fixed on the West Port (1689)

Charles Lord Fraser – accused of high treason. At the Mercat Cross of Fraserburgh he had proclaimed the late King James the lawful king, cursed King William, drank to his confusion; called him a Dutch Burgher, fired guns and pistols from the Cross and forced citizens to drink treasonable healths. He was fined £200 (1693)

George Cumming WS – hanged for the murder in the West Port of Patrick Falconer, a soldier in Lord Lindsay's Regiment whom Cumming had called 'sons of whores and bitches' (1695)

Robert Carmichael – schoolmaster, accused of the murder of one of his scholars. He had beaten him three times with his hand on the head and back. The boy died and stripes were found on his back, legs and thighs. Carmichael was sentenced to seven stripes and banishment (1695)

Captain Douglas – fined 300 merks for the rape of Christian Davidson (1695)

Thomas Aitkenhead – a 20-year-old student, accused of saying repeatedly in public that theology was nonsense, the Old Testament was composed of fables, that Christ learned magic in Egypt to perform his miracles. He preferred Mahommed to Christ and announced that God, the World and Nature were all one. He was sentenced on Christmas Eve – on 8 January between 2 and 4 in the afternoon he was hanged at the gallow lee and his body buried at the foot of the gallows (1696)

Captain Simon Fraser of Beaufort – accused of collecting an armed force, occupying and fortifying houses, raping a lady of distinguished rank (Lady Lovat) whilst bagpipes were played outside the bed-chamber; continuing in arms after being

MURDER, THEFT, TREASON and MISCARRIAGE of JUSTICE – continued

charged by a herald to lay them down. It was reported that the Fiery Cross was seen and the Coronach (war-song sung by women) was heard. He was sentenced to be executed as a traitor but in 1715 he supported the House of Hanover, receiving a pardon from King George. In the rebellion of 1745 he supported the Jacobites and after Culloden his house was burnt before his eyes. Simon Fraser is the only person on record to have been twice condemned, twice forfeited his estates and twice pardoned and restored (1698)

Captain Thomas Green of the English East India Company – commander of the 'Worcester', wrongly condemned for piracy and murder on a ship off the coast of Malabar – condemned to be hanged on the Sands of Leith with 13 of his crew. In the wake of the Darien disaster and the passing of the 1705 Alien Act by the English parliament the Edinburgh mob intimidated the Court of Admiralty into unjustly executing the captain and some of the crew of the English vessel (1705)

James Stewart of Aucharn – (whose estate had been forfeited after the '45), was hanged for the murder of the factor on the forfeited estate, Colin Campbell. Stewart was said to have instigated Allan Breck Stewart to waylay and shoot Campbell in Lettermore Wood. James Stewart was hanged on a gibbet at the side of Ballachulish ferry and his body hung in chains. During the execution a storm raged as if at the clear injustice of the proceedings at the Circuit Court of Justiciary at Inveraray (1752)

John Connocher – an Episcopal clergyman, accused of celebrating a clandestine and irregular marriage. He was banished for life under pain of death (1755)

John Maciver and Archibald Macallum – merchants of Greenock, accused of piracy (sinking ships and selling their cargo). They were condemned to stand for an hour in the pillory in Glasgow with labels on their chests saying they had bored holes in a ship in order to defraud the underwriters. The two were banished for life (1785)

Peter Greig – hanged for *hamesucken* (great violence to a person in their dwelling-house) in Glasgow (1800)

Peter McDougal – convicted of murdering his wife by throwing her into River Etive and hanged at Inveraray (last hanging Inveraray) (1807)

Archibald Begg – a resurrectionist banished from Scotland, whipped through the streets of Edinburgh for returning too soon (1807)

Alex Gillan – (aged 19) hanged for murder and rape in Inverness, his body later hung in chains (1810)

Two Irishmen, Kelly and O'Neil – hanged for highway robbery at Braidburn, Edinburgh (1815)

Matthew Clydesdale – a miner, hanged for murder in Glasgow. He was brought back to life by galvanic shock. He stood up before the students and professors of Glasgow University. The alarmed professor plunged his lancet into Clydesdale's jugular vein and the man fell back on the floor (1818)

John Ritchie – (17) hanged in Aberdeen for sheep stealing at Gordon Castle (1818)

John Baird and Andrew Hardie – hanged and beheaded in public (last execution in Scotland for treason) and 20 men transported in Radical Rising, Glasgow (1820)

Peter Heaman (mate) and Francois Gautier (cook of a schooner – hanged for piracy between Brazil and Gibraltar on Sands of Leith, Edinburgh (1821)

Edward Hand – whipped (80 strokes) through streets of Glasgow for criminal assault (1822)

Mary McKinnon – brothel-keeper of Edinburgh, hanged in front of 20 000 for stabbing a solicitor's clerk in her premises under the South Bridge (1823)

William Campbell – (9 years old) imprisoned for 18 months for theft in Edinburgh (most juvenile criminal sentenced in High Court) (1827)

William Burke (body-snatcher) – hanged and his body publicly dissected in Edinburgh (1829)

George Gilchrist – innkeeper of Edinburgh, hanged for robbing a coach of £5700 (18..)

nuel Waugh – hanged at Ayr for murder
of a special constable during the riots at
Girvan in 1831 (1832)

gh Kennedy – hanged for throwing vitriol
in the face of the boot-boy at the Buck's
Head Inn, Glasgow (1834)

s Jaffray – hanged in Glasgow for
poisoning two lodgers with arsenic at
Carluke (1838)

and Mrs Rosenberg – accused of fire-
raising in Aberdeen (only instance of a
Scottish trial extending into Sunday
morning) (1842)

liam Bennison (Holy Willie) – hanged for
wife murder and bigamy in Edinburgh
(1850)

ns McFarlane and Helen Blackwood – hanged
for murder of a ship's carpenter by
throwing him out of a window in
Glasgow (1853)

deleine Smith – accused of murdering her
lover. Not proven, Glasgow (1857)

orge Bryce – (30) a carter, hanged in
Edinburgh for the murder of a young
woman with a razor in a house near
Ratho (last public execution in
Edinburgh) (1864)

Edward Pritchard – hanged for murder of
wife and mother in-law by poison in
Glasgow (last public execution in
Glasgow – with 750 constables) (1865)

ene Chantrelle – a French teacher in
Edinburgh, hanged for poisoning his wife
(Calton Jail) (1878)

asgow Dynamiters' – (10 men) tried for
blowing up a gasometer and trying to
blow up the Canal Bridge at Possil. 158
crown witnesses. All sentenced to penal
servitude (1883)

red Monson – a shooting tenant at
Ardlamont, charged in Glasgow with
attempting to murder Windsor
Hambrough by boring a hole in his
rowing-boat. Also charged with shooting
Hambrough. Not proven (1893)

seph Calabrere – ice-cream merchant of
Glasgow, charged with murder of his
wife and family with a hatchet. Death
sentence commuted (1904)

sha Liffey – (20) a Basuto working in
travelling shows, executed in Glasgow for
the murder of a woman in the dark in
spite of an appeal for this former

dispatch runner and member of the 2nd
Scottish Rifles in the Boer War (1905)

James Connolly – (born in Edinburgh 1870)
executed in Dublin for leading the Easter
Rising (1916)

John Maclean – the Socialist activist, a
prisoner of war in Edinburgh Castle;
then a year in the Calton Jail. Later
joined by James Maxton, Jimmie
MacDougall and Jack Smith (1916)

Manny Shinwell (later Lord Shinwell) – serves
five months at Calton Jail as chairman of
the Clyde Workers Committee (1919)

Peter Manuel – the New York murderer of
eight people, hanged at Barlinnie Prison
(1958)

Henry John Burnett – last person to be hanged
in Scotland (at Craiginches Prison,
Aberdeen) for the murder of a seaman
(1963)

Capital punishment – abolished (1965)

FAMOUS LAST WORDS

Royalty

Robert the Bruce (1329) – Thanks be to God for
I shall now die in peace, since I know that
the most valiant, accomplished knight of
my kingdom will perform that for me
which I am unable to perform for myself

King Robert III (1406) – dying wish: to be
buried in a midden with the epitaph
'Here lies the worst of Kings and the
most wretched of men'

Queen Margaret (1445) – Fin de la vie! Qu'on
ne m'en parle plus (The end of life. Don't
mention it to me any more)

James V (1542) – It will end as it began: it
came with a lass and it will go with a lass

Henry Lord Darnley (1567) – It was even thou,
my companion, my guide and my own
familiar friend

Mary Queen of Scots (1587) – Into Thy hands,
O Lord, I commend my spirit. Sweet Jesus.

Nobility

Sir James Douglas [throwing the heart of Robert
the Bruce into the battle] (1330) – Now pass
thee onward as thou wast wont and
Douglas will follow thee or die

FAMOUS LAST WORDS – continued

James, Earl of Douglas at the Battle of Otterburn (1388) – My wound is deep, I am fain to sleep

George Gordon, 2nd Marquess of Huntly (1649) – You may take my head from my shoulders but not my heart from my sovreign [Charles I]

James Graham, Earl of Montrose (1650) – Ay God have mercy upon this afflicted Kingdom

Archibald, 8th Earl of Argyll (1661) – I die not only a protestant, but with a heart-hatred of Popery, Prelacy and all superstitions whatsoever

9th Earl of Argyll (1685) – Lord Jesus, receive me into Thy Glory

Thinkers

David Hume (1776) – I am dying as fast as my enemies, if I have any, could wish, and as cheerfully as my best friends could desire

Andrew Fletcher of Saltoun (1716) – I have a nephew who has been studyng law. Make him a judge when he is fit for it

Adam Smith (1790) – I believe we must adjourn the meeting to some other place

Thomas Carlyle (1881) – So this is death, well ….

Teachers

Dr Alexander Adam (1809) – The boys may dismiss

Ministers of Religion

Patrick Hamilton (1528) – Lord Jesus, receive my spirit

Cardinal Beaton (1546) – I am a priest. Fie, fie! All is gone!

George Wishart (1546) – I fear not this fire

John Knox (1572) – I wish to God you had heard them as I have heard them, and I praise God of that heavenly sound. Now it is come

James Guthrie (1661) – The covenants, the covenants shall be Scotland's reviving

Thomas Chalmers (1847) – A general goodnight

Soldiers

Captain William Kidd (1701) – This is a very false and faithless generation

Rob Roy Macgregor (1734) – Let the piper p 'Return No More'

General Charles Gordon (1885) – Where is the Mahdi?

Earl Douglas Haig (1928) – I hope to see yo on Tuesday at 10.30 am

Literary Men

Robert Fergusson (1774) – Oh, do not go ye mother. I hope to be soon … oh, do n go yet, do not leave me!

Robert Burns (1796) – Don't let the awkwa squad fire over me

George Gordon, Lord Byron (1824) – Let me a man to the last

Sir Walter Scott (1832) – God bless you all feel myself again

James Hogg (1835) – It is a reproach to the faculty that they cannot cure the hiccu

Sir James Barrie (1937) – I can't sleep

Sidney Smith (1845) – Bring me all the blotting paper there is in the house

Francis Lord Jeffrey (1850) – This is very cleverly thought out but there is a falla in it, for so and so …

Thomas De Quincey (Edinburgh 1859) – Siste sister, sister

Robert Louis Stevenson (1894) – My head, n head

Sir Arthur Conan Doyle (1930) – You are wonderful

Inventors

James Watt (1819) – I feel that I am now come to my last illness

Alexander Graham Bell (1922) – So little don So much to do

Politician and Philanthropist

Sir Henry Campbell-Bannerman (1908) – This not the end of me

Andrew Carnegie (1919) – I hope so

Sportsman

Jock Stein (1985) – Let's not lose our digni

SPORT

Olympic Games (Gold Medallists)

Date	Event	Name	Time/Distance
96	Weight-lifting (1 hand)	L. Elliot	
08	400 m	W. Halswelle	50.0
08	3 miles (4827m)	A. Robertson	
12	4 × 100 m	H. Macintosh	
20	4 × 400 m	R. Lindsay	
24	400 m	E.H. Liddell	47.6
52	Show-jumping team	Douglas Stewart	
56	Lightweight boxing	R. McTaggart	
76	200 m breaststroke	D.A. Wilkie	2:15.11
80	100 m	A. Wells	10.25

British Empire and Commonwealth Games (Gold Medallists)

Date	Event	Name	Time/Distance
30	Marathon	D.M. Wright	2:43:43
	Lightweight boxing	J. Rolland	
34	440 yd hurdles	F.A.R. Hunter	55.2
	Singles bowling	R. Sprot	
	100 yd backstroke	W. Francis	1:05.2
	200 yd breaststroke	N. Hamilton	2:41.4
50	Hammer	D.M. Clark	49.94 m
	Tower Diving	P. Heatly	
	Flyweight boxing	H. Riley	
	220 yd breaststroke	Helen O. Gordon	3:01.7
54	Marathon	J. McGhee	2:39:36
	Springboard Diving	P. Heatly	
	Flyweight boxing	R. Currie	
	Bantamweight boxing	J. Smillie	
	220 yd breaststroke	Helen O. Gordon	2:59.2
	Medley team race	P. Heatly	3:51.0
		Margaret Girvan	
		Margaret McDowall	

continued

British Empire and Commonwealth Games (Gold Medallists) – continued

Date	Event	Name	Time/Distance
1958	Flyweight boxing	J. Brown	
	Lightweight boxing	R. McTaggart	
	Light heavyweight weightlifting	P.M. Caira	
	220 yd butterfly swim	I. Black	2:2
	Tower diving	P. Heatly	146.76 poi
1962	Flyweight boxing	R. Mallon	
	Featherweight boxing	J. McDermott	
	Foil fencing	A.M. Leckie	
	Light heavyweight weightlifting	P.M. Caira	
1966	Marathon	J. Alder	2:2:0
1970	10 000 m	J.L. Stewart	28:11.
	5 000 m	I. Stewart	15:2
	800 m	Rosemary Stirling	2:6.
	Discus	Rosemary Payne	54.
	Light middleweight boxing	T. Imrie	
	Sabre fencing	A.M. Leckie	
1978	Small bore rifle shooting	A.M. Allan	
	200 m	A. Wells	20.
	4 × 100 m relay	D. Jenkins	39.
		A. McMaster	
		R.C. Sharp	
		A. Wells	
1982	100 m	A. Wells	10.05 (wind + 5.9m
	200 m	A. Wells	20.43 (wind + 0.4m
	Discus	M. Ritchie	62.
	Bowls (singles)	W. Wood	
	Bowls (pairs)	J. Watson/D. Gourlay	
	Air rifle shooting	A. Allan/W. Macneill	1137 poi
	Fullbore shooting	A. Clarke/H. Hunter	387 poi
	Smallbore 3-position	A. Allan	1146 poi
1986	10 000 m	E. Lynch	31:41.
	Badminton doubles	W. Gilliland/D. Travers	
	Bowls (pairs)	G. Adrain/G. Knox	
1990	10 000 m	E. McColgan	32:23
	Judo (under 56 kg) women	L. Cusack	
	Light welterweight boxing	C. Kane	
	Shotgun pairs skeet	I. Marsden/J. Dunlop	189 poi
	Bowls (men's fours)	D. Love/G. Adrain/I. Bruce/W. Wood	

gest stadia – Hampden Park (74 730 capacity); Murrayfield (53 000 capacity); Meadowbank (15 000 capacity); Kelvin Hall (2000 capacity)

orts Clubs

st skating club in Britain – Edinburgh Ice Skating Society (1778)

st club badge – Duddingston Curling Club: worn on jacket (1802)

st national sports association – Grand Caledonian Curling Association founded in Edinburgh with 36 clubs (1838)

st municipal bowling green – Edinburgh (1860)

st lacrosse club in Britain – Glasgow Lacrosse Club (1867)

n Soc of Edinburgh Boaters – Union Canal

ienteering in Britain – inaugurated by the Scottish Council of Physical Recreation at the 1962 Championships at Dunkeld

hletics

ngest world career – Duncan McLean (1884–80) set a world record for 100 m of 21.7 sec when aged 92 (1977), 73 years after his best sprint of 100 yd in 9.9 sec in 1904

rld professional 400 yd record – Alfred Downer (1897)

orge McNeill (1947–) – beat a pony and trotting-cart over 100 m; professional world record (120 yd) 11.4 sec (1970); Powderhall Sprint winner (1970); professional world sprint record (80 yd) (1972); Stawell Gift (Australia) 11.9 sec (1981)

ld Medal 800 m Europa Cup – Tom McKean (1989)

ld Medal 800 m European Championships – Tom McKean (1990)

ld Medal 3000 m European Championships – Yvonne Murray (1990)

rld 10 000 metres champion (1991) – Liz McColgan

wling

lie Woods (1938–) – Australia Mazda Masters (1983) 'William the Conqueror'

hard Corsie – World Indoor Champion (1989 and 1991)

Boxing

AMATEUR

Queensberry Rules in Boxing – drawn up by John Sholto Douglas and John Chalmers (1867)

First Scottish Olympic medal (bronze) – Hugh Roddin, bantamweight (1908)

Commonwealth Games Light-Middleweight – Tom Imrie (1970)

PROFESSIONAL

First Scottish Lonsdale Belt winner – James 'Tancy' Lee (1915)

First British and European lightweight title fight in Scotland – James Hall v Johnny Brown

First fight for British and Empire welterweight title in Scotland – Tommy Milligan v Ted 'Kid' Lewis (1924)

First Scottish British and Empire middleweight title fight – Tommy Milligan v Alex Ireland

First professional boxing contest filmed for cinema viewing – Industrial Hall, Annandale Street, Edinburgh

Winner of bantamweight Lonsdale Belt in record time – Jim Higgins

First top-class contest between American and Scotsman – Augie Ratner v Johnny Brown (1923)

Record attendance for Scottish boxing-match – 32 000 (Tommy Milligan v Frank Moody. Carntyne Stadium, 1928)

First Scotsman to referee a world heavyweight title fight – George Smith (Henry Cooper v Muhammad Ali, 1966)

Eugene Henderson – Freddie Mills v Gus Lesnevich (1946) Sugar Ray Robinson v Randolph Turpin (1951)

Welterweight Champion of Great Britain and Europe – Tommy Milligan (1924)

British, European and World Flyweight Champion – Benny Lynch (1913–46)

World Flyweight Champion – Jackie Paterson (1943)

European Bantamweight Champion – Peter Keenan (1929–) (1951)

World Lightweight Champion – Ken Buchanan (1946–) (1970/71)

World Flyweight Champion – Walter McGowan (1966)

World Lightweight Champion – Jim Watt (1948–) (1979)

SPORT – continued

WBC International Bantamweight champion –
Donnie Hood (1990)

Most boxing titles – 10: Alex 'Bud' Watson
(b 1914) of Leith who won the Scottish
Heavyweight title in 1938, 1942–3; the
Lightweight championship 1937–9,
1943–5 and 1947. Also ABA
Lt–Heavyweight title 1945 and 1947

Cricket

Captain of England (19 tests: 1973–5) – Mike
Denness who played 28 times for
England
Captain of Kent (1972–6) – Mike Denness
Winner of English Village Cricket Championship –
Freuchie (1985)
Batting record – Archibald Campbell
MacLaren (1871–1944) (424 in 7 hr 50
min for Lancashire v Somerset at
Taunton, 1895)
Most stumpings in an innings (6) – Henry
Yarnold for Worcestershire v Scotland
at Broughty Ferry (1951)
Most runs off a ball (11) – Lieutenant Philip
Mitford, Queen's Own Cameron
Highlanders in a Malta Governor's Cup
match (1903)

Cycling

Robert Miller – only Briton to be King of
the Mountains (1984)

Curling

Scotland – winner of World Junior Curling
Championships (1991)

Dancing

Kenny McKechnie and Beverley Rees – world's
No 1 Amateur Dance Champions (1990)

Darts

Jocky Wilson – World Professional Darts
Champion (1982/89)

Football

1457 – The parliament of James II passes
law forbidding football

Most postponements – 29 times (Scottish C
tie between Inverness Thistle and
Falkirk in winter of 1978–9)
First ever live TV coverage of League Football
Scotland – Hearts v Aberdeen (1986)
Most northern football team in Scottish League
Aberdeen
Team which won first three Scottish Cup finals
Queen's Park (1874–6)
Highest score in first class match – 36
(Scottish Cup tie between Arbroath an
Bon Accord, 36-0; 2nd highest score –
on the same day 35-0, 1885)
British goal-scoring record
 Scottish Cup – 13: (John Petrie for
  Arbroath against Bon Accord, 188
 Scottish League – 8: (James McGrory
  for Celtic against Dunfermline, 192
Highest number of goals by a British team in
professional League season – 142 in 34
matches (Raith Rovers, 1937/8)
Hibernian's record victory – against 42nd
Highlanders 22-1 (1881)
Most goals in League season in Britain – 66 i
38 games (James Smith for Ayr Unite
1927/8)
Greatest number of individual goals in one
season in junior professional league – 96
(Tom Duffy for Ardeer Thistle FC,
1960–1)
British Club record for goal-keeping – 1196 m
(Chris Woods for Glasgow Rangers,
1986–7)
Greatest number of Scottish FA Cup wins – 2
(Celtic, 1892–1989)
Most successive National League championshi
in Britain – Celtic (9) 1965/6–1973/4
Most Scottish League championships – 40
(Rangers)
Most Scottish League/Skol Cup wins – Rang
(17) (1947–88)

Most Scottish Cup-winners medals – 8 (Charles Campbell of Queen's Park, 1874–1886)

Rangers won Scottish League – 40 times (1989–90)

Celtic won Scottish Premier/First Division (to 1990) – 35 times

Most appearances for Scotland – Kenny Dalglish (1951–) (102)

Most appearances for Celtic – Billy McNeill (international, 1961–9)

Highest British attendance – 149 547 (England v Scotland at Hampden, 1937)

Highest attendance at Scottish Cup – 147 365 (Celtic against Aberdeen at Hampden, 1937)

Highest attendance at League match in Britain – 118 567 (Rangers against Celtic at Ibrox, 1939)

First Scottish Player to win 100 caps – Kenny Dalglish (1986)

Youngest footballer in Scottish League – Ronnie Simpson (15) (1946)

Youngest player in a Scottish League Cup final – Derek Johnstone (Rangers) aged 16 (1970)

Youngest footballer to be capped for Scotland – John Lambie aged 17 (1886)

Oldest footballer to make an international debut – R. Simpson (v England aged 36, 1967)

PLAYERS' NICKNAMES

Famous Five – Gordon Smith, Bobby Johnstone, Lawrie Reilly, Eddie Turnbull, Willie Ormond

Terrible Trio – Alfie Conn, Willie Bauld, Jimmy Wardhaugh

TEAM NICKNAMES

The Wasps – Alloa

The Warriors – Stenhousemuir

The Ton – Morton

The Bankies – Clydebank

The Dark Blues – Dundee FC

The Jags – Partick Thistle

The Doonhamers – Queen of the South

The Dons – Aberdeen FC

The Diamonds/the Waysiders – Airdrieonians

The Buddies – St Mirren

The Sons – Dumbarton

Only non-Scottish team in Scottish League – Berwick Rangers

Player of the Year (England) 1978 – Kenny Burns

English FA Cup final (1973) – winning goal scored by Ian Porterfield for Sunderland

English FA Cup final (1965) – winning goal scored by Ian St John for Liverpool

Captain of Leeds United – Gordon Strachan (1990)

Scottish manager of Liverpool – Bill Shankly (international 1938–9)

Scottish manager of Liverpool – Kenny Dalglish

Scottish manager of Liverpool – Graeme Souness (1991–)

Scottish manager of Arsenal – George Graham (international 1972–3)

Scottish manager of Manchester United – Alex Ferguson (1990 English FA Cup)

Scottish commentators – Bob Wilson, Scottish international goalkeeper (1972); Ian St John; Gordon McQueen

Rous Cup – Scotland 1st winners (1985)

First British club to win European Cup – Celtic (1967)

First British club to win European Cup and 2 senior domestic championships – Celtic (1967)

First British club to win European Champion Clubs' Cup – Celtic

First British club to win European Champion Clubs' Cup and three domestic championships (League championship, League Cup, Scottish Cup) in one season – Celtic

First British manager to win European Cup–Winners' Cup twice with two different Clubs – Alex Ferguson (Aberdeen 1983/ Manchester United 1991)

European Cup Final (1978) winning goal – Kenny Dalglish

Scored Celtic's 1st goal when 1967 European Cup won – Tommy Gemmell

European Cup Final 1981 (winning goal for Notts Forest) – John Robertson

Aberdeen – European Cup-Winners Cup at Gothenburg

First Scot to captain Italian First Division (four-in-a-row) – Rose Reilly

First Scot to win Women's World Cup – Rose Reilly (playing for Italy, 1987)

continued

SPORT – continued

FOOTBALL – continued
Earliest foreigners to play in Scotland –
Rangers inside forward: Carl Hansen
(Denmark) (1922–4); Rangers inside
forward: Mohammed Latif (Egypt)
(1934); Celtic reserve: Abdul Salim
(1936); Queen's Park goalkeeper:
Mustafa Mansour (Egypt) (1937–40)
Scotland's heaviest defeat in World Cup Finals –
Uruguay 7–0 (1954)
Record transfer fee – Trevor Steven to
Marseilles from Rangers for £5m (1991)

Golf

There are more than 250 first class golf
courses in Scotland
First mentioned – in prohibitive decree of the
Scottish parliament (1457)
Kings who played golf in Scotland – James IV
(1503), Charles I (1642), James VII
(1681)
Oldest golf clubs – Royal Burgess Golfing
Society of Edinburgh (1735);
Honourable Company of Edinburgh
Golfers (1744)
First 18-hole golf course – St Andrews
First professional golf tournament – won by
Willie Park of Musselburgh at Prestwick
(1860)
**Last home-based Scot to win Open Golf
Championship** – Willie Auchterlonie
(1883)
First women's golf tournament – Musselburgh
Golf Club (for the town's fishwives)
(1811)
First inter-club golf match – Edinburgh
Burgess Golfing Society against
Bruntsfield Golf Club at Bruntsfield
(1818)
First British Open winner – Tom Morris at
Prestwick (1861)
Lowest scores in Open – 63: Mark Hayes
(USA) at Turnberry (1977); Isao Aoki
(Japan) at Muirfield (1980); Greg
Norman (Australia) at Turnberry (1986)
Lowest total aggregate in Open – 268: Tom
Watson (USA) at Turnberry (1977)

Highest British golf course – Leadhills,
Strathclyde (457 m/*1500 ft* above sea-
level)
Longest championship hole in Britain – 6th at
Troon (528 m/*577 yds*)
Nicknames – *Valley of Sin*: Old Course St
Andrews (18th hole)
Only manufacturer of golf balls in Scotland –
Sonido

SCOTTISH GOLF PERSONALITIES
Tommy Armour (1896–1968) – British Open;
US Open; US PGA (1924); US PGA
Champion (1930)
Harry Bannerman (1942–) – Ryder Cup (1971)
Michael Bonallack (1934–) – Amateur
Champion; Walker Cup
Gordon Brand jr (1958–) – Scandinavian Open
Jane Connachan (1964–) – British Ladies
Stroke Play; Curtis Cup
Gordon Cosh (1939–) – Walker Cup
Bernard Gallacher (1949–) – Spanish Open;
French Open
Sandy Lyle (1958–) – Open Champion (1985)
US Masters (1988)
John Panton (1916–) – PGA Match Play;
Ryder Cup
Cathy Panton (1955–) – British Ladies (1976)
Dale Reid (1959–) – European Open (1988)
Isabella Robertson (1936–) – British Ladies
Open Amateur (1981)
Gillian Stewart (1958–) – European Open
(1984)
Muriel Thomson (1954–) – Curtis Cup
Sam Torrance (1953–) – Zambian Open
(1975); Spanish Open (1982)
Jessie Valentine (1915–) – New Zealand
Ladies (1935); French Ladies (1936)
Ronnie Shade – World Amateur Golf
Champion (1966)

Horse Racing

There are around 90 race fixtures in
Scotland
Scotland's oldest racecourse – Lanark (closed
in 1977)
Oldest horse race in the world – Lanark Silver
Bell dated from the time of William the
Lion (1143-1214)

Racecourses in Scotland – Ayr (flat/jumping all year round); Edinburgh (flat/jumping all year round); Hamilton (flat April-Nov); Kelso (jumping Aug-May); Perth (jumping Aug-May)

Trainers – Tom Dawson won the Derby twice (1856/1869); Matt Dawson won Derby six times and 23 other major classics

5th Lord Rosebery (1847-1929), Prime Minister of Britain – won the Derby three times, the 2000 Guineas twice and the St Leger

Racehorses –

Rockavon: winner of 2 000 Guineas (1961)

Peaty Sandy: first Scottish horse to win Coral Welsh National (1981)

Grand National winners: Merryman (1960); Lucius (1978); Rubstic (1979)

Willie Carson (1942-) – five times Champion Jockey

First woman in UK to be Clerk of the Course – Morag Chalmers (Ayr)

Record starting-price for a horse race winner – Equinoctial 250-1 at Kelso

First Soviet jockey to win a race in Britain – Mogamed Tokov, (Soviet Cham pion), on Macho Man at Maxwell Motors Glasnost Hurdle at Kelso (1990)

Judo

British Champion – George Kerr

World Champion (52 kilos) – Loretta Cusack (1982-4)

American Open Champion – Billy Cusack (1990)

Commonwealth Games Silver Medal (65 kilos) – Mark Preston (1990)

Motor Racing

World Land Speed Record – Richard Noble (born Edinburgh) in Thrust 2 (633.468 mph in Nevada's Black Rock Desert) (1983)

Most Grand Prix wins – 5: Jim Clark driving a Lotus (1962-5; 1967)

Motor-Racing – Jackie Stewart competed in 99 Grand Prix (winning 27)

Winner of first two places in Le Mans 24-hour race – Ecurie Ecosse (1956-7)

Winner of longest rally (London-Sydney) – Andrew Cowan (1977)

First British Truck Racing Champion – Heather Baillie (1990)

First British driver to win a World Rally Championship title – Louise Aitken-Walker (works Vauxhall Astra GTE 16v. 1990)

First Scot to be Stock Car World Champion (Formula Two) – Jimmy Wallace (1988-89)

Britain's top motoring teacher – Barbara Coverdale (1990)

Motor Cycle Racing

Isle of Man TT Circuit record – Steve Hislop (1962-) 123.48 mph (1991)

Isle of Man Race record – Steve Hislop (1962-) 1 hr 53 min 47.4 sec

World Side-car Champion (1980) – Jock Taylor (1954-82)

Mountaineering

Earliest recorded rock climb in UK – Stac na Biorrach, St Kilda (72 m/*236 ft*) by Sir Robert Moray (1698)

First Britons to climb Mount Everest – Douglas Scott and Dougal Haston (1940-77) (1975)

First ascent by SW face of Everest – Dougal Haston (1975)

First ascent of Mount McKinlay, Alaska – Dougal Haston (1976)

Scottish 24 hr Munro record – 28 Munros by Jon Broxap (130 km/*80 miles* in 23 hrs 20 mins (1988) Munros record (277 peaks) – Hugh Symonds (1953-) 66 days 22 hrs (1990)

Record for 4 000 ft peaks (8) – Martin Stone (21 hrs 39 mins (1987)

Record for 277 Munros and 222 Corbetts – Craig Caldwell (377 days) (1985-6)

Rowing

Oldest rowing Club in Scotland – St Andrews Boat Club, Edinburgh (1850)

Rowing length of Loch Ness – George D Parsonage

Rugby

First Seven-a-side Rugby Tournament – Melrose Rugby Football Club (1883)

First complete International Championship (England, Scotland, Ireland, Wales) – 1884

Most International appearances – 52: Jim Renwick (b 1952) 1972-84 51: Andy Irvine (b 1951) 1972-82

Most Tries in an International – 5: George Lindsay (1863-1905) for Scotland against Wales (1887) NB Ian Smith (1903-72) scored a record 8 consecutive International tries: 4 v France/4 v Wales (1925)

Scottish International Rugby record of points in a game – Gavin Hastings 21 (1986)

Record for International Scottish Rugby Football matches – Gavin Hastings (286 points in 27 Internationals)

Youngest International player – Ninian Finlay (1858-1963) and Charles Reid (1864-1909): both 17 years 36 days old when playing for Scotland v England in 1875 and 1881 (both Edinburgh Academy pupils)

Most wins in a Club Championship – 10 by Hawick in the Scottish League Division One (1973-81)

Most spectators – 104 000 (for Scotland's 12–10 win over Wales at Murrayfield) 1975

First rugby match televised – England against Scotland (Calcutta Cup) at Twickenham (1938)

Animal nicknames in Scottish rugby – Mighty Mouse (Ian McLaughlan), White Shark (John Jeffrey)

Shinty

Most titles – Newtonmore (won Camanachd Association Challenge Cup 28 times 1907-86)

Highest score – 11-3 (Scottish Cup Final: Newtonmore beat Furnace) 1909

Shooting

Highest score at Bisley – 295 (out of possible 300) for the final of the Queen's Prize (Lindsay Peden of Scotland) (1982)

Skateboarding

World endurance record – Tranent Youth Group (53 hours. 1990)

Snooker

Youngest winner of a major title – Stephen Hendry (b 1969) when 18 yrs 285 days winning Rothmans Grand Prix 1987

First player to win four consecutive ranking tournament titles – 21 year old Stephen Hendry (1990)

World record for consecutive tournament wins – Stephen Hendry (23 wins) (1990)

First to win five ranking tournaments in a season – Stephen Hendry (1991)

Squash

UK and European Champion – Mark Maclean (1991)

Swimming

Oldest person to swim the Channel – Ned Barnie (d 1983)

First man to swim the Channel both ways – Ned Barnie (1950)

First person to swim the Firth of Forth – Ned Barnie (2 double crossings) (1924)

Fastest Loch Ness (36.5 km/22.7 miles) swim – 9 hrs 57 mins (David Morgan) 1983

Fastest Loch Ness double crossing – 23 hrs 4 mins (David Morgan) 1983

Most lucrative sponsored swim – 'Splash '89' at Royal Commonwealth Pool, Edinburgh: raised £108 040 with 3012 swimmers (1989)

Tae Kwon Do

Oldest Black Belt in UK (1990) – Wallace McGregor (77) of Edinburgh

Some Internationals in Two Sports

Leslie Balfour-Melville (1854-1937) – Rugby (1892); Cricket (1874-1910) (36 year record); Scottish Lawn Tennis Champion (1879); British Amateur Champion Golf Champion (1895); Captain, Royal & Ancient (1906-7); recreation: Billiards

Eric Liddell – rugby and athletics

P.M.S. Gedge – rugby and fencing

G.P.S. Macpherson – rugby and long jump

Scott Symon – football and cricket

Andy Goram – football and cricket

J P Fisher – rugby and basketball (Olympics)

R H Lindsay-Watson – rugby and hammer throw (Olympics)

Alan Tait – Rugby Union Internationalist (1985-87) now playing rugby league for Widnes

35 individuals represented Scotland at both cricket and rugby

Unusual Sport and Events

Bruichladdich Islands Peak Race – 47 hrs 5 mins 13 secs by team of cata maran 'Two Hoots' skippered by Curly Mills (1989) (sail from Oban to Troon with 3 stops for runs of Ben More on Mull, 3 Paps of Jura and Goat Fell on Arran) Highland Cross Biathlon – 3 hrs 25 mins 6 secs by Jonathan Musgrave of Banchory (1988) (50 mile course from Kintail to Beauly, 20 miles of hill track and forestry trails on foot to Glen Affric, then 30 mile cycle to Beauly)

North of Scotland Inflatable Boats Race – (545 mile marathon)

Bed-pushing – 5204 km/*3233 miles 1150 yds* (a wheeled hosptal bed pushed by nine employees of the Bruntsfield Bedding Centre, Edinburgh from 21 June to 26 July 1979)

Haggis Hurling (min weight 600 g/*1lb 6 oz*) – 55.11 m/*180 ft 10 in* by Alan Pettigrew at Inchmurrin, Loch Lomond. 1984)

Largest litter collection in one day – 3641 bags and 25 skips (3510 volunteers on 'Clean Forth' project) 1988

Greatest Pancake Tossing (in 2 mins) – 262 (Philip Artingstall, Fordyce School) 1989

Largest Sandcastle – 8.37 km/*5.2 miles* long (staff and pupils of Ellon Academy, near Aberdeen) 1988

Oldest angling club – Ellem Fishing Club founded in 1829 by gentlemen from Edinburgh and Berwickshire

Oldest Archery Club – the Society of Kilwinning Archers (contested the Pa pingo Shoot since 1488)

Riding in Armour (longest ride) – 334.7 km/*208 miles* (Dick Brown left Edinburgh on June 10th 1989, arriving home in Dumfries four days later after a ride of 35 hrs 25 mins)

Longest Stamp-Licking – 328 stamps in 4 mins (John Kenmuir at the George Square Post Office, Glasgow) 1989

First Highland Games – St Fillans, Perthshire by the Highland Society (1819)

Braemar Caber – George Clark (1907-86) tossed the caber (5.86 m/*19 ft 3 in* and 54.4 kg/*120 lb*) in 1951 for the first time since 1891.

Throwing 56 lb Weight for Height (one hand) – 5.23 m/*17 ft 2 in* (Geoff Capes) 1982

Best Throw for Scots Hammer – William Anderson (46.08 m/*151 ft 2 in*) 1969

Oldest surviving Royal (Real) Tennis Court in Britain still used – Falkland Palace (built for James V in 1539)

Official British Duration Pigeon Racing Record – 1887 km/*1173 miles* in 15 days (C.S.O. owned by Rosie and Bruce, Wick) in 1976 Palamos Race

Pigeon Racing 24-hour Record into the UK – 1 165.3 km/*724 miles 219 yds* (E. Cardno's 'Mormond Lad' from Nantes, france to Fraserburgh)1977

Longest recorded Survival alone on a Raft – 133 days (2nd Steward Poon Lim of Merchant Navy: his ship the SS Lomond was torpedoed on 23rd Nov 1942 in the Atlantic. He was picked up off Brazil in July 1943)

Fastest Canoeing on Loch Ness (Fort Augustus to Lochend 36.5 km/*22.7 miles*) – 2 hrs 58 min 48 secs (Colin Simpkins from South Africa in a Jaguar K1) 1987

Highest Cribbage Score in 24 hrs – 111 201 points by Christine and Eliz abeth Gill, Jeanette MacGrath and Donald Ward at Grannie's Heilan' Hame, Embo) 1987

Earliest Curling Club – Muthill, Tayside 1739

Parchuting British title – Sergeant Ronald Alan 'Scotty' Milne of the Parachute Regiment won the title 5 times (1976-77; 1979-81)

Earliest Hang Gliding attempt – the Italian alchemist John Damian plunged from Stirling Castle making for France (1507)

First free-flight Balloon Ascent from British soil – James Tytler (Edin burgh) 1784

Mountain racing (Ben Nevis summit 1 346.6 m/4 418 ft and return) – Men: Kenneth Stuart. 1984 (1 hr 25 mins 34 sec) Women: Pauline Haworth. 1984 (1 hr 43 min 25 sec)

Mountain Endurance Running Scottish record for 28 Monro (mountains over 914 m/3 000 ft) – 128 km/80 miles with 10 700 m/35 000 ft of ascents and descents in 23 hrs 20 mins (Jon Broxap. 1988)

Highest Bivouac – 8 747 m/28 700 ft on summit of Everest (Douglas Scott and Dougal Haston) 1975

Traverse of 137 km/*85 miles* cross-country route of nine 1219 m/*4000 ft* Scottish peaks from Glen Nevis to Glen More – 21 hrs 39 mins (Martin Stone. 1987)

Long Run – 8 224 km/5 110 miles completed by Max Telford (b Hawick 1935) in 106 days 18 hrs 45 mins runing from Anchorage, Alaska to Hal ifax, Nova Scotia.

Highland Games Heavy Events records

Putting light ball or stone (16 lbs) – 65 ft 3 in (G Capes 1982)

Putting heavy ball or stone (22 lbs) – 53 ft 4 in (G Capes 1982)

Throwing light hammer (16 lbs) – 144 ft 2 in (K Rice 1985)

Throwing heavy hammer (22 lbs) – 123 ft 8.5 in (G Anderson 1983)

Throwing 28 lb weight for distance – 91 ft 5 in (G Capes 1983)

Throwing 56 lb weight for distance – 43 ft 7 in (H Davidson 1981)

Throwing 56 lb weight over bar – 17 ft 5 in (B Oldfield 1987)

Miscellany

Lastly, a dip into the quirkiness of the Scots – their nostalgia for vanished glory, their tall tales, their food, their music, books and drama.

Many an Englishman 300 years ago was astonished to find the Scots pint three times bigger than that south of the Border. The Auld Alliance with France produced a gallimaufry of Scots culinary terms.

The Scots are at heart dreamers, however much they fancy themselves as masters of technology. Indeed invention, whether in art or engineering, is the product of dreams and dreams are the result of hardship, disappointment and frustration. That perhaps explains why in Scotland football is such a popular sport.

ANCIENT KINGDOMS

Picts – Cape Wrath and John o' Groats to Perthshire and Angus
Scots – Argyll, Bute, Arran (Dalriada)
Britons – West (Strathclyde)
Angles – South-east

Caledonia: the Seven Pictish Provinces

Fife and Fothreve – Fife, Clackmannan, Kinross
Moravia – Moray, Ross and Cromarty
Atholl – Atholl, Breadalbane, Gowrie
Strathearn – Strathearn and Mentieth
Caithness – Caithness and Strathnaver
Mar – Mar and Buchan
Angus – Angus and Mearns
Dalriada – land of the Scots

Argyllshire settled by Fergus Mor from Ireland in 6th century

British Kingdoms

Votadini/Gododdin (Northumberland, Berwickshire, East Lothian)
Strathclyde/Cumbria
Rheged

MODERN REPUBLICS

Red-haired Brian Robertson (1947–), psychology graduate and member of MENSA, renounced his United Kingdom citizenship in 1977 to become 'Robbie the Pict' with an acre of land near Tote, south of Staffen on the Isle of Skye. This henceforth became the Pictland of Alba and was added to by his supporters until in 1990 there are some 400 ha/*1000 acres* in the Pictish Free State. After more than 300 prosecutions (such as occurred when in 1990 he was stopped in Alness driving an Audi owned by the Pictish Free State without a tax disc), Robbie the Pict is unmoved. He operates from the Pictish High Commission and drives with Diplomatic Corps plates which would normally ensure him freedom from prosecution.

Every year the members of the Pictish Free State celebrate Dunnichen Day, a national holiday to commemorate the victory of Nechtansmere (AD 685) when King Brude of Pictland defeated King Ecgfrith of Northumberland. A remembrance ceremony is held on Dunnichen Hill which overlooks the ancient battlefield. According to the official literature of the Pictish Free State the seat of ancient Greek learning was very probably in Strathclyde until a comet destroyed the lost continent of Atlantis, causing the Greeks to leave Scotland. The River Carron has been associated with the mythical Greek ferryman of Death, Charon and the River Styx is identified with the Kyle of Lochalsh.

Indeed, the ancient Greek hero Ulysses is likely to have been born in Keppel near Millport and the Shetlanders are descended from Gad, the lost tribe of Israel.

Little Sparta

The internationally-recognised concrete poet Ian Hamilton Finlay gave the converted cow-byre beside his home at Stonypath near Dunsyre the title of 'Garden Temple'. When in 1983 Strathclyde Regional Council attempted to levy a rate on the building as a commercial art-gallery Finlay with his supporters in art, the revolutionary Saint Just Vigilantes, organised a cunning resistance with camouflaged tanks, minefields, other weapons of war and much sparkling rhetoric.

Following this 'Little Spartan War' in which he used his love of Classical culture to best advantage, Finlay renamed his house 'Little Sparta' and the whole notorious episode became known as 'The First Battle of Little Sparta', a determined (if tongue in cheek) resistance against the heavy hand of bureaucracy.

King of Rockall

Tom McClean, former member of the
SAS, lived on Rockall, a tiny rock 386 km/
240 miles from the Outer Hebrides, for 40
days in 1985, to try and resolve a long
dispute between Britain, Ireland, Denmark
and Iceland as to fishing and seabed rights
around the rock. Since that time McClean
has been known as the King of Rockall.

MARVELS of the LANDSCAPE

Caves – Fingal's Cave, celebrated by the
composer Mendelssohn, is on the
uninhabited island of Staffa; Ossian's
Cave is on Aonach Dubh, a mountain
in Glencoe

Deepest cave in Scotland – Cnoc nan Uamh
(76 m/*249 ft*)

Second lowest hollow in Europe – Loch Morar
(328 m/*1077 ft*)

Deepest inland lake in Britain – Loch Morar
(328 m/*1077 ft*)

Longest glen – Glen Lyon, Perthshire (about
48 km/*30 miles*). Glen More (the Great
Glen) is not a true glen

Highest cliffs in Britain – Conachair cliffs on
St Kilda, Western Isles (425 m/*1397 ft*)

Electric Brae – an optical illusion between
Culzean Castle and Dunure produced
by the way in which the roadside hedges
are cut. From a car you seem to be
climbing when the road is really going
downhill

Magnetic rocks – Compass Hill on the island
of Canna, a basaltic rock with high
proportion of iron, affects ships'
compasses

Largest meteorite in Scotland – 10.09 kg/*22.25
lb* (Strathmore, Tayside) (1917)

Oldest rocks in Britain – NW Highlands and
Western Isles (gneiss and granulite)
formed about 2800 million years ago

Some Nicknames of Natural Features

Bullers of Buchan – 30 m/*100 ft* high cliffs
Colonel's Bed – cave in a gorge near
Inveraray
Devil's Beeftub – 152 m/*500 ft* deep for
hiding stolen cattle, near Moffat
Dumpling – Duncryne Hill, Gartocharn
Dutchman's Cap – one of Treshnish Isles,
west of Mull
Five Sisters of Kintail – hills surrounding
Loch Shiel
MacLeod's Maidens – pinnacles at entrance
to Loch Bracadale in Skye
Men of Mey – dangerous underwater reef in
Pentland Firth
Needle's Eye – subterranean passage near
Troup Head
Neptune's Staircase – series of eight locks in
Caledonian Canal at Banavie
Old Man of Hoy – 137 m/*450 ft* red sand-
stone sea stack (Orkneys)
Old Man of Storr – 49 m/*160 ft* rock on Skye
Seven Men of Moidart – seven beech trees at
Millhouse
Sugarloaf Mountain – Suilven
Sutors of Cromarty – headlands in Black Isle
Three Sisters – mountains in Glen Coe
Twelve Apostles – circle of 11 standing
stones at Holywood, Dumfries

GOLD and SILVER

When the Romans entered Strathclyde
they were met by 300 chiefs wearing
torques of pure gold around their necks
collected from the streams that flowed into
the River Clyde.

In 1153 David I granted all the gold
found in Fife to the Abbey of
Dunfermline. A century later we hear of
gold at Duriness while in 1424 the gold
from all the mines of Scotland was handed
over to the king by the parliament in
Edinburgh. James IV brought miners to
Leadhills (Crawford Moor) – known as
'God's Treasure House', while panning
took place at the Glengeber Burn in the
Vale of Yarrow. By the time of James V
there were 800 miners at Leadhills. By
1600 there were 200 different sites where

gold had been found, Wanlockhead in particular producing gold dust and nuggets. The silver mine at Alva dates from 1711.

The crown of the old kings of Scotland was made of native gold (that of James V had 1162 g/*41 oz* of the precious metal), while members of the aristocracy were also fortunate – the Marquess of Linlithgow, for example, being presented with Scotland's largest nugget which weighed 765 g/*27 oz*.

Private enterprise gold fever came to Kildonan in Sutherland last century. A nugget weighing 28 g/*1 oz* was found in the Kildonan Burn in 1853 and 15 years later there were 500 miners searching for gold. In 1870 the Strath Kildonan goldfield was shut by the landowners, some £100 000 worth of the yellow metal having been recovered.

Fresh interest in the area arose in 1969. The Irishman Hill, from which the Kildonan and Suisgill Burns flowed, became the focus of interest and there was fresh talk of 'Baile 'n Oir' (Gold Town). Today interest has shifted to Cononish Glen near Tyndrum, Argyll. There is thought to be £60m worth of gold in Beinn Chuirn, 457 m/*1500 ft* above Cononish village. Even Britain's first gold-panning course was started in Scotland – in Sanquhar, Dumfries in 1990.

British gold-panning champion (1991) – Vince Thurkettle

MINERALS and NORTH SEA OIL

Mineral Production (1988)

	(Tonnes 000
Igneous rocks	16 219
Sand and gravel	10 753

Mineral Production – continued

	(Tonne 000
Sandstone	1 70(
Limestone	1 64
Clay and shale	1 54
Industrial sands	52(

Waste Disposal by Method (1988)

	(Tonne 00(
Direct to landfill	2 57(
Baling	42
Compacting	30(
Incineration	19
Pulverization	178
Transfer to loading site (with tipping/landfilling)	15

First oil exploration licences granted for North Sea – 1964
First oil/gas discovery in North Sea – 1965
First oil production platform installed – Forties Alpha (1974)
First Scottish oil-field – Argyll (1975)
First North Sea oil landed – 1975
First North Sea oil terminal – Sullom Voe
Cumulative oil production to 1989 – 1282 million tonnes (7.5 barrels per tonne)

Oil Pollution Incidents Reported (1988)

Offshore North Sea	26
East Scotland	5(
Orkney/Shetland	3(
West Scotland	1

EXTINCT and THREATENED SPECIES

Extinct Species

Aurock – (urus: 2 m/*6 ft* wild ox) extinct in Scotland in prehistoric times

Beaver – extinct by 11th or 12th century

Caledonian Bear – used in Roman arenas, survived to 10th century

Elk – (moose) disappeared in 9th century

Giant Fallow Deer – (3.7 m/*12 ft* high) disappeared in prehistoric times

Great Auk – exterminated on St Kilda (1840)

Lynx – disappeared in prehistoric times

Reindeer – disappeared in 9th century (re-introduced in 1950s)

White-tailed sea eagle – disappeared in 19th century

Wild Pig – existed until early 18th century

Wolf – last one killed in Morayshire (1743)

Threatened Species

Osprey (disappeared in 19th century but reintroduced in 20th)

Goshawk (disappeared in 19th century)

Capercailzie

Wild Cat

Pine Marten

Monsters

Highland lore tells of strange beasts in nearly every loch. There are two main species – the ferocious kelpie (water-horse) in league with the devil, bent on destroying mankind, and the peaceable water-bull.

Beasties have been sighted in Loch Assynt (1857), Loch Arkaig, Loch Shiel, Loch Lochy and Loch Quoich. In Loch Canisp it had a long neck, a head like a hind's and no ears; in Loch Oich (1936) it was black with two humps, a snake-like neck and a shaggy head; in Loch Morar (1887) it was an attractive sea-serpent known as 'a-Mhorag'.

'Nessie' (an Niseag) on Loch Ness was first recorded in AD 565 when St Columba drove away a water-monster by the power of prayer. Since that time the Loch Ness monster has been the subject of feverish speculation. Mussolini tried to bomb it, the BBC to photograph it, but all in vain. It seemed to prefer revealing itself to local worthies driving from Inverness to Fort Augustus late on a Saturday night!

PEARLS

History records that it was the Roman legions who first made jewellery with pearls from the River Tay. The first king to wear a Scots pearl was Alexander I in 1120. Robert the Bruce had one in his crown and James V had the largest ever found set into his sceptre. The fame of Scots pearls spread south of the Border – Henry V of England had one stolen from his tent at the Battle of Agincourt. Queen Victoria had a collection and Edward VII was a proud owner. Most of the ladies in the royal family today have a Scots pearl.

The Scots pearl is found in the freshwater mussel (Margaritifera Margaritifera Linn), which lives for 60 years. In 1865 a pearl was found which weighed 30 grains but the largest is 'Wee Willie', the 44.5 grain Abernethy Pearl, taken from the River Tay by Bill Abernethy in 1967.

EATING and DRINKING

Some Scots Meat Cuts

Collop – thin slice of fried or stewed meat

Gigot – leg of mutton or lamb

Heukbone ('pope's eye') steak – rump steak for frying/grilling

Hoch (hough) – joint cut from rear of shin

Loin – mutton (two loins joined together are a chine)

Spalebone – bladebone steak

Scots Culinary Words From the French

Ashet (*assiette*)
Gigot (*gigot*)
Haggis (*hachis*)
Hotch-potch (*hochepot*)
Petticoat tails (*petits gastels*)
Sybo (*cibo*)

Some Traditional Scots Dishes

Athole brose – oatmeal, honey, whisky,
   water (and cream)
Bannocks – oatmeal cakes
Black bun – spicy fruit cake for Hogmanay
Bridie – minced steak and onion pie
Cock-a-Leekie soup – broth made of leeks
   and chicken with onions or prunes
Cranachan – dessert of beaten cream and
   oatmeal
Crowdie – soft cheese
Cullen skink – smoked haddock soup with
   potatoes, onions and milk
Finan haddie – smoke-cured haddock
Friars chicken – chopped chicken, boiled
   with parsley, cinnamon and eggs
Haggis – lungs, liver, heart of sheep minced
   with oatmeal, suet and onions with
   pepper and salt, placed in a sheep's
   stomach
Largest haggis – 274 kg/*603 lb* contained in
   eight ox stomach linings (David Hall of
   Broxburn, 1986)
Kale (colewort) – green vegetable
Petticoat tails – triangular shortbread
   biscuits
Scones – cake made from flour and milk
Sheep's heid – boiled sheep's head with the
   wool singed off
Solan goose – gannet (from Bass Rock)
Sowans – a flummery (light pudding) made
   from fermented husks of oat grain

Towns Associated with Food

Arbroath pippin (apple)
Bridies (Forfar: invented by local butcher,
   Mr Jolly)
Dundee (jam)
Dunlop cheese (Ayrshire village)
Edinburgh fog (creamy dessert)
Eyemouth pales (smoked haddock)
Falkirk raisins (green peas)
Hawick balls (sweets)
Jeddart snails (Jedburgh toffee)
Moffat (toffee)
Musselburgh pie (steak cooked with
   mussels)
Rutherglen cream (milk and sugar)

Whisky

Scotch whisky – over 2000 brands (blends
   and single malts)
**Valley with largest concentration of whisky
   distilleries** – Spey valley
Single malt whiskies – 100
Scotland's smallest distillery – Edradour near
   Pitlochry (227 280 l/*50 000 gal* a year)
Scotland's most southerly malt whisky distillery
   – Bladnoch, near Wigtown, Galloway
**Largest distillery (largest blender and bottler of
   Scotch whisky)** – United Distillers
   Shieldhall plant, Glasgow (capacity for
   144 million bottles a year)
Largest bottle – 185 l/*41 gal* of William
   Grant's Family Reserve Finest Scotch
   Whisky (1.8 m/*6 ft* tall) 1987
Smallest bottle of liquor – 5 cm/*2 in* high
   holding 1.3 ml/*22 minims* (Whyte and
   Mackay Scotch)
Most expensive spirits – 60-year-old The
   Macallan sold by the Rotary Club of
   Elgin in 1988 for £6000
Largest whisky collection – Whiskeyteca in
   Salo, Lake Garda, Italy (3100 different
   labels)

Alcohol and Tobacco

**Highest consumption in Britain of alcohol and
   tobacco** – Scotland (8.7% of weekly
   income, 1988)
**Country with highest percentage of smokers in
   Britain** – Scotland (37%)

PLACES

Nicknames of Scottish Places

Auld Reekie – Edinburgh
Capital of the Highlands – Inverness
The Fair City – Perth
Hielandman's Umbrella – Argyll Street under Central Station, Glasgow
The Honest Toun – Musselburgh
Khyber Pass – street in Stromness, Orkney
The Lang Toun – Auchterarder, Perthshire
  Kirkcaldy, Fife
The Misty Isle – Skye
Paddy's Milestone – Ailsa Craig, Firth of Clyde
Queen of the South – Dumfries

Places with Similar Names

Aberdeen – port of Hong Kong
Alexandria – five miles north of Dumbarton
California – Stirlingshire village
Dallas – near Forres
Houston – Renfrewshire
Kelso – USA
Leith Harbour – South Georgia
Moscow – village north-east of Kilmarnock
Patna – Ayrshire
Portobello – near Edinburgh
Rome – group of houses south-west of Kilmarnock
Sodom – Shetland
Washington – village near Coupar Angus

Longest and Shortest Place-Names

Longest single word placename – 18 letters: Coignafeainternich (Inverness-shire)
Second longest single word placenames – Claddochknockline (Outer Hebrides) Claddochbaleshare (Outer Hebrides)
Longest multiple word placename – 32 letters: Meallan Liath Coire Mhic Dhubhaill (hill in Loch More area)
Shortest place names –
  I (Gaelic for Iona)
  Ae (Dumfries and Galloway)
  Oa (Island of Islay)
  Bu (Wyre, Orkney Islands)

A Miscellany

Most northerly town on Scottish mainland – Thurso
Britain in Bloom competition (most often won) – Aberdeen
Britain's oldest working post office – Sanquhar near Dumfries
Scotland's only Buddhist temple – Eskdalemuir
Follies – McLaig's Folly, Oban; Pinneapple, Stirlingshire
Scotland's first major aluminium plant – Fort William
Scottish Hydros – Crieff and Dunblane, Perthshire
Town which has been both Scottish and English – Berwick-upon-Tweed
Oldest structure in Scotland – hearth from Mesolithic period (c 6013 BC) on Island of Jura, Argyll
Oldest continuously inhabited house – Traquair House (built in 10th century)
Narrowest house frontage in Britain – 50 Stuart Street, Millport, Great Cumbrae (1.2 m/ *47 in*)
Largest house in Scotland – Hopetoun House, West Lothian (1696–1756) whose west façade is 206 m/*675 ft* long
Highest village in Scotland – Wanlockhead, Dumfries and Galloway (420 m/*1380 ft* above sea-level)
Village with steepest access road in UK – Applecross (626 m/*2053 ft*)
Most northerly habitation in Scotland – the Muckle Flugga Lighthouse
Narrowest hotel in Britain – Star Hotel, Moffat (6.1 m/*20 ft* wide)
Most remote hotel in Britain – Garvault Hotel by Kinbrace, Sutherland
Highest restaurant in Britain – Ptarmigan on Cairngorm
Oldest seafood restaurant in Scotland – Oyster Bar, Café Royal, Edinburgh
Longest bar in a British pub – The Horse Shoe, Drury Street, Glasgow (31.8 m/ *104 ft 3 in*)
Loneliest pub in UK – Old Forge Pub, Knoydart (11-km/*7-mile* sail or 30-km/ *18-mile* trek)
Only Japanese carry-out in Scotland – Little Japan Delicatessen, Edinburgh
Largest dome in Britain – Bell Sports Centre, Perth (67 m/*222 ft* diameter)

MISCELLANY – continued

Longest stairs in Britain – Cruachan Power Station, Argyll (324 m/*1063 ft*)
Largest maternity hospital in Britain – Simpson Memorial Maternity Pavilion, Edinburgh (218 staffed beds)
Largest hospital in Britain – Hartwood Hospital, near Shotts (1600 staffed beds for the mentally ill)

OLD SCOTS MEASURES

CURRENCY
merk – silver coin worth two-thirds of pound Scots
bawbee – copper, pewter, lead, silver coin (1539–58)

MEASURE

Scots	Imperial
1 mutchkin	= 1 pint (1/4 pint Scots)
1 choppin	= 1 quart (1/2 pint Scots)
1 pint	= 2 quarts
1 quart	= 1 gallon

Scots Weights and Measures Abolished by the Treaty of Union (1707)

Pint – 26 200 English Troy Grains of the clear water of Leith, when of the Temperature 50 degrees of Fahrenheit's Thermometer which is equivalent to 3 pounds 7 ounces of the Lanark Trois weight declared by Statute 1618 to be the contents of the Scots pint [the Scots pint was three times larger than the English]
mile – 1984 yards
ell – 37.0598 inches

TARTANS

Tartans – over 2000 identified by the Museum of Scottish Tartan, Comrie, Perthshire
Only some 60 tartans are officially recognized by the Lyon King of Arms and recorded in the Lyon Court Books or the Lyon Register
Oldest tartan – the Falkirk tartan (from around AD 245: discovered inside a jar of coins in Bell's Meadow, Falkirk)
First named clan tartan – Murray (1618)
Stewart tartan – 22 separate tartans
Biggest kilt – 135 cm/*53 in* round the waist (made in 1840 for the 1.9 m/*6 ft 3 in* Earl of Inverness in his own tartan and worth around £30 000 today)
First tartan on the moon – Macbean (Alan Bean on Apollo 12 lunar module Nov 1969)

CLAN ORGANIZATION (17TH CENTURY)

Chief
Tanist (heir to chiefship)
Commander (warleader)
Near Kinsmen of Chief
Heads of Houses
Gentry of the Clan
Dependants

Chief's Household
Gentlemen; Sennachie (Genealogist); Bard; Harper; Seneschal; Spokesman; Treasurer; Standard-Bearer; Piper; Sword-Bearer; Henchman; Bodyguard; Quartermaster; Cupbearer; Warder; Forester; Porter; Stabler; Guide; Baggage-man; Privy Counsellor; Train-Bearer; Harper's Attendant; Piper's Servant; Running Footman; Jester

WRITING, PUBLISHING and PRINTING

Literature – a Miscellany

First detective story to be published in Britain – in Chambers Journal (1844)

World's first historical novelist – Sir Walter Scott (1771–1832)

First sequel to a novel – Further Adventures of Robinson Crusoe, Defoe (1719)

First Scottish printing works – Walter Chepman and Andrew Myllar, Edinburgh (1507)

Smallest bound and printed book – Old King Cole (1 × 1 mm or 1/25 × 1/25 in) published by Gleniffer Press, Paisley, 1985)

Oldest Biblical text discovered – around 587 BC from Numbers 6:22-7 (inside two silver amulets found under the Scottish Church, Jerusalem)

Popular Fictional Characters Created by Scots or Created in Scotland

Humphrey Clinker – Tobias Smollett (1721–71)

Robinson Crusoe – Daniel Defoe (1660–1731)

Sherlock Holmes – Sir Arthur Conan Doyle (1859–1930)

Rip van Winkle – Washington Irving (1783–1859)

Lucia di Lammermoor – used by Donizetti (1797–1848), the Italian composer of Scots descent in his opera of that name (based on Scott's novel)

Wee Willie Winkie – William Miller (1810–72)

Dr Jekyll – Robert Louis Stevenson (1850–94)

Frankenstein – Mary Shelley (1797–1851)

Dracula – Bram Stoker (1847–1912)

Big Brother – George Orwell (1903–50)

James Bond 007 – Ian Fleming (1908–64)

Toad of Toad Hall – Kenneth Grahame (1859–1932)

Peter Pan – Sir James Barrie (1860–1937)

Jean Brodie – Muriel Spark (1918–)

Don Juan – Lord Byron (1788–1824)

Libraries

Oldest subscription library in Britain – Leadhills (1741)

Largest public reference library in Europe – Mitchell, Glasgow (capacity for 4 000 000 volumes)

Largest academic library in Europe – Edinburgh University Library

First mobile library (motorized) – Perthshire and Kinross County Library (1921)

Library foundations

1412	University of St Andrews
1451	University of Glasgow
1494	University of Aberdeen
1505	Royal College of Surgeons (Edinburgh)
1580	University of Edinburgh
1680	Innerpeffray Public Library (near Crieff)
1681	Royal College of Physicians (Edinburgh)
1684	Leightonian Library (Dunblane)
1698	Royal College of Physicians and Surgeons (Glasgow)
1709	Advocates Library (Edinburgh) with the right of legal deposit
1722	Signet Library (Edinburgh)
1783	Royal Society of Edinburgh
1796	Strathclyde University
1821	Heriot-Watt University (Edinburgh)
1876	Mitchell Library (c 1 080 933 volumes 1990)
1881	Dundee University
1883	Dunfermline – first Carnegie Public Library
1925	National Library of Scotland (from the Advocates Library c 4 500 000 volumes 1990)
1966	University of Stirling

Europe's biggest school library (floor space) – Leith Academy

Newspapers

First newspaper printed in Scotland – Diurnal Occurrences, printed in Edinburgh (1642) but dealing mainly with matters in England

First newspaper wholly produced in Scotland – Mercurius Scoticus, printed in Leith (1651) by Englishmen for the English garrison

First true Scottish newspaper – Mercurius Caledonius, printed in Edinburgh (1661)

Most read newspaper – Sunday Post (established 1914) estimated Scottish readership 57% (2 613 654)

Scottish newspapers

1651	Mercurius Scoticus
1661	Mercurius Caledonius
1680	Edinburgh Gazette
1705	Edinburgh Courant
1715	Glasgow Courant
1718	Edinburgh Evening Courant
1720	Caledonian Mercury
1721	Dumfries Mercury
1741	Glasgow Journal
1747	Aberdeen's Journal (now Press and Journal)
1755	Dundee Weekly Intelligencer
1759	Edinburgh Chronicle
1764	Edinburgh Advertiser
1777	Dumfries Weekly Journal
1783	Glasgow Advertiser (became Glasgow Herald, 1805)
1805	Kelso Chronicle
1791	Glasgow Courier
1797	Kelso Mail
1817	Scotsman
1820	Stirling Journal
1822	Fife Herald
1824	Paisley Advertiser
1827	Elgin Courier
1836	Stirling Observer
1847	North British Daily Mail (Daily Record, 1901)

SCOTTISH NEWSPAPER CIRCULATION
(estimated 1989)

Sunday Post	2 613 654
Sunday Mail	1 769 058
Daily Record	1 550 036
Glasgow Herald	249 450
Aberdeen Press and Journal	218 07(
Scotsman	176 52.
Scotland on Sunday	146 52.

JOURNALS AND NEWSPAPERS FOUNDED BY SCOTSMEN

Spectator (1711)

Scots Magazine – oldest surviving magazine in Britain (1739)

Edinburgh Medical Journal – oldest medical journal in Britain (1773)

Glasgow Herald – oldest daily newspaper in English-speaking world (1783)

Economist – founded by Robert Owen (1821)

New York Tribune (1841)

New York Herald – founded by James Gordon Bennett (1840)

Mind (1876)

Political Quarterly (1916)

Forbes Magazine – founded by B.C. Forbes (1917)

Dictionaries

First English concordance to the Bible – Alexander Cruden (1701–70)

First editor of the Oxford English Dictionary – James Murray

First dictionary published in Britain to back up its definitions with dated and referenced quotations – An Etymological Dictionary of the Scottish Language (Jamieson, 1808)

Earliest British historical dictionary – An Etymological Dictionary of the Scottish Language (Jamieson, 1808)

Greatest lexicographer – James A.H. Murray (born Roxburghshire) who worked on the Oxford English Dictionary (1884–1928)

Dictionaries in Scotland –
Glossary of Thomas Ruddiman to first modern edition of Gavin Douglas's translation of Vergil's Aeneid into Scots
The Exposition of the Termes and Difficill Wordes [Dictionary of Ancient Scottish Legal Terms] (Sir John Skene, 1597)

An Etymological Dictionary of the
Scottish Language (John Jamieson, 2
vols, 1808)

English Dialect Dictionary (Joseph
Wright, 6 vols, 1898–1905)

Dictionary of the Older Scottish
Tongue (4½ vols, 1980)

Scottish National Dictionary (10 vols,
1976)

Scots Dialect Dictionary (A. Warrack,
1911)

Lallans (J.N. Jarvie, 1947)

The Scots Word Book (W. Graham,
1977)

The Concise Scots Dictionary (M.
Robinson, 1985)

The Scots Thesaurus (I. Macleod, ed,
1990)

Five out of six of Dr Johnson's assistants
in the compilation of his Dictionary of
the English Language (1755) were Scots
– MacBeans (2), Shiels, Stewart,
Maitland

British crossword champion (1991) – Norma
Maclean

Encyclopaedias

Earliest British encyclopaedia – Liber
Exerptionum by the Scottish monk
Richard (d 1173) made at St Victor's
Abbey, Paris around 1140

First edition of Encyclopaedia Britannica –
(Andrew Bell, Colin Macfarquhar, Wm
Smellie) 1768–71

Most comprehensive encyclopaedia in English –
The New Encyclopaedia Britannica
(1768)

A MUSICAL MISCELLANY

Earliest Scottish song – Ex te lux oritur
(wedding-hymn of Princess Margaret of
Scotland and Eric II of Norway, 1281)

First musical society in Britain – Edinburgh
Musical Society (1728)

First musical society hall – St Cecilia's Hall,
Edinburgh (1762)

Most frequently sung songs – Auld Lang
Syne/Happy Birthday/For he's a jolly
good fellow

Largest carillon in Britain – 48 bells (St
Nicholas Church, Aberdeen)

Oldest bell in Europe – St Nicholas Church,
Lanark (1110)

Longest one-man-band playing – 199 hr on 17-
25 Feb 1989 (Dave Sheriff of Garve,
Highland at the Eastgate Shopping
Centre, Inverness)

Most song titles played by a DJ in Scotland – 35
titles in 2 min at Sweeney Todd's Disco,
Anstruther, Fife by John Murray (1990)

Most song titles played by a DJ in Britain – 37
titles in 2 min in UK at BBC TV Centre
by John Murray (1991)

Fastest live recording into the shops – 'Dear
God' single by Midge Ure (81 hr after
performance at the Venue, Edinburgh
(1988))

First British concert with 10 pianos – Bute
Hall, Glasgow (1990)

**First pop artist to have US Top 5 hits in Pop,
Country, R & B, Dance and Adult
Contemporary Charts** – Sheena Easton

**First British female pop singer to appear behind
Iron Curtain** – Lulu

British Brass Band Champions (1990) – Co-op
Welfare Society (Glasgow)

British Brass Band Youth Section winners (1990)
– West Lothian Schools Brass Band
(youngest player 10 years old)

Winner, Young Musician of the Year (1988) –
David Horne (1968–)

BBC Choirgirl of the Year (1990) – Susan Gray
(1974–)

SCOTTISH COUNTRY DANCING

Reel
Eightsome (set dance with 4 couples in the round)
Dashing White Sergeant (set dance with 2 men and 4 ladies in groups of 3, each half set progressing round the room in opposite directions)
Jig
Strip the Willow (line dance with 4 couples)
Hamilton House (line dance with 4 couples depicting a flirtation)
Strathspey
Monymusk (line dance with 4 couples)
Foursome Reel (set dance with 4 couples – mixture of strathspey and reel)
Waltz Country Dance
(square dance for 3 couples, each couple progressing round the room in opposite directions)
Shetland Reel
(line dance with 4 couples danced to Shetland-style hornpipe reels)

Most complex Scottish country dance – 256-some reel in Vancouver, Canada (1988)

SCOTS SONGS ARRANGED by FOREIGN COMPOSERS

An Thou Wert My Ain Thing – Joseph Haydn (1793)
Auld Lang Syne – Joseph Haydn (1804); Beethoven (1793)
Auld Rob Morris – Joseph Haydn (1803); Max Bruch (1863)
Bessy Bell and Mary Gray – Joseph Haydn (1807)
The Birks of Endermay – Joseph Haydn (1803/1804)
Bonny Dundee – Gay (The Beggar's Opera); Weber (1826)

The Braes of Bellenden – J.C. Bach (1779); Joseph Haydn (1803)
The Broom of Cowdenknows – Gay (Beggar's Opera); Geminiani; J.C. Bach (1770); Joseph Haydn
The Bush Aboon Traquair – Geminiani; Joseph Haydn (1804); Boïeldieu (overture to La Dame Blanche) (1825)
Cold and Raw – Purcell (1692)
Corn Riggs Are Bonny – Joseph Haydn (1804)
The Country Lass – Geminiani; Joseph Haydn (1795)
De'il Tak The Wars – Joseph Haydn; Beethoven
The Drunken Wife of Galloway – Joseph Haydn
I'll Never Leave Thee – J.C. Bach (1770); Joseph Haydn (1804)
Kinloch of Kinloch – Beethoven (1818)
The Lass of Patie's Mill – Gay (The Beggar's Opera); Geminiani; Joseph Haydn
The Last Time I Cam O'er The Muir – Gay (The Beggar's Opera); Geminiani; Joseph Haydn (1803)
Maggie Lauder – Joseph Haydn (1808)
Peggy, I Must Love Thee – Purcell; Joseph Haydn
Saw Ye My Father – J.C. Bach (1777); Joseph Haydn (1808); Max Bruch (1863/1876)
Scots Wha Hae – Joseph Haydn; Berlioz (1832); Max Bruch (1865/1880)
She Rose And Let Me In – Geminiani; Joseph Haydn (1793)
Thro' The Wood, Laddie – Joseph Haydn; Max Bruch (1880)
'Twas Within A Furlong of Edinburgh Town – Purcell (1695)
When Phoebus Bright – Geminiani; Joseph Haydn
Will Ye Go To The Ewe-Buchts, Marion? – Joseph Haydn (1803); Max Bruch (1876/89/92)
The Yellow-Hair'd Laddie – J.C. Bach (1777); Joseph Haydn (1804); Boïeldieu (La Dame Blanche) (1825)

Burns Songs Set by Foreign Composers

The Bonie Lad That's Far Awa – Robert Schumann Op 25/20 (1840)
The Captain's Lady – Robert Schumann Op 25/19 (1840)
For The Sake O' Somebody – Robert Schumann Op 25/4 (1840)

The Highland Balou – Robert Schumann Op 25/14 (1840)

The Highland Widow's Lament – Robert Schumann Op 25/10 (1840)

I Hae A Wife O' My Ain – Robert Schumann Op 25/22 (1840)

Let Me In This Ae Night – Robert Schumann Op 34/2 (1840)

My Heart's In The Highlands – Robert Schumann Op 25/13 (1840)

O My Luve's Like A Red, Red Rose – Robert Schumann Op 27/2 (1840); Alban Berg (1902)

Who Is That At My Bower Door? – Robert Schumann Op 34/3 (1840)

O Wert Thou In The Cauld Blast – Felix Mendelssohn Op 63/5 (1842); Dimitri Shostakovich Op 62/4 (1942)

Auld Lang Syne – Robert Schumann Op 55/4 (1846)

Highland Lassie O – Schumann Op 55/1 (1846)

I'll Ay Ca' In By Yon Town – Robert Schumann Op 55/3 (1846)

Address To The Tooth-ache – Robert Schumann Op 55/2 (1846)

Cock Up Your Beaver – Robert Schumann Op 75/4 (1849)

I Look To The North – Robert Schumann Op 25/23 (1849)

John Anderson, My Jo – Robert Schumann Op 67/5 and Op 145/4 (1849); Richard Strauss (1880)

Rattlin, Roarin Willie – Robert Schumann Op 146 (1849)

Green Grow The Rashes, O! – Arnold Bax (1918)

Comin Thro' The Rye – Dimitri Shostakovich Op 62/2 (1942)

McPherson's Farewell – Dimitri Shostakovich Op 62/3 (1942)

O Poortith Cauld – Michael Tippett (1965)

Afton Water – Benjamin Britten Op 92/5 (1975)

Leezie Lindsay – Benjamin Britten Op 92/7 (1975)

Phillis The Fair – Benjamin Britten Op 92/2 (1975)

Wee Willie Gray – Benjamin Britten Op 92/3 (1975)

What Will I Do Gin My Hoggie Die? – Benjamin Britten Op 92/4 (1975)

Winter – Benjamin Britten Op 92/6 (1975)

Music Inspired by the Ossian Poems of James MacPherson

Les Bardes, ou Ossian – Lesueur (Ossian was Napoleon's favourite poet. He awarded Lesueur the Legion d'Honneur) (1804)

Uthal – Mehul (1806)

Fingallo e Comala – Pavesi

Oscar and Malvine – ballet d'action, William Reeve (1791)

Ossian's Lied nach dem Falle Nathos – Franz Schubert

Ossian's Song in Werther – Jules Massenet (1892)

Gesang aus Fingal (Op 17/4) – Johannes Brahms

Darthulas Grabesgesang (Op 42/3) – Johannes Brahms

Nachklange von Ossian Op 1 – Niels Gade (Danish) (1840)

Schottische Ouverture, Im Hochland – Niels Gade

La Chasse d'Ossian – Georges Bizet (1860)

Cantata, Leaves from Ossian – Liza Lehmann

Works Inspired by Scotland

Fantasia in F sharp minor Op 28 (Sonate écossaise) – Felix Mendelssohn

Hebrides Overture – Felix Mendelssohn (1830)

Scotch Symphony – Felix Mendelssohn (1842)

Marche écossaise sur un thème populaire – Claude Debussy (1908)

Chanson écossaise – Maurice Ravel

Four Scottish Dances – Malcolm Arnold

Scottish Fantasies – Max Bruch

Also:

Edvard Grieg (1843–1907) – the Norwegian composer was of Scots descent, his forbear Greig having come from Aberdeen

Erik Satie (1866–1925) – the eccentric French composer had a Scots mother. He is reputed to have been conceived in the Highlands of Scotland where his parents were on honeymoon

OPERA

Opera Companies

Scottish Opera (1962) – based at the Theatre Royal, Glasgow

Haddo House (1945) – choral society founded by Lady Aberdeen

Ayr Intimate Opera/Opera West (1972) – patron: Elisabeth Schwarzkopf

There are around 173 amateur companies in Scotland affiliated to the National Operatic and Dramatic Association (NODA)

Operas Based on the Novels of Sir Walter Scott

More than 40 operas are based on Scott's works. These include:

Guy Mannering – La Dame Blanche by Boeïldieu (1825)

Old Mortality – I Puritani di Scozia by Bellini (1835)

The Bride of the Lammermoor – Lucia di Lammermoor by Donizetti (1835)

The Fair Maid of Perth – La Jolie Fille de Perth by Bizet (1867)

Ivanhoe – by Rossini (1826)

Kenilworth – by Donizetti (1829)

Maria Stuarda – by Donizetti (1834)

Operas Based on Shakespeare's 'Macbeth'

Macbeth – by Verdi is based on Shakespeare's play which in turn was taken from Holinshed's Chronicles (1847)

Lady Macbeth of Mtsensk – Dimitri Shostakovich (1934)

BALLETS on SCOTTISH THEMES

La Sylphide – choreographed by Bournonville with music by Herman Lvenskjld: (the first great romantic ballet) (1836)

Dances on a Scotch Theme (The Tartans) – choreographed by Frederick Ashton with the music of William Boyce (arr by Constant Lambert) (1930)

Scotch Symphony – choreographed by Balanchine with music by Mendelssohn (1952)

An Cl Mor (The Big Cloth) – choreographed by Stuart Hopps (1972)

Embers of Glencoe – choreographed by Walter Gore (1910–79) (1973)

Mary Queen of Scots – choreographed by Peter Darrell; music by John McCabe (1976)

THEATRES/SHOWS

Smallest repertory theatre in Scotland – Byre Theatre, St Andrews (audience of 74), founded 1933

Smallest public theatre in the world – Mull Little Theatre at Dervaig, Mull (audience of 43; stage 2 × 4 m/7 × 14 ft) founded 1966

Smallest touring theatre in the world – Mull Little Theatre

Biggest temporary stage ever built – Scottish Exhibition Centre, Glasgow (for the visit of the Bolshoi Opera and Dance Company, 1990)

World's biggest stage – Forth Rail Bridge birthday (2582 m/2765 yd wide, 1990)

Oldest surviving music-hall theatre in Scotland – The Britannia, Argyle Street, Glasgow (1860)

Oldest surviving theatre in Scotland – Theatre Royal, Dumfries (1792)

World's largest firework – Forth Rail Bridge birthday (107 m/350 ft wide and 12 m/40 ft high) (1990)

World's largest floodlighting scheme – Forth Rail Bridge (1990)

Major Theatres

Adam Smith Centre, Kirkcaldy
Brunton Theatre, Musselburgh
Byre Theatre, St Andrews
Citizens Theatre, Glasgow
Clyde Theatre, Clydebank
Cumbernauld Theatre, Cumbernauld
Dundee Repertory Theatre, Dundee
Eden Court Theatre, Inverness
Gaiety Theatre, Ayr
His Majesty's Theatre, Aberdeen
King's Theatre, Glasgow
MacRobert Arts Centre, Stirling
Magnum Theatre, Irvine
Mitchell Theatre, Glasgow
Palace Theatre, Kilmarnock
Perth Repertory Theatre, Perth
Pitlochry Festival Theatre, Pitlochry
Royal Lyceum Theatre, Edinburgh
Theatre Royal, Glasgow
Tramway Theatre, Glasgow
Traverse Theatre, Edinburgh
Tron Theatre, Glasgow
Village Theatre, East Kilbride

Theatre Companies

Borderline Theatre Company
Brunton Theatre
Byre Theatre
Communicado Theatre Company
Cumbernauld Theatre Company
Dundee Repertory Theatre
Perth Repertory Theatre
Pitlochry Festival Theatre
Royal Lyceum Theatre Company
Scottish National Association of Youth
    Theatre, Glasgow
Scottish Youth Theatre
7:84 Theatre Company (Scotland),
    Glasgow
Theatre Alba
Tag Theatre Company, Glasgow
Theatre Workshop, Edinburgh
Traverse Theatre, Edinburgh
Tron Theatre
Wildcat Stage Productions, Glasgow
Winged Horse Touring Productions

FILM, TV and VIDEO

World's first panorama – created by Robert Barker in Edinburgh (1784)
Developed motion in pictures – David Brewster (1781–1868)
First Scottish films – Queen Victoria at Balmoral filmed by a Mr Downie (1895); Gordon Highlanders leaving Maryhill Barracks (1895)
First advertising film – Haig's Scotch Whisky (1897)
First in-flight movie – based on Sir Arthur Conan Doyle's 'The Lost World'
First commercial film – included in film 'Highland Fling'
Scenic director for MGM – George Gibson (1939–64)
Founded documentary film movement – John Grierson (1898–1972)
First motion picture to use actors – Mary Queen of Scots (1895)
First horror movie – based on R.L. Stevenson's 'Dr Jekyll and Mr Hyde'
Floors Castle – used in 'Greystoke', the legend of Tarzan, Lord of the Apes
Slains Castle – inspired Bram Stoker's 'Dracula'
First film of total eclipse of the sun – Duke of Montrose (1878–1954)
Highest fee for comedian in silent films – Harry Lauder (£10 000 to play a grocer in Huntingtower, 1927)
First Scots feature film – McNab's Visit to London (1905)
First Scottish Gaelic feature film – Hero (1982)
Laurel and Hardy film – Bonnie Scotland (1935)
Father of documentary film-making – John Grierson (1898–1972)
Largest independent film and television studios in Scotland – Blackcat (Glasgow)
Most successful Scottish films – Tunes of Glory (1960); Seawards the Great Ships (1961): Oscar winner; The Prime of Miss Jean Brodie (1968); The Dollar Bottom (1980): Oscar winner; Chariots of Fire (1981): 4 Academy awards
Most portrayed character in films – Sherlock Holmes (70 actors in 197 films) created by Edinburgh-born Sir Arthur Conan Doyle based in part on his teacher Dr Joseph Bell (buried in the Dean Cemetery, Edinburgh)

Film Versions of Shakespeare's Macbeth ('The Scottish Play')

1915 – directed by D.W. Griffiths with Sir Herbert Beerbohm Tree
1948 – directed by Orson Welles (who also starred)
1956 – directed by Ken Hughes with Paul Douglas
1957 – Throne of Blood (Japanese) dir by Akira Kurosawa
1960 – directed by George Schaefer with Maurice Evans and Judith Anderson
1971 – directed by Roman Polanski with Jon Finch and Francesca Annis

Television Landmarks

First televised film in Britain – made by John Logie Baird (1888–1946)
First public TV service – BBC 30 Sept 1929 (John Logie Baird)
First suggested electronic TV through cathode ray tubes – Alan Campbell Swinton (1863–1930)

Video

Largest documentary video production company in Britain – Lamancha Productions, Edinburgh

A MILITARY MISCELLANY

Only man to hold officer's rank in the British, American and Russian navies – John Paul Jones (1747–92)
First campaign medal – Dunbar Medal 1650 (after Battle of Dunbar)
Nicknames – Curse of Scotland (Nine of Diamonds). Three possible explanations are given for the term: the order for the Massacre of Glencoe written on it; the order 'No Quarter' given at Culloden; it is in the shape of the 'Corse' (cross) of Scotland

Biggest death-toll in Scottish air-raid – 1200, attack on Clydeside by 300 German aircraft (13-14 March 1941)
Finest prisoner-of-war church – Italian Chapel, Lamb Holm, Orkney, built by Italian prisoners (1943)
First aerial propaganda raid – Admiral Thomas Cochrane (1775-1860)
Last shot at the Battle of Waterloo – by 71st Highland Light Infantry
First German pilot shot down over Britain – Helmut Pohle (pilot of Junkers Ju88), shot down on 16 October 1939 over the Forth Bridge by Scots Spitfire pilot George Pinkerton
Oldest infantry regiment in British army – Royal Scots (1535)
Oldest Highland regiment – Black Watch (1739)

MAJOR DISASTERS and TOTAL NUMBERS KILLED

1689–1700 – Darien Disaster (over 300 died from disease or killed)
16 July 1832 – The Bad Day – 31 Shetland fishing-boats lost (105)
2 July 1879 – Blantyre Colliery explosion (25)
28 Dec 1879 – Tay Bridge collapse (75)
20 Jul 1881 – ten Shetland fishing-boats lost (58)
14 Oct 1881 – Eyemouth fishing fleet lost (189)
3 Jul 1883 – SS Daphne sinks at launching (124)
28 May 1887 – Udston Colliery explosion (73)
5 Sept 1889 – Mauricewood Pit (70)
19 Nov 1905 – Glasgow lodging-house fire (39)
22 May 1915 – Gretna rail crash (277), worst rail accident in UK
9 July 1917 – Scapa Flow: HMS Vanguard explodes (804)
31 Jan 1918 – 'Battle of May Island' fiasco (103)
1 Jan 1919 – Naval yacht Iolaire sunk off Lewis (205)

21 Jun 1919 – Scapa Flow: scuttling of German High Seas Fleet (52 ships)

25 Sep 1923 – Pit disaster, Redding, Stirlingshire (40)

31 Dec 1929 – Glen Cinema fire, Paisley (70)

14 Oct 1939 – Scapa Flow: HMS Royal Oak sunk (833)

28 Oct 1939 – Valleyfield Colliery, Fife (35)

March 1941 – Glasgow Blitz (1200)

May 1941 – Greenock, Gourock, Dumbarton Blitz (280)

21 Oct 1947 – KLM crash, Auchenweet Farm, Ayrshire (39)

31 Jan 1953 – Princess Victoria ferry sunk (133)

18 Sep 1959 – Auchengeich Colliery, Lanarkshire (47)

2 Jan 1971 – Ibrox football stadium tragedy (66)

6 Nov 1986 – Chinook helicopter crash near Shetland (45)

6 July 1988 – Piper Alpha oil rig explosion (167)

21 Dec 1988 – Lockerbie Pan Am jumbo crash (270)